Our Unknown Ex-President

A PORTRAIT OF HERBERT HOOVER

Books by Eugene Lyons

OUR UNKNOWN EX-PRESIDENT:
A Portrait of Herbert Hoover

THE RED DECADE

STALIN, CZAR OF ALL THE RUSSIAS

ASSIGNMENT IN UTOPIA

WE COVER THE WORLD (*Editor*)

MOSCOW CAROUSEL

SIX SOVIET PLAYS (*Editor*)

THE LIFE AND DEATH OF SACCO AND VANZETTI

Our Unknown Ex-President

A PORTRAIT OF HERBERT HOOVER

by Eugene Lyons

1948

Doubleday & Company, Inc.

Garden City, New York

Acknowledgments

The photographs used on end-sheet papers are by courtesy of the Hoover Institute and Library on War, Revolution and Peace.

TOP ROW, *left to right:*

Herbert Hoover with his brother Theodore and sister May

Mr. Hoover with Prince Leopold, Queen Elizabeth, and King Albert of the Belgians, ferry dock, San Francisco Bay, 1920

Mr. Hoover receiving an honorary degree, Doctor of Humanity, Lincoln Memorial University, June 1939

Mr. and Mrs. Hoover, February 12, 1933

MIDDLE ROW, *left to right:*

Herbert Hoover, 1898

Herbert Hoover, 1947, at the Bohemian Grove (courtesy of Leon Lazarian)

BOTTOM ROW, *left to right:*

The "Old Swimming Hole," West Branch, Iowa, 1928

Mr. Hoover accepts nomination for presidency, Stanford University Football Stadium, 1928

Mr. Hoover at the New York Automobile Show, 1940—with Governor Alfred E. Smith

Mr. Hoover receiving a degree at Charles University, Prague, 1938

Contents

Our Unknown Ex-President

A PORTRAIT OF HERBERT HOOVER

CHAPTER I

A Sort of Dedication

A FANTASTIC HOOVER MYTH, FACTU-
ally false and humanly unjust, has been industriously promoted
during many years by hordes of official and volunteer propagandists and is still very much in circulation. It presents our
thirty-first President as a heartless ogre, inept and callous and
reactionary, who "caused" a depression, then "did nothing" to
mitigate its horrors.

Anyone who doubts the magnitude and the virulence of the
myth might test it, as I did, through young people who have no
personal memory of the Hoover period, having grown up during
three and a half Roosevelt terms. Only the least critical among
them, I found, have swallowed the anti-Hoover legend whole.
But nearly all of them have accepted as historical fact some portion of the fable of a President who "brought" economic disaster
to his country and stubbornly refused to undo the mischief or
succor the victims.

And why not? How could anyone avoid absorbing some part
of the great myth? It was in the press, on the radio, in the very
air we breathed. Legions of experts on the government pay rolls
were engaged in "selling" the New Deal which, inevitably, meant
unselling the Old Deal.

A thousand times children in their most impressionable years
heard offhand references to the "Hoover depression" and weighty
warnings against return to "Hoover breadlines." They saw a
President mocked and caricatured in endless ways. And they

knew little more about that President than that he was Very Rich, allied with Big Business and Monopoly Capital, opposed to taxing his wealthy friends, and content to "let them starve" after he had pushed the bottom out of American economy.

Take Betty, for example, a bright college girl with a lively social conscience. The political clichés of her high school years— about planned economy, economic royalists, cradle-to-grave security, pump-priming for full employment, and the rest of it—roll easily and honestly from her tongue.

She has read a great many articles and pamphlets about Roosevelt and the New Deal, in most of which Hoover played the role of villain and menace, but nowhere has she read a comparable defense of Hoover. She came repeatedly under the influence of what she calls "liberal" teachers and radio commentators, all of whom pronounced the word "Hoover" in tones of mockery or with a slight grimace, as if it tasted sour.

Impatient, like so many young intellectuals, for drastic and immediate solutions of all mortal problems, she has listened in sympathy to the "line" of the Youth Congress, American Youth for Democracy, and other such campus organizations.

Then there has been the obsessive subject of Soviet Russia and its Great Experiment, and that, too, is somehow mixed up with her feelings about Hoover. Betty is too intelligent to be unaware of the seamier and even horrifying side of life in that particular Utopia and too honest to deny it. But for reasons which she cannot quite explain she resents those who "harp" on it. After all there are sharecroppers and lynchings and unemployed in America and black injustices everywhere, so why take it out on Stalin?

And Hoover—not the man, about whom she is profoundly misinformed, but the name, the symbol—figures in all her adolescent yearnings for a better world. In a vague way that defies logic he has become a synonym in her emotional vocabulary for reaction, fascism, red-baiting, depression; in short, for Evil obstructing the path of Progress.

Solemnly Betty explained to me one day that President Hoover, in contrast with his successor, had "done nothing" to help the unemployed and the distressed, since it was against his wicked principles for government to intervene in economic affairs. She did not present this as a debatable opinion but as a fact learned by rote, like Columbus discovered America in 1492.

To feed the poor, she said, Hoover would have had to tax the rich and that self-evidently would not have been tolerated by his Wall Street bosses. No, he did not exactly "cause" the great collapse. The point was that he refused to go in for National Planning, the one thing that could have prevented the collapse or ended it instantaneously when it did come.

Betty suspected I was pulling her leg when I tried to assure her that Hoover, far from opposing government intercession, was the first American President to act on the principle of federal responsibility in meeting an economic crisis, instead of letting it take its course as in past depressions; and that he did this against the advice and over the honest opposition of more conservative elements in his party.

Her credence in my good faith suffered a further shock when I went on to claim that Hoover had organized effective relief on a scale without precedent before his administration; that the tall tales of refusal to care for the destitute were later inventions— they had not even been featured in the 1932 election campaign indictment.

Hoover, I said, as she stared in puzzlement, had warned against the speculative boom and overproduction before he became President, and after the crash fought valiantly to cushion the shocks and to head off panic; in fact, a few of the New Deal measures were first undertaken by Hoover, and others he had tried in vain to put over against the opposition of a Democratic Congress.

By that time the last shreds of Betty's respect for my veracity were blown away. I could practically see them floating off into space. But doggedly I went on to apprise her that the New Deal had no more "ended the depression" than Hoover had started it; that there were almost as many unemployed at the zenith of the Roosevelt era as at the nadir of the Hoover era, and vastly more families dependent on relief; that, indeed, only the fortuitous advent of a great war in Europe, which made us the "arsenal of democracy," finally wound up the depression.

"But let's put aside politics and policies and economic theories for the moment," I suggested. "Those are so often matters of opinion and interpretation. Let's consider Herbert Hoover the man.

"How much do you really know about his life story, his career, the steps by which he rose to eminence? How much insight do you have into his character and his philosophy of life and government and human relations? You know, my dear Betty, these are not really deep mysteries. There have been a number of excellent biographies of the man, and he has explained himself pretty clearly in several books, not to mention half-a-dozen volumes of his more important speeches and articles."

I wish I could record that her knowledge on this score was zero. Unhappily it was minus zero, since the scraps and tag ends of Hoover biography she had picked up here and there were lamentably false or twisted out of shape.

She was astonished to learn, for instance, that our thirty-first President was born into a poor Quaker family in a cottage almost as humble as the one in which Lincoln was born; that he was orphaned as a child, knew poverty and hard work in his teens, and worked his way through college; that his first job after graduating was underground in a mine as a common laborer.

Because she had always connected his name with Money and Profits, she was particularly amazed to learn that money meant exactly nothing to Hoover; that he had deliberately brushed aside chances for incalculable fortunes to serve mankind and that he has never accepted payment, not even his salaries, for these services.

Despite herself—because now we were on human rather than politico-economic ground and her sales resistance therefore relaxed—she became interested in, and after a while fascinated by, this President's life history. She asked pertinent questions and contributed exclamations like, "Well, I never! I thought he was born a plutocrat!"

It is, after all, an authentically American success story, this rise of the son of an Iowa village blacksmith to wealth and a position as the world's leading mining engineer in his thirties; to world fame as a humanitarian in his forties; and ultimately to the White House in his fifties. It is a story to thrill and inspire American youth and give them a deepened pride in their country as the land of opportunity. Here were three careers in one lifetime—in business, social work, and politics—and the topmost peak achieved in each of them! That it has been neglected in a country so appreciative of rags-to-riches epics is a commentary on the virulence of political passions in our time.

Every American, I had supposed, was at least familiar with the magnificent saga of a fellow American's prowess in saving millions of Belgians and Frenchmen, then scores of millions of other Europeans, from famine and pestilence. But I discovered that I was mistaken. A generation has grown up to whom World War I and its dramas are so much ancient history, scarcely related to living men and living problems.

Besides, so far as Hoover is concerned, partisan emotion has operated retroactively, blotting out what it could not conveniently distort.

It is for Betty, for thousands of young Americans like her, that I am writing this book; and for those of their elders who innocently, casually, repeat about Hoover the products of malice though there is no malice in their own hearts. It is written for those, young or old, who continue to treat the political libels of the 1930s as if they had any relevance to the living facts of those years; who light-mindedly continue to vilify a great American whose major sin was to be President in a time of universal trouble. I shall be well pleased if a few of them here and there read it and view Herbert Hoover for perhaps the first time from a new vantage point.

What follows was started modestly as an article, but somehow it grew. . . . I was intrigued as I went along, digging into the literature on Hoover and talking to his friends, by facets of his career and his personality about which I had not known. But this work is still modest in design and intention, no more really than an outsize article. It makes no pretense to completeness or to the scholarship rightly demanded of a real book.

I shall conclude this introductory chapter with a personal note. For a long time I counted myself among those intellectuals who would rather be caught stealing than caught on the un-liberal, conservative, let alone "reactionary" side of any political debate.

The mortal sin in our milieu was not to be wrong but to be Right.

In 1936, it happens, I took a leave of absence from my business of the moment to throw myself actively into the campaign to re-elect Franklin D. Roosevelt. To be specific, I acted as publicity director of the newly formed American Labor party which that year did help swing the balance that put New York in the Democratic electoral column. Though the Republican candidate was Alf Landon, the chief targets of my publicity, as of the Democratic offensive generally, were Hoover and the "Hoover depression." Naturally, I was not encumbered with too much knowledge or any understanding of the man.

Shortly before that I had lived and worked in Soviet Russia and had come reluctantly to hate Communism and all its works. I was under attack among people who had been my friends as a "renegade" who had "sold out to the enemy." That's another story which I have told elsewhere in excessive detail. But looking back to 1936, I suspect that my eagerness to support the New Deal and castigate Hoover was an unconscious retort to the name callers. I was demonstrating to myself that, despite my deep disillusionment with Stalin's Utopia, I was still "on the right side," which is to say the Left side.

Be that as it may, I did join the pack howling at Hoover's heels. It was in part, no doubt, because of that memory that the article grew into the book. It is written for Betty and some of her elders—including myself.

CHAPTER II

America's Uneasy Conscience

FOR MORE THAN A DECADE OUR ONLY living ex-President had been so persistently maligned, so expertly misrepresented, so recklessly lampooned, that a further decline in his personal stock seemed impossible. But just before the United States was pushed into the war by the Pearl Harbor outrage, the impossible came to pass: his stock did touch a new low.

Herbert Hoover is indifferent to prevailing intellectual fashions. In this there is no snobbishness, no nose-thumbing defiance. He is no more capable of improvising or trimming opinions to shock the herd prejudices of the moment than to flatter them. In his mental and moral make-up there is no trace of the perverse or frivolous or paradoxical. Right or wrong, his views flow from the depths of his nature; they are integral with the whole man. At this time, as always, they were consistent with his philosophy of life.

But had he chosen perversely to make himself the focus of the largest irritations and hatreds of the moment, he could scarcely have done much better.

With war fevers mounting steadily, he remained stanchly opposed to military intervention. With the Roosevelt administration reaping credit for the new war-boom employment and prosperity, he continued to attack the New Deal methods. A new tolerance of Soviet Russia was sweeping the country, but Hoover felt it necessary to underscore the totalitarian, anti-democratic essence of the Kremlin regime. In defiance of the most clamorous of the competing public opinions of the time, he was demanding that America feed the starving children of France, Greece, and other Hitler-held countries.

As a bid for unpopularity, his program was truly a masterpiece. He seemed on the "wrong" side of every great issue and wrong-headed in proclaiming the fact. At that low ebb only a journal specializing in faith and divine rectitude, I suppose, could have risked the prophecy that Hoover "is only now approaching the summit of his career."

This is precisely what the *Christian Century* did. It referred, of course, to a moral rather than a political summit. Its editors had been moved by the spiritual grandeur of the former President's tireless accent on Christian charity—in its concrete form of bread for hungry children—in a world riven by hatreds.

Time has justified their daring faith. At this writing, in the seventy-fourth year of Hoover's crowded life and the sixteenth year since he went directly from the White House to the dog-house, he again enjoys tremendous popular esteem and an influence in public affairs second to no other private individual. As a matter of course he is referred to as our First Citizen and Elder Statesman: titles to which no man is elected and which no party bosses can cancel out. Not since his presidency have his opinions and his advice weighed so heavily in the scales of national policy.

Fragments of this book having been published in advance in The *Reader's Digest,* I received a vast number of letters from all parts of the country and all kinds of people. Nearly all of them offered variants on the same theme: "Thank God the truth about Herbert Hoover is coming out at last. . . . About time someone spoke up for a great man and a great American. . . ." I felt, reading those letters, that multitudes of Americans had a feeling of guilt about the long ordeal of Herbert Hoover.

The tone of the press and radio suddenly turned deferential. Even those who still disliked Hoover or still mistrusted his ideas seemed awed by his moral stature. In asserting that they considered him wrong, they no longer implied that they considered him wicked. Except in the Communist propaganda, where he is still the reigning demon, slander gave way to respectful disagreement.

A left-wing columnist, Samuel Grafton, recently prefaced an attack on certain Hoover proposals with this revealing comment: "I wonder why I stick my neck out in this way, for I realize that Mr. Hoover is one of the three or four elder statesmen before whom we customarily abdicate our function of criticism." Customarily? Decidedly a new custom, though catching on fast. Only yesterday writers of his political coloration would have felt it necessary to apologize for praising Hoover, not for lambasting him.

The leftish *New Republic,* in taking exception to some view or other of the former President, conceded wryly that "at heart . . . Hoover is an honest, soul-searching humanitarian." And Dr. Alvin Johnson, a ranking liberal, in an open letter to the ex-President in June 1947 declared:

"The place of Hoover in history, a most honored place, is that of the man who extended American neighborliness to the world. . . . I do recognize that among the Americans of my time you have been the greatest, by virtue of your extending the concern of Americans to the whole world."

Trivial in themselves, these and a thousand other expressions and incidents reflected the change in the mood of the nation in relation to Hoover. They signalized the fact that our thirty-first President was out of the doghouse. His virtual ostracism from public life, roughly coinciding with the New Deal era, was ended.

Let me cite a few little things of large symptomatic import:

In May 1947 Hoover attended the Gridiron Club dinner in Washington for the first time since he moved out of the White House. The club's tradition did not allow direct quotation of what was said. But Charles T. Lucey of the Scripps-Howard chain, who was present, later wrote: "It violates no rule to report that his presence here brought him acclaim among today's national leaders such as he has not known in many years. Party leaders on both sides paid him tributes."

In the course of the annual newspaper publishers' convention in New York, some time later, Hoover attended one of its dinners. His presence evoked a huge and spontaneous ovation. "So spontaneous," George Sokolsky reported, "that he could not and did not respond to it except in an expression on his face that might have been the struggle to withhold a tear." The publishers gathered in the Waldorf ballroom rose and cheered and cheered. It has been the established custom of the convention dinner to toast only the President of the United States. This night the custom was broken; an ex-President, too, was toasted.

For fifteen years Hoover's birthday had been ignored, or at most acknowledged briefly and grudgingly. But when he reached seventy-three, on August 10, 1947, it was front-page news for many leading newspapers, and the occasion for warm and even affectionate editorial tributes in nearly all newspapers. I have examined a fistful of those editorials. Running through them was the same pleased sense of a wrong being redressed at long last that ran through my letters. I may be mistaken, but I am convinced that America has an uneasy conscience over its treatment of Hoover; there are overtones of embarrassment in its belated acclaim.

In October 1935, on the eve of a presidential year, an article by George Creel in *Collier's* quoted top Republicans as saying, "Lord, if only Hoover would get out and leave us alone." In a spirit of charity I skip over the implications of the remark as an index to Republican loyalty and gallantry and to political morals in general. I quote it only to point up the contrast. On the eve of yet another presidential year, in 1947, it occurred to no prospective candidate to disown him. Hoover, indeed, had become one of the great party assets.

In that year Republicans sought his guidance, demonstratively, on domestic and foreign affairs. And not only Republicans. There was hardly a day during the sessions of Congress when its members, of both parties, did not solicit Hoover's advice. Individually and in groups they came to consult him. A dozen House and Senate committees invited him to give his views on as many subjects.

The ex-President, a Washington *Post* special writer reported, "packs more weight on legislation today than any Republican leader outside Congress." To exemplify the point he cited the $350,000,000 foreign relief bill that had just been passed. "It was Hoover's word that saved the President's relief bill from defeat," he showed, and "most of the safeguards written into the bill by the House were Hoover's." An Associated Press dispatch similarly attested that the former President "is emerging as one of the top economic counselors" of that Republican Congress. It was not without significance, as a sign of balmier weather, that a bill was introduced to make all retired Presidents members of the United States Senate; the only living ex-President, of course, was Hoover.

In placing Hoover at the head of a bipartisan twelve-man commission to study ways and means of rationalizing the structure of the executive branch of the national government, Speaker Martin of the House of Representatives said it may "well prove to be the greatest job of his career." In the light of the gigantic enterprises Hoover has generaled in the course of that career, this was claiming a great deal.

Reform of the federal administrative setup had been one of Hoover's most insistent projects when he was in the Harding and Coolidge cabinets. He returned to it repeatedly as President, only to be stymied by inertia and greed for patronage. That he should be entrusted with the job after the long banishment from public life made drama as well as justice. At this writing Hoover is devoting himself to the task with his familiar zeal and thoroughness.

A new appreciation of its former occupant also prevailed in the White House. It soon ceased to be a secret that in his second month in office President Truman sent for Hoover and that their meeting was mutually satisfactory. The two men are worlds apart in experience, intellectual scope, and grasp of world affairs. But they found that they had essential human decency and a certain guilelessness in common and it sufficed to make them friends.

At the Gridiron dinner, which I have already mentioned, Hoover's neighbor on the dais reached over and inscribed his speech manuscript: "With regards to a great American." It was signed Harry S. Truman.

The zooming spiral of the ex-President's new popularity was touched off by Truman's action in asking him to make an intensive world survey of food stocks and relief requirements. Through Dr. Julius Klein the White House reached the ex-President in the midst of a fishing holiday in the Florida Keys and Hoover, though fully aware of the physical hardships involved, accepted.

Accompanied by experts of his own selection—largely men who had worked with him on famine relief in the past—Hoover girdled the globe, flying 35,000 miles to gather data in twenty-five countries of Europe and Asia. Then, without a breathing spell, he flew another 15,000 miles and visited eleven more countries in a swing through Latin America.

The very gallantry of such an undertaking by an aging man somehow bridged three decades. It helped restore Herbert Hoover to his essential historical role as the most effective instrument of America's idealistic conscience and humanitarian instincts. Again he became, in the phrase of *Newsweek*, "the symbol of hope and sympathy" for a distracted world. Benevolence, rather than party politics, seems to be the real sphere of Hoover's genius.

2

On his way from his home in Palo Alto, California, to Washington in November 1932, President Hoover paused to inspect the great dam bearing his name then going up on the Colorado River.

It was only a few days after his decisive defeat by the Democrats. The sight of the magnificent structure in progress—"the greatest engineering work of its character ever attempted by the hand of man," as he described it next day—must have been balm for his battered spirit. Here was a solid, indestructible achievement, symbol of a thousand other visions he had translated into reality in the preceding twelve years. Here was something the snipers and vilifiers could not easily take away from him—something they could not easily twist out of shape with mockery and slander.

It had been a brutal, dirty, and largely one-sided campaign. His detractors had spared no vitriol or smear stuff. Those were weapons with which Hoover had no skill, even if his nature had allowed him to employ them. Besides, he was still President of the United States; in the sawdust of a political slug fest he found himself muscle-bound by his profound respect for the dignity of that office. He had responded to sizzling slogans and pyrotechnic accusations with sober arrays of facts and figures; he had answered lies with logic; he had, in short, been ineffective.

If it be a fault in a political leader to be hurt and insulted under a barrage of malodorous mud, then Hoover is blameworthy. For under his stoic exterior he *was* hurt and insulted. His good-natured comment on the election results covered a great sadness that was not wholly or even primarily personal.

Week after week he had heard himself denounced and mocked as a heartless blunderer, callous to the agonies of his fellow men. He had heard himself charged with direct personal responsibility for economic earthquakes that had been gathering force for the break-through ever since World War I. He, who had devoted his every waking minute during three terrible years to an uneven struggle with piled-up disasters, to breaking the force of their impact, to caring for their victims, heard himself blamed, amazingly, for "doing nothing."

So it must have been good to look at the huge skeleton of the Hoover Dam upon which flesh was being put. If there was one project in all the land which was clearly and overwhelmingly the product of Hoover's mind and energies it was this dam. He had planned it, fought for it, from his first day as Secretary of Commerce to these last days as President.

For ten years, as chairman of the Colorado River Commission, he labored as an engineer and a political leader to clear away the tangled underbrush of legal and technical obstructions, to obtain the necessary money, to adjust the conflicting claims to water rights of six southwestern states. He helped to draft the legislation authorizing the construction. He provided the basic plan, embodied in the Sante Fe compact after three years of negotiation, apportioning the interests of the six states in the harnessed river.

As the first engineer in the White House, he even passed on the technical plans. The project, when completed, would cost more than $400,000,000, but Hoover had so managed it that every dollar would eventually be returned to the Treasury. His Secretary of Interior, Dr. Ray Lyman Wilbur, negotiated the power contracts, the largest in all history, to govern the use of the dam.

It was against this background that President Hoover spoke next day to a gathering in Boulder City. "This is not the first time I have visited the site of this great dam," he said. "And it does give me extraordinary pleasure to see this great dream I have long held taking form in actual reality of stone and cement." He traced a little of the history of the undertaking and summarized its purposes.

"But the whole of this," he went on, "translates itself into something infinitely more important. It translates itself into millions of happy homes for Americans out under the blue sky of the West. . . . I hope to be present at its final completion as a bystander. Even so I shall feel a special personal satisfaction.

"The waters of this great river, instead of being wasted in the sea, will now be brought into use by man. Civilization advances with the practical application of knowledge in such structures as the one being built here in the pathway of one of the great rivers of the continent. The spread of its values in human happiness is beyond computation."

It had become custom to name such works of man for Presidents. There was the Roosevelt Dam for Theodore Roosevelt; the Wilson Dam, the Coolidge Dam. In those instances the use of their names was a gesture of respect; their interest in the structures had been casual. In Hoover's case it was vastly more, since he had fathered the project and nurtured it. In line with precedent, Secretary Wilbur therefore named the Colorado dam for his chief on September 8, 1930. Congress confirmed and legalized the christening when it appropriated funds for the "Hoover Dam."

But early in the reign of Hoover's successor a strange and almost incredible thing happened. Secretary Harold Ickes changed the name to Boulder Dam! Legalities aside, viewed in its purely human aspects, it was a piece of pettiness to make normal people blush. Having attached the ex-President's name arbitrarily to the Hoover depression, Hoover breadlines, Hoovervilles, certain men now tried to erase it from the Colorado River and other products of Hoover's labors, perhaps to keep the score even.

In some cases the ex-President's name, engraved on the cornerstone of postoffices and other public buildings begun in the Hoover administration, was actually chiseled out and the name of his successor inscribed in its place. Obviously Mr. Roosevelt cannot be blamed for such excesses of zeal on the part of subordinates.

Secretary Ickes is a man of many real gifts, the most conspicuous of which, alas, is his talent for bitter and long-sustained personal animosities. Having dug his fingernails into a victim, he did not let go for months, for years, forever. The very syllables of Hoover Dam seemed to upset him. One of his first acts in office, in May 1933, was to suggest to the Commissioner of Reclamation that the Colorado structure thereafter be referred to as Boulder Dam in his publications.

This he followed up by years-long efforts to maneuver the United States Board on Geographical Names into formally rechristening the dam. According to the New York *Sun,* this board deserves "a delayed citation for deft broken-field running" in evading the Ickes pressure. When the board disowned jurisdiction, insisting that its authority did not extend to man-made items in the geographical landscape, the Secretary obtained a ruling from the Acting Attorney General to the contrary. The board, however, stuck to its view. Meantime Ickes simply decided on his own authority that Boulder Dam was a more suitable designation; he attested the decision in a letter dated May 17, 1935.

When the dam was finally completed, Hoover was not invited to the dedication ceremonies conducted by President Roosevelt. His hope "to be present at its final completion as a bystander" apparently was adjudged presumptuous by those who issued the invitations. The embarrassed mayor of Boulder City asked Hoover to come anyhow, but the former President decided to stay away. "I somehow did not feel like making myself so public an exhibit of vindictiveness," he explained subsequently.

But in 1947 a Republican Congress and a Democratic President acted to wipe out that piece of political vendetta of which no one —including, one prays, its authors—was too proud. Congress passed and President Truman signed a bill restoring the original name of Hoover Dam.

Our ex-President has a Quaker-bred disinterest in worldly honors. He had watched the juggling of the name of the Colorado dam more in sorrow than in anger; in the aggregate of insult it was a very minor item indeed. But to his friends the official restoration of the name meant a lot. They had resented the arbitrary erasure as an attempt to anticipate the verdict of history on an American President. The action of Congress and Truman, and especially the eloquent approval it evoked in the country, seemed to them proof that the verdict was still history's secret.

3

Hoover would be less than human if he were not gratified by the clear shift in popular sentiment in recent years. Man's hunger for understanding and affection is the most human of our appetites and one in which vanity is not necessarily involved. Besides, uninterrupted abuse, as some of us have learned the hard way, can become more boring than offensive with familiarity; it tends to become so standardized and banal.

The increased flow of friendly letters; editorials which "thank God that the nation and the world begin to see in him a shelter in time of storm" (the quotation is from a clipping before me); the cordiality of Republicans who used to think him "poison"— such things are naturally welcome to Hoover after a steady diet of contumely.

He has a humility that is inborn, Quakerish—a humility that is not proud of itself. It is genuine, and therefore without alloy of mock modesty. Hoover has an engineer's respect for facts— including the quite obvious facts of his own special abilities. Surely no man could undertake colossal jobs like salvaging vast mining empires or feeding a continent or reorganizing a government with the confidence he always brings to big enterprises if he derogated his own qualities.

The implied vindication seems to have given a visible "lift" to his mood, an unwonted springiness to his personality. He radiates again the self-assurance of his most active periods. Meeting him after an interval of several years, he seemed to me actually younger looking, more buoyant.

He is tall, robust, and vigorous in appearance; his face remarkably unlined; his eyes clear and bright. He carries his years easily, as the expression goes. And mentally they seem to have deepened his intuitions and heightened his clarity of perception and analysis.

To hear Hoover discuss some subject to which he has given thought—and he is reluctant to enlarge on subjects where his knowledge is sketchy—is an experience. It is a little like watching a precision instrument in the hands of an expert. He cuts through non-essentials, avoids tempting tangents, and is almost at once at the heart of an issue.

The most helpful tonic for Hoover's spirits is big and vital work. It is the renewal of that tonic after so many years of denial that really accounts for his new buoyancy. The point is not that a "new Hoover" has emerged, as those who write of his "comeback" imply, but simply that the old Hoover can be discerned more clearly now that the fumes of obsessive hatred around him have thinned out.

When I pressed him to explain the kindlier winds of opinion playing around his head, he said with a characteristic chuckle, "Look at the last election—there's your answer." He was referring to the election of 1946, when America went Republican for the first time since the stock-market crash of 1929 and the Democratic party itself sloughed off some of its more disfiguring barnacles on the Left.

No doubt he was right. The change was primarily in the country, not in himself. Certainly he had not run away in panic from any of the reasoned opinions and instinctive attitudes which contributed to his loss of popularity. At no point had he adjusted himself to the propaganda pressures. Neither had he—and this is the greater temptation for men under political assault—taken up the role assigned to him by opponents yelling "Reactionary!"

The New Deal and Communist propaganda, he said in effect —I am not quoting his exact words, of course—had made him the symbol of depression, unemployment, hunger, and reaction. It made a kind of political shorthand, convenient and profitable. Why bother to deal with these things intelligently as social forces when you can personify them in two tiny syllables?

It is fair to say that Hoover has run for President three times since 1932. The candidates of record may have been Landon and Willkie and Dewey, but the attacks were centered on

Hoover. This was not accident but shrewd design. In every one of those elections the orders went out to renew the anti-Hoover offensive. As a flesh-and-blood summation of everything hateful, he was too valuable a political property to be discarded and forgotten.

Then, roughly around 1946, the symbolism began to function also in reverse. On the whole, he said, there was no more logic in the credit he was being given today than in the debits that were being loaded on him yesterday. He stands, after all, pretty much where he always stood. He did not catch up with the people; the people were streaming back to him after some hectic wanderings.

Hoover does not believe in what is called the middle way. He sees no special glory in a cautious centrism. You cannot compromise with evil and error and thereby achieve approximate virtue or approximate truth. The logic of the modern tendency to strike an average between two extremes, Left and Right, revolution and reaction, is altogether spurious. It may make good politics but it never makes good sense. A point equidistant from two admitted horrors may be as horrible as either of them.

I shall discuss Hoover's philosophy in another chapter. For the moment suffice that he remains what he was from the outset, long before the public had heard of him. He remains an individualist of a peculiarly American brand and an uncompromising partisan of personal freedom—not because that's the middle of the road but because for him it is the whole road, the American road.

Those who described Hoover in the years of his eclipse as an embittered man were making a natural assumption. They simply reflected their awareness that he had plenty of cause for bitterness. The people closest to him (most of whom *were* bitter) know that the assumption was false. They have told me that his temper was remarkably equable, his attitude even toward his most virulent detractors remarkably tolerant. At least one of them complained with some spirit about Hoover's inability to sustain a good healthy grudge; not without chagrin he described, for instance, the cordiality with which Hoover received Raymond Moley after that brain truster's retreat from Washington.

The fact is that Hoover was psychologically prepared for the worst even in his best days. Referring to the years just after World War I, when he was extravagantly idolized, he wrote one of his former secretaries:

"I could establish by contemporaneous documents that I was not fooled by all this adulation. While my period of popularity lasted for nearly twelve years, and my real friends never deserted me, I was at no time under any illusions. I knew that if a man continued in public life he was bound to create opposition . . . that he was fated to accumulate enemies; that in the United States the laws of libel and slander had little potency, and that the customary form of reply to sober argument was aspersions on one's parentage or assumption of corrupt motives. I knew from the bitter experience of all public men from George Washington down that democracies are fickle and heartless. When the ultimate bump came, I was well fortified to accept it philosophically and, in fact, to welcome it, for democracy is a harsh employer."

A reading of his speeches and writings since he left the White House bears out this claim that he took mass ingratitude gracefully. If he was bitter he did an amazing job of dissimulation.

His opposition to the New Deal was earnest, consistent, searching; taken together it constitutes the most impressive criticism of the Roosevelt era yet produced. But it showed little of the acerbity and captiousness to be found, say, in the Liberty League or Manufacturers Association critiques of the New Deal; and none of the name-calling that marred journalistic opposition to the Roosevelt administration. Here and there Hoover allows himself a dash of irony, which is native to his muted kind of humor, but always he prefers a barbed fact to a barbed adjective.

With every year after the removal of the presidential burdens from his shoulders, moreover, his addresses seemed to have more sparkle, less austerity. They were never really so dull as the Hoover legends pretend; certainly not so dull as they sounded, since the fault was so often in his delivery. Yet one needs only read a sampling of his speeches ten years apart to be conscious of a lighter tone and a defter touch.

True, the change which this chapter has tried to indicate is less in Hoover than in the times. It is still a fact, however, that there has been a distinct mellowing of his personality, a certain easing of his manner. Some of the reserve and the stiffness has crumbled. More of the affectionate, often droll, and always sympathetic Hoover known to his immediate circle is getting through to the American people.

It is this truly startling contrast between the private Hoover and the public image of him that provides the most useful key to his strange and contradictory reputation. It helps explain why so much of the absurd, far-fetched smear stuff manufactured by his detractors has stuck. It helps explain why, after more than three decades in public life, he remains almost unknown to his countrymen.

CHAPTER III

"No Politician"

ANYONE WHO WINS THE HIGHEST PO-litical prize this side of Paradise, the presidency of the United States, might reasonably be presumed to possess large, varied, and effective political talents. Yet the one thing on which Herbert Hoover's devoted friends and ardent foes seem agreed is that he is "no politician."

Whether that is an insult or a compliment depends on the tone and intent with which it is offered. In the mouth of detractors the allegation sounds like an important item in their inventory of the man's failings. In the mouth of admirers it sounds like clinching proof of a lofty character far removed from the vulgar trickeries, compromises, and public posturings of the political vocation. But on the core of fact there is something like unanimity.

We can accept the fact without accepting either set of implications. It is neither the gold of virtue nor the dross of defect, but contains a lot of both. It is simply an element reflecting and inseparable from Hoover's total personality; one of the defects flowing from his finest qualities.

Those who place most value on his public services have most reason to regret a flaw which has limited and thwarted those services by giving a great advantage to Hoover's more adroit opponents. To reduce the matter to the lowest commonsense denominator: lack of political mastery, even if explained by other and nobler attributes, is highly inconvenient for a man in politics.

There is little doubt that Hoover himself recognizes and very likely deplores the paucity of certain political gifts in his equipment. There is even less doubt that he would never knowingly pay the price demanded for some of those gifts in the coin of integrity as he conceives it.

The implication is not that our thirty-first President is deficient in sound political judgment or in the grasp of political trends and strategies. He is a shrewd enough judge of men and over-all situations; a thousand times he has demonstrated in vital matters that he is an executive, administrator and negotiator with few equals in his time. He has dealt ably and effectively with simple miners and complex prime ministers the world over.

Where he falls short is in dexterity—in maneuvering people and making "deals" on the political plane; in selling himself and his policies to the crowd; in playing on mass emotion.

The prototype of the American politician is all too familiar in our national life and literature. He is a hail-fellow extrovert, ready with the broad smile and the intimate slap on the back; more concerned about first names than first principles; with a flair for flattering the masses that is in part contempt. He thrives on publicity and controversy, and has more in common with the showman than the statesman, the actor than the activator.

This portrait has no point of contact with Herbert Hoover. It is pretty much a summation of what he is not himself and what he rather despises in others. Small wonder, therefore, that the garden-variety politicos feel out of place with him, at a loss to comprehend his ethical vocabulary. They are thrown off balance by the discovery that for him all their catch phrases about "public welfare" and "the people" have literal and inviolate connotations.

It is no accident that among Hoover's closest friends there are no real politicians. They include industrialists and labor leaders, journalists and professors, economists and diplomats, but no party bosses or political hacks. "He has been more successful with those high in industry, business, and labor than with men in public life," a White House associate attests. That was, he explains, because Hoover deals with a sure hand with genuine problems but seems unnerved by "cheap partisan politics."

Hoover knows better than any of his friendly critics that he is less able to sway man in the mass than individual men. The very calm persuasiveness of fact and knowledge which impresses a dozen men around a table depresses a mass meeting.

Inspiring blind loyalty in millions calls for a histrionic proficiency that is no part of his natural endowment. Where the born politician expands and luxuriates in the limelight, Hoover contracts and grows uneasy. His instinct is to run away from the applause which other men crave and stir up artificially.

"I have never liked the clamor of crowds," Hoover has remarked. "I intensely dislike superficial social contacts. I made no pretensions to oratory and I was terrorized at the opening of every speech."

Which is not precisely a glowing recommendation for an applicant for high political office. In extenuation it can be said that he was not applying. These candid words of self-appraisal, though set down much later, harked back to memories of 1919–20, when presidential boomlets, Democratic as well as Republican, were being launched for him. But the launchings did not have his consent and in some cases took place over his protests.

It was a time when America was doing handsprings of adulation for Hoover. His world reputation was tall, incandescent, dazzling. He had just returned from Europe, where he was universally regarded as a "savior," an American savior. For nearly six years his name had spelled bread and soup and medicine for tens of millions from Belgium to Poland, from Finland to the Balkans. It had spelled life, in the literal sense, for millions of children who were his special wards. The mechanism of his labors might be called Commission for Relief in Belgium or American Relief Administration; to the world at large, and the beneficiaries in particular, it was simply "Hoover relief."

Every nation had its particular hero, but Hoover was a hero to nearly all nations, victorious and defeated alike. President Wilson's halo was askew. Men such as Clemenceau and Lloyd George made friends at home by making enemies abroad. None of them, in the nature of the case, could expect anything but detestation in the beaten and humiliated countries.

Hoover was the exception, the sole exception, as popular in Germany and Austria as in Belgium or Serbia. His own country went overboard in expressing an overflowing pride in his achievements. It was in large measure self-acclaim: America saluted in Hoover the effective agent of its own most humane and disinterested impulses.

For a natural politician it would have been a setup made to order. For Hoover it was first of all a reminder that he must brace himself for the unwelcome "clamor of crowds" and a lot of terrifying speeches. The excitement and the hurrah shouting seemed to him almost an intrusion on his privacy. He evaded all of the decorations and as much of the plaudits as he could without being offensive. He accepted honors and invitations only in the measure that they might serve the interests of the great charitable works— especially the continuing feeding of children—still in progress.

In the years ahead he was able to overcome most of his terror in the face of speechmaking, but not his aversion to noisy crowds and shallow social contacts.

2

The late Charles Michelson, who from 1929 forward, as Democratic party press chief, made Hoover-baiting his life's work, classed Hoover among "the amateurs of the art of politics," as one who "did not know how to chart the process of overcoming opposition." And another veteran Washington reporter, Herbert Corey, who wrote a passionate book in defense of the President in 1932, remarked at one point that Hoover "seems not to have the least appreciation of the poetry, the music, and the drama of politics." He did not put on a good spectacle, that is to say, for the correspondents and the country.

Michelson had disparaged Hoover as a politician on an earlier occasion, before he was hired to disparage the man in general. The future President was then in his second term as Secretary of Commerce. In his Washington column, *Political Undertow,* Michelson wrote:

"The Old Guard of the Senate, most concerned as to who is going to win the next presidential nomination, don't like Hoover, don't understand him, and are doubtful of their ability to deal with him. . . . It is bad enough to have Coolidge in the White House with his reticence and the uncertainty where his favor lies;

but Coolidge at least is a politician, thinking their language, if he does not speak it much; *while Hoover revolves in a different orbit. . . ."*

In other words, Hoover was no politician, in the Old Guard and Coolidge sense. He was not, and by reason of his whole psychological make-up never could be, "one of the boys" at the public feeding trough. The professionals could never feel at their ease with this stern amateur and his strange moral fixations.

The Old Guard, Michelson went on to report, feared "the Hoover organization." By this they did not mean a party machine fueled by give-and-take patronage; that was an animal they could tame or bribe or beat. They meant the groups of devoted friends, not one of them an ordinary politician, who had shared Hoover's lifesaving adventures in European relief and his labors as Secretary of Commerce: "the small but efficient army . . . that still calls him Chief and is ready to mobilize at a word." How could they deal with supporters moved not by lucre but by love?

In due time this Michelson was to become as annoyed with Hoover's rigid code of conduct, with his special moral orbit, as the Republican Old Guard. Alone among political leaders, Michelson complained in his autobiography, Hoover took "campaign asperities" and smears on his motives seriously. He was not sporting enough to brush off ten years of filth-mongering for a fee as one of democracy's little jokes. Bennett Clark, Burt Wheeler, and others were also attacked by Michelson in line of duty and attacked him in return, but in "private" life they remained good friends.

"In fact," Michelson boasted, "all the Republican leaders call me by my first name, regardless what they have been saying on the Senate or House floor as to my wickedness. *We are all like actors who, having wiped off their make-up, forget the villain-and-hero struggles on the stage."*

Only Hoover failed in this test of political amiability, or shall we say cynicism. He was a maverick in that herd of actors. He did not play a villain-and-hero farce to win the galleries; he could not remove the make-up because he did not wear any. The lines he spoke were not written by some Michelson of his own. Hoover's opinions, enthusiasms, worries, and indignations were not stage effects but in deadly earnest. For him politics was not a game for stakes of power or loot.

All of which the authentic mummers on the political stage accounted a grievous fault and very nearly a left-handed insult, as perhaps it was.

A more charitable view on this failing as an actor is conceivable, however. A book on Hoover by Earl Reeves published in 1928, with only his performance as a cabinet member to draw on, voiced an opinion not much removed from Michelson's, except that it rang more like a tribute than an aspersion.

Hoover, he wrote, "does not 'dress up' his statements or his acts; he is not on dress parade before correspondents. . . . A 'press agent' would say that he overlooks a million chances no politician should overlook."

I ran across supporting evidence of the no-politician thesis from another source, significant as the spontaneous impression of an impressionable lady far from the American political scene.

Secretary Hoover had addressed a banquet of the National League of Women Voters in Baltimore, to convey the greetings of President Harding. A foreign guest, Lady Astor, was moved to offer some impromptu remarks. Having aimed some pleasantries at Governor Ritchie, she turned to—or turned on—Hoover. "Why, all Europe looks upon him as a sort of savior of mankind!" she announced. The fifteen hundred women in the hall thereupon exploded in applause, cheers, and a waving of napkins and handkerchiefs. The Hoover moon face blushed crimson; he was so palpably embarrassed that the demonstration was mixed with laughter.

"Look at him!" Lady Astor pursued her quarry. "He is not an ideal politician. He lacks the glad hand and the perpetual smile, thank goodness."

More earnest and academic corroboration is at hand. In a history of *American Parties and Elections,* E. M. Sait wrote of Hoover:

"Unfortunately, he had been trained as an engineer, not a politician; his contact with public life had been limited to his service as Secretary of Commerce under Harding and Coolidge; and his temperament, like his training, did not accommodate itself to the peculiar rules of the great game of politics."

According to another historian, Allan Nevins, Hoover "can run a department or a set of departments with great skill; he can organize forces to meet an emergency; but he cannot direct a party, lead a parliamentary group, or guide public opinion."

Random samples, these, of the prevailing view. Most of the men most closely associated with the former President, some of them for thirty or forty years, are inclined to concur in the general verdict, though taking violent exception to this or that specific detail. Hoover, one of them told me, has always seemed to him "out of character" in the political arena. Another said that "the ways of the politician were never quite clear, and, on the whole, distasteful, to the Chief."

3

Having conceded that he lacks popular glamor, they usually add in fond irritation that he would never do anything to remedy the matter. Worse, he would not allow them, his friends, to do so. I am indebted to Arch W. Shaw, one of the men who can be "mobilized" by the Chief at a word, for two illustrative anecdotes in this connection.

The first refers to an early stage in Hoover's political career. Some of his backers prepared for newspaper release a dramatic account of Hoover's role in the siege of Tientsin during the Boxer uprisings at the turn of the century. It was a true story and told, among other things, how the youthful American engineer had rescued a child trapped in the line of gunfire. They made the tactical mistake of showing the text to Hoover before releasing it. He read the story, frowned, slowly tore the sheets into the tiniest fragments, and dropped them into a waste basket.

"You can't make a Teddy Roosevelt out of me," he said quietly in a way that foreclosed argument.

The second anecdote refers to the pre-convention campaign. Hoover's associates were chronically worried by his tendency to keep "important callers" waiting, or even to refuse to see them, when he had what he deemed in his unpolitical way more pressing work on hand. Their concern came to a head when their candidate let an influential politico from a doubtful state cool his heels in the outer office and finally spared him only a few minutes on the way out to keep an appointment.

Arch Shaw was delegated to apprise the Chief of the political facts of life. Tactfully he tried to point out that Hoover had not always shown the kind of tenderness for the personal feelings of callers expected from a man seeking office. Hoover was impressed. He paced the floor for several minutes in thought. Then he turned to his friend abruptly and said,

"All right! But I'll kiss no babies."

Baby-kissing, obviously, was to him sign and symbol of the kind of clowning for votes and favor that went against the grain of his innermost nature.

From another source I gathered an episode of the same genre. On the eve of Hoover's first campaign, in 1928, some Republican stalwarts met in a New York hotel to outline a program for "humanizing" their candidate. It was a good program, but in the end they decided there was no use presenting it to Hoover—he simply would not lend himself to their bright public-relations stunts.

Always he edged away in alarm from the devices of publicity build-up because, he insisted, he did not want a synthetic picture projected on the public mind. The result has been profoundly ironical. What was in due time projected was a sort of photographic "negative," in which Hoover's whitest attributes somehow showed up black.

If Hoover had had a better eye for personal glorification—had he been a better politician—his heroic efforts to stem the tide of calamity in the early depression years would have provided a four-ring circus for an avid press. He might easily have dramatized his almost unprecedented burdens of office, his inhumanly long hours of work, his continuous struggle against political obstruction and pork-barrel demagoguery.

But he chose to work in semi-secrecy. Reporters had to dig hard for news which another President would have blown up for them with the help of battalions of public-relations officials at the taxpayers' expense. He insisted that his colossal exertions be played down instead of up, because he was anxious not to stampede an alarmed public into a state of disastrous panic.

Doubtless there was much justice in this view. But it is also true that he recoiled from the spectacular. At a time when Congress and the press were making him the scapegoat for tragic events not of his making, President Hoover told one of his secretaries, Theodore G. Joslin, "This is not a showman's job. I will not step out of character."

I believe he was wrong. The chances are that by this time he knows he was wrong. The presidency is very much of a showman's job. Leadership from the White House must appeal to the heart no less than to the mind; it must arouse faith and fervor and courage beyond cold calculations. In insisting that it was not a showman's job Hoover was rationalizing his distaste for showmanship and his ineptitude behind the footlights.

There was more than occupational irritation in the complaint of newsmen during his administration that he was not "good theater." As one of them put it:

"He has never, so far as my observations have informed me, attempted to add to his personal popularity by the usual methods of the guild. It would be physically impossible for him to put his right hand on the left side of his chest and repeat Fourth-of-July platitudes."

Yet it is clear in retrospect that greater personal popularity would have helped him over many a barrier when he, and the nation, needed most urgently to get to the other side. The usual methods of the political guild, however vulgar in themselves and unpalatable to a man of Hoover's type, have a democratic logic rooted in experience.

Let me tell in brief an episode which Joslin rightly tells in full. On May 28, 1932, three children came to the White House door. They had hitch-hiked from Detroit to the capital in childlike faith that the President could and would restore Charles Feagan, their father, to his family. Feagan, it appeared, had been jailed for stealing an automobile while in search of work.

"Three children resourceful enough to manage to get to Washington to see me are going to see me," Hoover said.

By the time the youngsters, a girl of thirteen and her two younger brothers, were in Hoover's study telling their story, Joslin had phoned Michigan and obtained the facts. Though it was not a federal matter, Hoover risked a promise.

"I know there must be good in a man whose children are so well behaved and who show such loyalty and devotion to him," the President told his visitors. "I will use my good office. You may go home happy." He gave them each a little gift. "Now run along and go straight home. Dad will be waiting there for you."

When Joslin was summoned to the President's study, he found him standing by a window, his back to the room. In a strangely thick voice he said, "Get that father out of jail immediately." The secretary pleaded for permission to give the facts to the press. Here was a perfect human-interest story at a time when his Chief's humanity was being impugned. But Hoover would agree "only to the barest announcement." "Let's not argue about it," he said. "That will be enough. That is all I will say about it. Now we will get back to work."

The thirty-first President represents the paradox of a great political figure who never became acclimated to the harsh world of politics and political publicity. Whether a debit or a credit in the bookkeeping of his career—and probably it should figure prominently on both sides of the ledger—this limitation was summed up aptly by an editorial in the *Christian Century* some years ago:

"Mr. Hoover was never in his proper place as a politician. His trouble in office was not merely that he lacked political dexterity; there is in him none of that glibness, none of the superficial good fellowship, especially none of those arts of accommodation which mark the political craftsman."

It is frequently said that Hoover failed to build a personal political machine. In truth he did not fail, because he never tried. He had a fanatic respect for the office of the presidency, regardless who held it, that made it impossible for him to exploit its powers for merely political advantages, to put politics ahead of policy. How to use the potent levers of patronage seems to be one of the things he never learned in his engineering courses.

I have been told the story—it is typical of scores of the same sort—of the two Midwestern senators who came to urge the appointment of a party hack to a vacant federal judgeship in their state. What were his qualifications, the President wanted to know. Chiefly, it appeared, that he was a Republican whose influence was badly needed in the next election. "Well, put that in writing," Hoover suggested with a straight face, and the interview was over.

In filling jobs he reached out repeatedly for experts, in conscious disregard of the political payoffs normally governing these matters. He ignored "deserving" party hacks in favor of men more suited to the particular duties involved. This he did knowing full well that he was making political enemies. His sense of duty simply outweighed his sense of party.

The very fact that he has a deep aversion to ghost-written speeches seemed to the typical politicians around him as old-fashioned as his collars. He has discarded his collars but not his allergy to literary ectoplasm. *Harper's* magazine, having published an article in which there was an allusion to his alleged ghosts, later, after investigating the subject thoroughly, made a handsome public apology.

Louis B. Mayer, the movie mogul, once offered to put his most expensive wordsmiths at Hoover's disposal in the hope of injecting some Hollywood glamor into his campaign speeches. Nothing came of the proposal. Be it ever so unglamorous, there's no speech like your own, Hoover insisted in effect.

He will read suggested drafts and accept correction of his own efforts. But his every address, article, or book (except where collaboration is frankly acknowledged) is the product of his own mind. Ideas to him are not externals, to be cooked to the taste of some current diners, but part and parcel of the man; though he admits readily that his dishes lack some of the vote-getting vitamins expert cooks might have injected.

He scrawls the first draft of a speech in pencil, edits it laboriously, then has it copied. Then he works on the typewritten version until it looks like a futurist design only his own secretaries can decipher. The result is set up in type by a printer—not any printer, but one accustomed to his corrections upon corrections—after which he will mangle half a dozen or more successive sets of printer's proofs before the final okay. From the penciled rough to the final reading draft there are rarely less than a dozen versions.

No, Hoover is "no politician." The first and the only office for which he ever ran was the presidency, and that, possibly, was the most serious error of his amazing career.

CHAPTER IV

Unknown Character Traits

THERE IS NEARLY ALWAYS A GREAT gap between the popular image of a prominent man and his private, everyday self. It was in this sense that G. K. Chesterton in his memoirs attested that almost every time he met someone he met someone else, "a private man oddly different from the public man." If this be true for celebrities generally, it is doubly true for political celebrities, since their reality is doubly falsified; by friends and dependents in one direction, by foes and competitors in the other.

In the case of Herbert Hoover, the distance between the man and his shadow on the public mind is astronomic, the contrast startling. Most of the prevailing notions about his personality and character are not simply untrue but in vital respects the contrary of the truth.

Americans as a whole think of him as austere, monumental, and rather cold. Few of them have any inkling of the warm, whimsical, and tender Hoover known to his intimates, the very human and deeply humane Quaker behind the solemn façade.

Even those who share his political and economic outlook are inclined to see him as an unemotional engineer-statesman rather than a sentient human being. They tend to credit some if not all of the myth of an impersonal, almost machine-like administrator. The myth happens to be a sad caricature of a sensitive, softhearted person who craves affection, enjoys congenial company, and suffers under the slings of malice.

The caricature cannot be blamed on hostile misrepresentation or on misunderstandings growing out of his years in the White House. It was fairly widespread long before he ran for President; one finds references to it in books written before 1928. Its main lineaments appear even in British memories of Hoover dating back to World War I.

"His personality never 'got across' in this country," an Englishman who worked with Hoover and therefore knew the falsity of the caricature, is quoted as saying by Earl Reeves. "He was always too busy to talk 'sweet nothings' to society ladies; and to those who only met him occasionally he seemed preoccupied, dour, reserved. . . . Those who did not understand him even accused him of a 'damping' influence in ordinary life. He was said not to be able to smile. Consequently, the people on the outside admitted his genius and his great work, and left it at that. . . . I should say that it was entirely his own fault, due to his shrinking from personal publicity."

The forbidding picture of Hoover painted by people who have never met him unfortunately seems confirmed when first you meet him. To this I can testify personally. Usually a second and a third confrontation, a process of acquaintance, are required before the wrappings of diffidence and inhibitions are peeled from his character.

We have considered some of his shortcomings as a politician. When traced to their source in his psychological make-up, they appear to derive from character quirks of which the public is largely unaware. They are, in fact, quirks so rare in a successful political figure that they seem exotic and a bit incredible.

The most striking of these, everyone who knows Hoover at close range asserts, is shyness—an almost physical shrinking from strangers, crowds, and demonstrations. He is at his best in talking informally, in a friendly setting. His voice is rich, his features light up, and he achieves an artless kind of eloquence. Once started, he can be fluent and epigrammatic, drawing easily on a phenomenal memory for the apt anecdote and episode and funny story.

But on the platform, or in front of a radio microphone, he seems to stiffen. His voice is somehow drained of color and his features of expression. Only the intense earnestness remains and it is rarely relieved by those sly asides and good-natured digs which enliven his intimate conversation.

Probably his upbringing in a stern and self-contained religious community that frowned on worldly pride, pomp, and pleasure has a lot to do with it. Yet most of us know Quakers who are the opposite of dour and reticent. Hoover's father, from all reports, was a man of lively spirit and cheerful, gregarious charm.

But whatever the cause, there is not much doubt of the fact. "The crown of that personality is shyness," one of Hoover's admiring biographers, Will Irwin, has recorded; Irwin was his classmate at Leland Stanford and his friend ever after. The emphasis on shyness is repeated by all who have tried to plumb the paradox of Hoover's nature.

"God's grace blended courage and faith and humility and tenderness in Herbert Hoover," John Spargo, the great liberal publicist, once wrote. And Lester Hinsdale, a college chum who remained a lifelong associate, in recalling his earliest impressions of the tall, slim, aloof lad he met on the campus, declared:

"He seemed shy to the point of timidity—rarely spoke unless spoken to. It wasn't until later, when we got into politics on the same side, that I realized how much it was possible to like him." He was referring, of course, to campus politics.

Those who encounter Hoover for the first time, unless they are forewarned or bring a saving insight to the experience, run the risk of mistaking his shyness for hardness. There is no glibness, no facile friendliness about him. He rates friendship too highly to dispense it lightly to all comers.

He is likely to wait with lowered eyes for the other fellow to start the conversational ball rolling. When people called on President Hoover in the White House there were sometimes long and embarrassing pauses while he waited for them to state their errands without ice-breaking preludes. He has not been known to comment on the weather unless the information was pertinent to fishing or crop prospects.

Hoover has little talent for small talk and persiflage—none at all for the back-slapping, glad-handing, first-name familiarity one associates with the political trade. And matters are hardly improved by his one intolerance, which is intellectual: an intolerance for beating around the bush, fuzzy thinking, and vague facts.

What seems outwardly a lack of cordiality is usually the result of excessive reserve. Facing people whose co-operation he needs, he does not attempt to "soften them up" with empty compliments before stating his problem. He prefers to appeal at once to their social conscience, if they have one, and to their intelligence. Joslin, having served as his secretary for press relations, found this aspect of the President's character a serious handicap.

"Hoover lacked the ability to win people over to his side by pleasantries, as other Presidents have been able to do," he wrote. "He either won people by the force of his arguments, or he lost them. He couldn't tell a funny story, talk about baseball, golf, poker, or participate in gossip.

"If he could do these things, it would have served him on many occasions, when he needed to line up people outside his circle of intimate friends. He could be a fascinating conversationalist among his friends when he put weighty issues aside, but he could not do it on demand. When advised to try, he would say: 'I have other things to do when the nation is on fire.'"

The element of pathos in this introverted nature is evident in Joslin's further comment: "Yet few of our chief executives ever desired companionship and friendship more sincerely than did Mr. Hoover." He went on to record that the President, far from withholding himself, was always inviting people for breakfast, dinner, week ends in his Rapidan camp. "During the four years there were almost 10,000 of these guests—to be exact, 9,769—most of them people who could be helpful to the country." And he quoted a comment by Mrs. Hoover when he had suggested that the usual contingent of guests be omitted from one of the Rapidan trips.

"Oh no," she said, "that would not do at all. He always wants to have people around him. The more he has, the happier he is."

The greater the pity, therefore, that breaking the ice in social intercourse with Hoover can be such a chilling process. But once broken "it is a warm and very human Hoover" who stands revealed. The quotation is from a friend who has known him for half a century or more.

I have been told of instances when men and women came to seek help—and Hoover is if anything too accessible—and departed crestfallen, sure that they had failed, only to discover later, in amazement, that he had acted quickly and generously on their particular requests.

A domestic scene in Hoover's New York residence was described to me by a newspaperman whose affection for the Chief borders on adoration. The man's children were paying Uncle Hoover a holiday visit during Christmas week. The ex-President was sprawled on the floor with his young guests with their new toys, and having fun in a big, hearty way. Just then a stranger who had an appointment was announced. Instantly Hoover "froze up." The formal, solemn Hoover whom the caller confronted did not seem even remotely related to the playful, uninhibited Hoover of a few minutes earlier.

This tableau pretty well sums up the self-consciousness that has stood like a wall between our thirty-first President and the great mass of the American people. Your typical officeholder shows the new visitor his best face first, and it is too often a false face. Hoover shows his worst face first, and it is always a false face.

Stories pointing up his shyness are legion. When his unexpected entry, or unsuspected presence, at some public function is discovered and evokes an ovation, he looks positively unhappy, like a guilty intruder.

Hoover accompanied President Wilson to Belgium in the course of the latter's European sojourn. A visit to the House of Parliament in Brussels was one of the incidents of that triumphal visit. The President's entry evoked a huge demonstration, of course. Hoover, according to an eyewitness, "waited until this was over and guests and members alike were preoccupied about regaining their seats; then he sidled in, turning his head away and making himself as inconspicuous as possible."

But he was observed. A second demonstration was touched off, as loud and prolonged as the one for Wilson.

"Hoover had no option but to turn and acknowledge the ovation, which he did with very evident embarrassment. He nodded, a bob of the head. It was the awkward, even painful, bow of a schoolboy of West Branch, Iowa. He blushed. The cheering continued. He shook his head, first at demands for a speech, and grew pinker. Then he shook his head as if to stop all this fuss, and grew red. Minute by minute he seemed to grow still redder: he was the most embarrassed man anyone had seen."

It was not entirely modesty that prompted him to avoid advance announcement when his duties as European relief head required a journey to some country. It was largely shyness, an attempt to escape the cheers and parades and banquets which would otherwise be his heavy portion.

The authorities in the new Poland, though of necessity apprised of his coming in 1919, were given less than twenty-four hours' notice of the event. It was thus that Hoover hoped to shield his diffidence against another instalment of adulation. The officials and the populace of Warsaw were heartbroken. A sentimental folk, they would have liked to stage a memorable show of their affection and gratitude for the American who had kept nearly a million of their children fed and healthy since the armistice.

What they did do, however, was superbly fitting and has become one of Hoover's most cherished memories. A deep love of children and a vibrant sympathy for their sufferings have always been at the heart of his character. In the reports of conditions in Poland brought to him at the end of the war he had been touched to the quick by a casual observation that there were no signs of children playing on the streets of Warsaw. It meant they were too weak, undernourished, and dispirited to play like normal children.

This day in Warsaw some fifty thousand boys and girls were mobilized hurriedly for a parade and review in his honor on an old race track. Hour after hour they passed before the foreigners in untidy formations, until twilight fell and after—boys and girls from three to twelve years of age, most of them in tattered nondescript clothes, but laughing, cheering, spirited. Here was the noisy living proof that a year of American care had taught the children of Warsaw to play and laugh again.

Thousands of them, having come directly from their American hot lunch, brought their tin cups along and waved them aloft like banners. Thousands of others carried improvised little American flags. Never before or since has there been a stranger, more moving parade, or one more happily in consonance with the nature of the man being greeted. The head of the French Military Mission, General Henrys, was so overcome with emotion that he left the stand to hide his tears. He paused to remark to Hoover in a choked voice, "There has never been a review of honor in all history that I would prefer for myself to that which has been given to you today."

At one point in the march of the tiny tots an astonished rabbit leaped out of the grass and started down the track. That was too much of a test for the decorum of the little paraders. Thousands of them broke ranks and dashed wildly after the rabbit, laughing and shouting. Having caught the animal, they brought him triumphantly to Hoover as their gift of love. Vernon Kellogg tells the rest:

"But they were astonished to see, as they gave him their gift, that this great, strong man did just what you or I or any other human sort of human being could not have helped doing under the circumstances. They saw him cry."

2

Few occupants of the White House have curtained their private lives from public scrutiny as conscientiously as the Hoovers. Mrs. Hoover, who died in 1944, was a gracious, good-looking, highly intelligent woman. She was constantly doing useful and noble things which, in the case of other first ladies, would have made the front pages. But except for her leadership in the Girl Scouts, which in the nature of the case involved public notice, she always remained in the background.

The two Hoover sons, Herbert, Jr., and Allan, are both personable and capable men; they have become independently successful in engineering, farming, and business. The Hoover grandchildren who swarmed over the President were as cute as any youngsters who ever graced the White House. Yet the private life of a Scottie named Fala in the subsequent administration received more press, screen, and radio attention than the private lives of the whole Hoover family combined.

The elder of the boys, Herbert, Jr., was taking post-graduate courses in the Harvard School of Business Administration while his father was President. One summer he decided to get himself a job. He did, with the Baltimore Electric Company—under the assumed name of Watson to avoid exploiting the paternal position. The secret leaked out, as secrets will, but the episode is symbolic of the family's attitude.

On another occasion, when Herbert, Jr., was offered a post on the West coast pretty obviously too big for him, he turned it down indignantly. "My father's name is not for sale," he explained to a family friend in describing the incident.

I have already alluded to the half secrecy in which Hoover shrouded his extraordinary labors as President. Whatever justifications he may cite, his deep-running shyness in considerable measure helped along the fantastic charge that he was "doing nothing" and that he remained "indifferent" to mass distress. It flourished in an ugly legend of presidential callousness because Hoover failed to convey to the American people a sense of his self-sacrificing devotion to the unequal struggle.

Another element in his make-up which has seriously limited Hoover as a political leader is his inordinate sensitiveness, which is in part the same shyness in another dimension.

He "was always the thinnest-skinned executive in Washington," according to Michelson. Under the kind of paralyzing partisan opposition he met after 1930, the Democratic press agent wrote, "A stronger President would have browbeaten the politically minded Congress . . . if necessary would have carried his fight to the people." But Hoover's "instinct in this untried field recoiled from conflict."

The ex-President's admirers put the matter more generously, in terms of his distaste and incapacity for public brawling. Where an Al Smith or an F.D.R. actually enjoyed a slugging match in the blazing limelight, Hoover suffered insults and abuse in stolid silence—without so much as a durable grudge. His ability to take brickbats without retaliation and his strange lack of vengefulness have been a continual trial to his friends.

He will defend his views and policies to the limit; his fifteen-year war on the New Deal improvisations and practices is an epic of fortitude under adverse conditions. But attacks on his motives and character are another matter. He is likely to treat them with a hurt contempt which the average American, being a combative animal, often misunderstands.

Hoover tackles gigantic impersonal forces that would scare the bravest men—whether it be the rescue of a starving continent or the rehabilitation of a wrecked world—with amazing self-assurance. Indeed he is happiest, most himself, when dealing with a great task or challenge. But personal feuds, double-dealing, mud-gunning contests leave him disarmed and rather bewildered.

To this day he finds it difficult to comprehend the magnitude and ferocity of the hatreds to which he has been subjected by detractors. He understands disagreement but not persecution, and is inclined to assign better motives to the persecutors than they merit. You can ignore attacks "if you're right with God," according to a Quaker precept. It is not a precept too well suited to the profession of politics.

Naïveté is a strange word to apply to a completely self-made and supremely successful man; to a man who amassed a fortune in international mining before he was forty and has dealt as an equal with the top statesmen and financiers, dictators, and potentates of his time; who knows the peoples and the nations of this planet more intimately than any other American in political life. But it is a word that obtrudes itself in appraising Herbert Hoover.

Despite piled-up evidence that politicians are not exactly incorruptible, he continued to deal with them on the level of disinterested patriotism which is his own natural habitat. He stared in pained disbelief when leaders broke their solemn pledges; when congressmen failed to keep confidences involving public welfare; when senators made agreements only to break them at the crucial moment; when reporters occasionally put a scoop above the national interest as Hoover saw it.

"Naïve? Why, the Chief even trusted the stock-exchange boys to live up to promises to reform their practices!" a man close to the ex-President summed up the matter for me.

His basic trouble, a member of the Hoover cabinet told me, is that he won high office at one big bound, without passing through the rough-and-tumble of precinct politics. Those lusty, rowdy, "humanizing" regions, he said, remained an alien and rather repugnant world to him.

Its free-and-easy morals, the opportunism that it took for granted, its guiding principle of the main chance, offended his Quaker assumptions. The denizens of that untidy world, even after they reached the top rungs, sensed Hoover's squeamishness—his moral snobbery, as one phrased it—and sometimes resented it in a very personal way.

The set of values to which Hoover has adhered must seem quixotic to men acclimated to ward politics. To put duty above personal interests and rectitude above tactics must seem to them even a bit pretentious. Mark L. Requa, another devoted Hoover-ite, once said, "I have seen Mr. Hoover at close quarters, in trying circumstances, and I never have known him to waver for a moment between right and wrong." A strange and alarming human phenomenon, surely, for people who trade votes and swing states and delegations!

3

In the period after Hoover's defeat for re-election he was often described—by people who did not know him—as a "lonely old man." That, like his supposed "bitterness," was unalloyed assumption. The truth is that few men have been so richly blessed in loyal friendships.

During World War II, when unexampled pettiness in high places kept him from contributing his special genius to the national effort, Hoover was one of the best informed men on public affairs notwithstanding. He was frequently in the know on secrets and strategies and plans reserved for the insiders among insiders in Washington. I know this from journalists who considered Hoover a primary source of information and briefing.

This happened because in every department of government there were men and women, Democrats and Republicans, New Dealers and Old Dealers, who had for the former President a devotion that can only be described as filial, since it is unsullied by political motivation or any other hope of gain. Though he solicited no information, they kept him apprised in confidence of developments which seemed to them of interest to a man like Hoover.

I asked several of the men who accompanied Hoover on his fact-gathering missions for President Truman in 1946 how he managed to gather so much detailed data in such a short space of time. Part of the answer, of course, was in Hoover himself: his encyclopedic backlog of knowledge, his careful planning in advance, his unerring instinct for the relevant question in interviewing experts.

But part of the answer was also in the extraordinary number of loyal Hoover friends deployed throughout the world. In virtually every capital, I was told, there were a few diplomatic, commercial, and military men, humbly placed or eminent, for whom a request from Hoover was a sight draft on loyalty on which they never defaulted. In effect he drew on the services of an unofficial but effective world-wide Hoover organization.

It is impossible to write about Hoover without writing about his friends. The Old Guard was justified in not discounting the "small but efficient army" that "calls him Chief." To have worked under Hoover once, it would seem, is to become a reserve officer in that army for life.

They are an amazing lot, these friends. Because of their intense devotion to Hoover, they are devoted to one another, forming a kind of loose fraternity. For each of them the Chief's suggestion has the effect of a command. On his part, he takes it for granted that they will drop whatever they are doing, at whatever sacrifice in time and money, to rush off on some errand at his request, paying their own expenses to boot.

I became increasingly aware, in talking to a great many of these friends, that I was dealing with fanatic initiates of a cult—a cult that rested solely on affection. John Spargo wrote some years ago: "This Herbert Hoover his friends love with a love that has in it some of the qualities of worship." A man who went through the Belgian job with him—and therefore, it goes without saying, has been available for Hoover jobs ever since—once declared, "Attachment to Hoover tends in the end toward fanaticism."

All of which sounds exaggerated until one meets his acolytes face to face. One of them, trying to convey to me how they all feel about the Chief, used the word "veneration." Another, when I alluded to his supposed coldness, all but lost his temper. "Cold?" he exclaimed. "How can anyone who inspires such loyalty and generates such warmth be cold?"

Once a year as many of these initiates as can manage it get together with him for dinner. There are usually more than two hundred. It is a purely sentimental occasion, a family gathering, and no one knows just how it got started. A "silver" loving cup made of high-quality tin is presented to the guest who has come the longest distance; it has been won by men from Europe and China, Africa and Australia. In 1946, because Hoover was away on the Truman food missions, the dinner took place without him, an empty chair at table symbolizing his presence in spirit.

Probably no one in our times, unless it be Franklin D. Roosevelt, has been under such terrific attack. But the Hoover cultists point out proudly that no attack has ever come from people close to him. A spate of vicious anti-Hoover books polluted the national atmosphere in the last year of his presidency—they were written, without exception, by people who did not know him personally, the ugliest by those who had not even met him.

Here, for the record, is a fact that should be known and savored: Hoover has a multitude of enemies but no ex-friends. It seems to me significant that those who know him best love him best.

In fifty years of business and public service not one major associate of Hoover has turned against him. Whatever the general public may think of him at any given moment, as the mercury of popularity moves up or down, the people closest to him have loved him consistently in all political seasons. They have loved him largely for those qualities of warmth, kindness and humor about which the mercurial public knows almost nothing.

4

I discovered, too, in talking to Hoover's lifelong associates, that their affection has in it a large element of protectiveness, an eagerness to shield him against a heartless world. His main fault, as they see it, is one which they discuss with pride: an excessive faith in people that leaves him defenseless against the grosser varieties of ill will. They feel that they must guard him against his inclination to credit others with his own disinterestedness, to underrate human cussedness and greed.

When they take it upon themselves to fight his battles, they get little encouragement from their Chief. Hoover has always been remarkably restrained, considering the towering provocations, in discussing the late Mr. Roosevelt, as distinct from Roosevelt policies. His friends have no such inhibitions. They are unanimous in the judgment that no American President has ever been so shabbily treated by his successor and tell tales out of school to support that opinion.

Their indictment begins with the day of Roosevelt's inauguration. Traditionally the departing President continues to be guarded by Secret Service men as long as he deems it necessary. That tradition was broken on March 4, 1933.

Anti-Hoover sentiment was then inflamed. Some crackpot act of violence was quite conceivable. But Hoover's secretaries were informed that on orders from higher up all his federal guards had been withdrawn, much to the chagrin of the Secret Service officials themselves. At the Washington end, railroad police, having learned of the insult, took on the job. At the New York end, the chief of police, having been apprised of the sad state of affairs, showed up personally and placed his own men at the ex-President's disposal.

Their indictment ends, of course, with the notorious refusal of the White House to use Hoover's services during the war, though he offered them repeatedly. Secretary of War Stimson, Secretary of State Hull, Bernard Baruch, and others, it is known, pleaded that Hoover's talents as an organizer and administrator be put to work. If only for appearance sake, as a gesture to historical seemliness, as a token of the national unity celebrated by all orators, some of them urged, our only living ex-President should be given a role in the country's effort. Pleas and arguments were of no avail.

Nevertheless, the Hoovers did not tolerate personal vilification of the Roosevelts in their home. One night some years ago a guest at dinner became heated and picturesque in assailing the character of F.D.R. Possibly he thought he was pleasing his hosts. Mrs. Hoover turned to her neighbor (on whose authority I have the story) and whispered, "Please, please talk loud and fast about something else, anything else!" He did, and his stentorian voice drowned out the Roosevelt hater.

From Raymond Moley's book of memoirs I excerpt the following:

I'm reminded of an incident that took place in 1938, when accidentally I happened to meet Herbert Hoover traveling to New York from California. We were sitting in a dining car together when the steward, who was not only an entrepreneur of food but of gossip, stopped by the table.

"Do you think," he said to me, "that Mr. Hoover would like to hear the latest story about Mr. Roosevelt?"

Hoover then gave expression to one of the most brilliant pieces of unconscious humor that I have ever heard. Glowering at the menu, he rumbled, "I don't like stories about Presidents."

It was not humor, unconscious or otherwise. It was genuine, and in character for the man who before he became chief executive himself once declared: "The presidency is more than an executive responsibility. It is the inspiring symbol of all that is highest in American purpose and ideals."

But to return to his friends. In bringing him a fierce, unswerving loyalty they are dealing in his own native coin. Without exception they recount examples of the Chief's quiet, unobtrusive, but vigilant concern for the men and women in his unofficial family. Not the big and dramatic things, but small acts typical of the man, like the one Edgar Rickard took such relish in the telling:

In the summer of 1946 Rickard was in a San Francisco hospital for an operation. Somehow Hoover surmised what his friend did not say: that he yearned to have with him his married daughter, then in Massachusetts. A few days later, on the eve of the operation, the door opened and there she was! Hoover, it appeared, had telephoned her and suggested that it would do her father good to see her. By the time she reached New York, Lucius Boomer of the Waldorf-Astoria, who was another in that circle of Hoover cultists, had arranged the transportation and at the San Francisco airport Hoover himself drove her at once to her father's bedside.

Another friend told me about the time when a subordinate in Hoover's Food Administration wrote an indiscreet letter in which he said something to this general effect: "To hell with the boys on Capitol Hill!" Naturally, the letter fell into the hands of a senator who immediately rushed to Hoover to demand that the man be disciplined. "When I appoint men I take responsibility—even for their mistakes," the Food Administrator informed him.

And nearly all of them alluded to a phase of Hoover conduct with which I must deal though I suspect he will not thank me for giving it notoriety.

There are people who practice sin in secret—but Hoover is that rarer individual who has reversed the process. When I was very young I thought up a character whom I called Bruce Prindle for a sketch published in the New York *Post* of those days. Prindle was a man with a fabulous reputation for wickedness who practiced virtue in secret and concealed this "weakness" with all the artifices other men use to conceal their vices. I had not thought that a generation later I would learn of a man who approximated that character in real life.

The fact is that Hoover goes to extraordinary lengths to hide his benevolences, especially from those who benefit through them. He avoids facing the people he helps, as if fearing to burden them with the obligation of gratitude.

"The beginnings of his extensive and well-concealed philanthropies," the late Will Irwin wrote, go back to his college days. Much of Hoover's summer earnings went for "loans" to classmates poorer than himself. When he began to earn his first substantial salary, in Australia, he sent a large monthly slice to his friend Lester Hinsdale for distribution among Hoover relatives and needy students. The fact was disclosed by Hinsdale; it's not one that Hoover would tell or admit. To this day he runs away from questions about his personal charities as if they were clandestine vices.

"For twenty years," Irwin wrote in 1928, "I have in California or New York observed men and women of our common acquaintance sliding smoothly through a crisis like a long illness or unemployment. Then, years later perhaps, I will learn by some impulsive confession or through the process of dovetailing two remote facts, that the solvent was—Hoover."

He will wangle a loan, a job, or some other help for distressed friends and acquaintances. Only years later, if ever, they may discover who was behind the timely miracle. Hoover is not the sort to greet waiters, servants, obscure clerks with breezy inquiries about the wife and kiddies. But he has frequently helped the wives and kiddies of such people in his orbit through trying periods on the quiet.

One instance of this concealed helpfulness was recounted to me in some detail, save for the names involved. My informant was made a confederate in a Hoover "plot." His role was to turn over money to a person in financial straits in such a way that he would not suspect the real source of the gift! As far as he is aware the recipient still does not know that the saving sum came from the ex-President.

The paternal concern which he extends to the people around him is implicit in one story out of dozens which have come to me. It concerns Admiral Lewis Strauss. Lewis, then a young college graduate, offered his services to Hoover when he was Food Administrator in World War I. The only job open, alas, was that of office boy. Lewis accepted. His abilities were too obvious to remain long neglected; he soon became personal secretary to the Chief. In that capacity he went with Hoover to Europe at the end of the war. When the European relief work was being wound up, Hoover had occasion to discuss weighty matters with Paul Warburg, head of Kuhn, Loeb & Co. But he did not forget lighter matters. At the end of the conference he said in effect:

"Mr. Warburg, I have with me a young co-religionist of yours of amazing abilities. If you take him into your organization in any capacity whatsoever, I guarantee he will be a partner in your firm in ten years."

Hoover was mistaken. Lewis Strauss was given a full partnership in Kuhn, Loeb within eight years. He did not know about the "guarantee" for a long time after he was hired by Warburg.

It is because this quintessential nature of Herbert Hoover—his private charms, his shyness, his naïveté, his generosity of spirit—is so little recognized; because his own aversion to "humanizing" publicity has interfered with that recognition, that I have ventured to call him "our unknown ex-President."

CHAPTER V

Hoover's Humor

MEN MAY BE FORGIVEN THEIR LACK OF a sense of justice or decency or probity or gratitude. They may be forgiven their lack of just sense. But they cannot hope for absolution in this world or the next if they lack a sense of humor.

Which is probably as it should be: a distillation of all human experience. I mention the matter not in complaint but to justify what follows: a whole chapter in refutation of the most shameful of all the failings imputed to our ex-President.

The tragic idea that in the geology of Hoover's ample spirit there is no vein of the comic is so widespread that unless arrested it threatens to become a permanent part of the American folklore. The idea happens to be a libel on a President whose sense of humor and ironic perceptions have saved him from the effects of souring experiences. They have helped him to live through locust years of abuse without permanent scars on his essential optimism or lesions on his love of the human animal with all its faults.

Humor, of course, is as personal a mark as one's fingerprints. No two people laugh in quite the same way or about quite the same things. Hoover's brand of the jocular and his fashion in laughing are authentically his own. Some, at least, of those who doubt his abounding sense of the funny, the grotesque, the whimsical in life are simply saying that it does not happen to match their own.

His cronies are familiar with Hoover's laugh. "A deep, rich chuckle which seemed to originate far down in his chest and psychology," one of them has described the indescribable, "and to lose most of its force in inner mirth before it came to the surface." It is the kind of laughter that shakes a man's frame with a series of inner explosions.

Part of the new, almost guilty, appreciation of Hoover shows itself in belated credit for flashes of humor and drollery. I have before me two recent articles about him, for instance. Both make the point—the discovery, I might say—that Hoover can laugh and make others laugh.

"He can bring himself," says one, "to display the deft, highly polished sense of humor he formerly reserved for a few of his intimates." By way of illustration both of them refer to a recent Gridiron Club address which sparkled with wit, and to some amusing comments on the philosophic implications of fishing in a recent broadcast.

The joke within the jokes in that broadcast is that Hoover was largely plagiarizing some hilarious observations on matters piscatory made many years ago—by Hoover. They drew laughs in their day and were forgotten, though they are on record in print. As for the Gridiron talk, his addresses under the same auspices during his four years as President are available in book form, under the title *Hoover After Dinner*. They make delightful reading, being as witty as the recent one, and in spots much wittier.

My point is that his humor is not a flower that bloomed in the winter of his life. It has flourished in all seasons, even when it was not sufficiently observed and appreciated. Why, then, has it been so little recognized?

The first answer is in the fact that his public services have been related primarily to serious and tragic events: to famines, wars, revolutions, economic earthquakes. His reputation, in consequence, has taken on some of the coloration of the events. Because the public came to expect portentous appeals and serious announcements from Hoover, it rarely caught the overtones of mirth.

The second answer is provided by Hoover's admitted deficiencies as an orator. Apparently he hasn't that special instinct for timing, pausing, and inflection without which the point of a joke is blunted before a large audience. Reading the texts of his speeches, one finds highly entertaining passages which must have been lost in the delivery, since so little of them remains in popular memory.

The third and most important answer is in the special quality of Hoover's humor, which for the most part does not conform to the popular patterns. It steers clear of slapstick, profanity, clowning. It does not sneer at the sacred or make fun of individuals. Hoover's wit aims at the mind and the imagination of the listener, not simply at his solar plexus. It is subtle, cerebral, and sometimes even literary—the kind of humor that must be savored and makes some demands on the receiving intelligence.

2

There is not exactly a belly laugh in his discovery that "all men are equal before fish," but its flavor lasts.

When the New Deal was loud in its concern for the Forgotten Man, Hoover quietly appealed for "the Forgotten Woman—the Statue of Liberty."

Having met Mahatma Gandhi in his most recent visit to India, he informed pressmen that "As a common mark of our humility Gandhi and I each carry a dollar watch."

In the period when Henry Wallace was tearfully plowing under little pigs, Hoover remarked, "It is the more abundant life—without bacon."

Apropos of certain agricultural proposals he paid his respects to "politicians who live by the sweat of the farmers' brow."

When the country abandoned the gold standard he summed up the event in one sentence: "We devalued the dollar 41 per cent under the hypnosis that if we reduced the length of the yard to 21.2 inches we would have more cloth to the bolt."

Because the wing flaps in the plane that took his mission around the world recently made a mooing sound when lowered, Hoover kept referring to the machine as "our faithful cow." Faithful Cow —a winking allusion to the Sacred Cow which had flown other Presidents—remained the name of the plane to the end.

Not the kind of humor, I admit, that has 'em rolling in the aisles, but the kind that lingers in memory and reveals new depths of meaning on repeated savoring.

"Incidentally," Hoover once interrupted a statistical analysis to remark, "when I comb over these accounts of the New Deal, my sympathy arises for the humble decimal point. His is a pathetic and heroic life, wandering around among regimented ciphers trying to find some of the old places he used to know." The pathos of that old-fashioned dot in the brave new world grows on one. "Those who judge progress by the size of figures will agree," he added on the same occasion, "that great improvements have taken place in the national debts. . . ."

In his second campaign President Roosevelt rebuked critics of his economic improvisations with a story. He told of a nice old gentleman who fell off the dock in 1933 and was grateful to be rescued, but now, three years later, was complaining because he lost his hat in the process. The parable evoked a nationwide guffaw of laughter.

Hoover's retort went unlaughed. But without venturing into the science of comparative humor, I submit that it was at least a match of the Roosevelt story.

"I have some inside information about that incident," Hoover said in Philadelphia. "The old gentleman was surreptitiously pushed off the dock in order that the hero could gain the plaudits of the crowd as a lifesaver."

The allusion, of course, was the refusal of President-Elect Roosevelt, in the months before his inauguration, to co-operate in preventing the bank panic. The image of the old man being shoved into ultimate danger to heighten the value of the rescue deserves to rank among the gems of political repartee.

If it is a token of the comic spirit to detect lurking laughter under the surface of the commonplace, Hoover qualified in the course of a speech in St. Louis in December 1935. He was commenting on the Administration's tendency to abandon experiments halfway and launch new ones. In that connection he had found a revealing press dispatch which he shared with the audience.

Datelined Los Angeles, November 28, the dispatch announced that a street had been christened New Deal Avenue. "The new street," Hoover read with relish, "is located near the Tugwell resettlement colony. . . . Because New Deal Avenue comes to a dead end, the county supervisors will arrange ample room . . . to turn around."

It was in the same address that he pictured how the distressed were being buffeted by the growing bureaucracy from the FERA or PWA to SERA, then to CWA and FRSC, back to FERA and over to WPA. "When all are buried," he concluded, "their spirit will live on in IOU."

He was not the only one to press a few chuckles from the proliferating agencies, but he alone among the chucklers offered a practical suggestion for the occasion. Observing that four letters of the alphabet seemed to be missing in the array, he proposed establishment of "The Quick Loans Corporation for Xylophones, Yachts, and Zithers, after which the alphabet of our fathers will be exhausted—but of course the New Russian alphabet has thirty-four letters."

The speech in which this practical step was recommended was delivered in New York on November 16, 1935. The subject was not exactly frivolous: "The Consequences of 'Economic Planning' and Some Remedies for It." Yet I dare guarantee that anyone who thinks Hoover has no sense of humor will be cured of that misconception by reading it. I touch on a few more of its light moments lightly:

Hoover said at the outset: "I explained [to your committee] that even if I were simply to read the Ten Commandments it would be interpreted as critical by the Administration in Washington." Plunging into the subject, he charged that the miracle billed as "Planned Economy" had become in practice "Planned Extravagance"; now another glittering panacea was being advanced, the Third Economy, and he added, "I trust it is not so expensive as the others."

Having outlined various categories of criticisms directed against White House planning, he pointed out that "Any of these views could be confirmed by the writings of a dozen charter members of the New Deal who have now turned against the order." As to the huge blank checks being voted by Congress, he conceded that the system did have one virtue: "This method of planning avoids exhaustion from congressional debate."

The transfer of relief distribution from local and state authorities to a centralized bureaucracy in Washington, he noted, "has added nothing to the security and care of those deserving in distress—except expense." Though opposed to the vagaries of "managed currency," he admitted that "as potent devices for destroying confidence they have merit." The stock-market boys, he suggested, were already "peeking into that Bluebeard's cave," inflation. The picture he drew of our silver policies would be funnier if it were not so sad. No doubt it was "part of our good-neighbor policies that we have joyfully subsidized every foreign speculator in silver. . . . Apparently 'Planned Economy' aims to become a bi-metallic Midas."

It was one of those supposedly dull Hoover speeches loaded with facts and figures and, dullest of all, reasoned argument. Its purpose was not to amuse or bemuse but to enlighten. Yet in reading it one strikes veins of irony and big nuggets of humor. This is more or less the case with all his speeches. The intention of their humor is likely to be to make listeners wince rather than guffaw.

When Hoover described "the effervescence of righteousness which bubbles through the intoxicating waters of the finer life" projected by New Deal theorists he could have had little expectation of shouts of glee. But there is in it a delicate ribbing of pretentiousness that rates as comic in my book. It reflects what Will Irwin, who knew his Hoover through and through, called "a sense of humor too delicate for anything but literal quotation."

That same delicacy I find in the ex-President's discussion of certain policies which were urged on his administration: "We could have adopted the methods later adopted by the New Deal. These have proved wrong ever since they were first tried by Emperor Diocletian. And he was about the last of the Roman emperors." Or in his aphorism: "Demagoguery abhors arithmetic, except when it adds zeros to its expenditures." Or to his commentary on those who give lip service to American principles while smashing them in practice:

"All this reminds me of the small girl who said, 'Mother, you know that beautiful jug you said has been handed down to us from generation to generation?' Mother replied, 'Yes, Ann, what of it?' And Ann answered solemnly, 'This generation dropped it.'"

Those in his audience at Colorado Springs on March 7, 1936, who knew as a fact that the speaker was devoid of a sense of humor, may have been a bit disturbed in their belief. Hoover was celebrating the march of inventions in our time. He listed the steam engine, electricity, the automobile, telephones, airplanes, et cetera, then cracked quietly, "I might include the adding machine but its present use by the New Deal raises doubts as to its contribution to the welfare of mankind."

3

In any "documentary" biography of Hoover two curious documents quite unlike the rest will have a place.

One was composed in his Palo Alto home soon after he returned from Europe in 1919. America seemed determined to frustrate his plans for a quiet life with his wife and two sons. Urgent invitations to speak, to accept degrees and awards, to dedicate things and to grace assemblages poured in upon him in unending flood. Hoover decided to say No to all of them in a statement—again I quote biographer Irwin—"whose humor proceeded from its mild burlesque of an engineering report or a college syllabus."

With mock solemnity he drew up a five-part set of rules. Rule (a) in Part the First attests: ".That I will reply to no telephone calls, and my secretary has directions to explain in the most amiable manner that I am spending a month with two vigorous small boys. . . ." Rule (b) is "solely for his own good" and specifies that he will not read any communication longer than one page. Rule (c) by contrast is "for the public good," and provides that he will decline the honor of making any and all speeches.

There were serious passages in the document; Hoover rarely indulges in humor for humor's sake—for him it is functional. In particular he used the burlesquerie to review some of the jobs ahead of him, such as continued feeding of some four million children in eastern Europe. And he concluded with this explanation:

"I offer this intimate disclosure of my private affairs in order that no further inquiry on this subject will be needed, and so that it may be seen that I contemplate no mischief against the commonwealth. . . ."

The second document he wrote—again in the mock-serious style of a formal report—some months later and distributed to correspondents troubled by some of the early partisan accusations against him.

"I have noted your feeling that I should answer some of the solemn discourses on my private life and crimes," it began. "Some of the things that have been said of me cause me a sense of financial oversight. For instance, I have made quite careful inquiries and I regret that so far I cannot find:

(a) The $10,000,000 I am said to have made in my early youth, or even middle age, or altogether, or any respectable part of it.
(b) The investments I am supposed to have in Great Britain.

Like the Negro porter who was asked to change ten dollars, I am grateful for the compliment. I am sorry that these funds do not exist, for they would be useful for Children's Relief.

He then announced that he has also given deep thought to certain other items. Is he a British subject or did he ever apply for such citizenship? "No," he replied. "Many generations of persecuted Quaker ancestors rise in their graves at such a discovery. They should remain quieted, however, for no Californian could live three months in London climate and become a British citizen if he knew it."

On another of the charges:

(c) I gather also that it is moral turpitude to have managed large enterprises. The hope to rise from the ranks of labor to the ranks of management will, however, probably not be crushed from the heart of the American boy even by this onslaught.

In the first years of the Belgian Relief undertaking, Hoover shuttled continually across the submarine-infested and mine-strewn North Sea between England and the continent. To fill the interstices of time in those crossings he wrote the story of his early life in considerable detail for his young sons. While the manuscript is serious enough in content and intent, it abounds in foolery of the sort that must have delighted the hearts of growing boys. I can cite only a few examples.

In recounting his experiences as an apprentice surveyor during college vacations, he told his sons of his weeks and weeks on horseback:

"In those long mountain rides I arrived finally at the conclusion that a horse was one of the original mistakes of creation. I felt that he was too high off the ground for convenience and safety on mountain trails. He would have been better if he had been given a dozen legs so that he had the smooth pace of a centipede. Furthermore, he should have scales as protection against flies, and a larger water tank like a camel. All these gadgets were known to creation prior to the geologic period when the horse was evolved. Why were they not used?"

When he tested another means of transportation a few years later, in crossing the ocean for the first time, he again had some difficulties. "The White Star ship of 7,000 tons," he confided to the manuscript, "proved unable to overcome the waves to my satisfaction."

As a sidelight on life in the Mt. Leonora district in wildest Australia in his first year as head of a mining enterprise, he recorded the following:

"The sodden conditions of life at 'The Gwalia' were perhaps expressed by a foreman who had a habit of getting drunk about once a month. Good foremen were too scarce to discharge for such sins and on one occasion when I reprimanded him violently he said, 'Well, if you live in this place you just have to get good and drunk once in a while.' I inquired how he knew when he was 'good and drunk.' He replied, 'When Mt. Leonora whisky begins to taste good, then I know.'"

4

Let's leaf through the Gridiron addresses, eight of them delivered during his administration. The club is composed of top Washington correspondents. Its semi-annual dinner is dedicated to sticking pins into public figures, in particular the current President, through lively skits and songs. As a test of a President's susceptibility to humor, both at the receiving and dispensing ends, it has no equal.

For fear of floating this book off into space with excessive persi-flage and pleasantry, I shall limit myself to a very few samples of Hoover's contributions. They may suffice to convey the general idea that the lighter style is no recent eruption.

In the very first of those addresses President Hoover acknowl-edged that he had received "much political education from those dinners." He had found the press representatives helpful in unex-pected ways, he said:

"For instance, they daily assist me beyond my greatest hopes by their suspicious research work in new implications for my most carefully formulated phrases. I discover by the time an idea of mine has filtered through the clear and crystal minds of one hun-dred different correspondents that particular idea throbs with a sense of courage and public service, that it has sinister implica-tions, that it is impractical, that it spells malevolence, that it is weak and vacillating, that it is filled with political bias, that it bristles with idealism, sanity, and progress. When I take refuge in silence, the gentlemen of the press again assist me by the work-ings of their own speculative minds to the extent of Column 1, Page 1; and promptly extend to me the privilege of denial. I do not wish to seem ungrateful for this co-operation, but I decided some time ago that I ought not to destroy the confidence of managing editors in their correspondents nor to dull the spirit of imaginative writing."

Another of these speeches he launched by explaining "why Presidents seldom worry about anything." Presidents, he said, "have so many troubles in the closet or stowed away in the icebox that when one of them gets tiresome they can always send for another, and by great variety maintain interest and a high cheer-fulness of spirit."

Kidding the correspondents gently on a propensity to make big stories out of little facts or rumors, Hoover said at another of these dinners: "One's taste for Roquefort cheese can be perma-nently destroyed by a microscope. And a cheese mite amplified a few thousand times is one of the most sensational and terrifying beasts exhibited to man."

In December 1930, having sat through an evening of typical Gridirony, Hoover, as the final speaker, said that some parts of the program reminded him of a rhyme current in his youth, and proceeded to recite it:

> *"If all good people were clever,*
>   *And all clever people were good,*
> *The world would be nicer than ever*
>   *We thought that it possibly could.*

> *But somehow, 'tis seldom or never*
>   *The two hit it off as they should;*
> *The good are so harsh to the clever,*
>   *The clever so rude to the good."*

He followed this with a fanciful description of the "joyous enterprise" government would become if it were revised to suit the rightful needs of the press and its correspondents. Official life, he said, would be limited strictly to news-producing materials; and government would be dedicated to the generation of excitement. Only officials "who start something by way of attack and combat" suitable for the front page would be tolerated. Opportunity would, of course, be given for "denial on the inside page provided the denial is peppy enough to maintain the combat." At least two fights would have to be developed daily, "one for the afternoon papers and one for the morning . . . on a strict schedule, with advance release."

My own favorite passage in these addresses is Hoover's discourse in April 1931, on "the abuses which have arisen in the land from bells." It is a minor classic of humor, yet alas too long to be quoted in full here.

He described the proliferation of bells in modern life as "a malevolent force . . . which invades liberty, stimulates grief, terror, and hate; it is more all-embracing, ever-present, nation-wide, and terrible than the Power Trust." Yet, he complained, no champions of the people have arisen to combat this menace. Once upon a time we had only the spiritual church bells and the sweet-voiced cowbells. These have declined; in their place we have ten million telephone bells—and "there is no noise in the world that so fills one's heart with alarm and foreboding as the telephone bell." This, he added, "is especially true for officeholders, for good tidings always come by mail." The telephone bell breaks honest sleep and "interrupts free speech."

In this wise he analyzed alarm-clock bells: "To interrupt a man's sleep and jerk him from the realm of real bliss into the cold realities of another day is a greater invasion of human liberty than any yet wrought by the Eighteenth Amendment." Then there were the front-door bells; the bells on "Stop" and "Go" signs; ambulance and fire bells—each an insult to man's nature and a limitation on his liberty. He recommended that the Gridironers take up this issue which, trivial though it might seem at first glance, seemed to him "more important than a vast number of reforms now agitating Washington."

From which it must not be deduced that Hoover underrated the correspondents. He appreciated that their dinners contributed to national unity "by rubbing the salt of wit, the vinegar of hyperbole, and the iodine of satire into the raw wounds of politics." "Their streams of humor," he assured them, "refresh the political soul and their streams of ridicule quench the fires of ambition. I would not say that the Gridiron Club is the gyroscope of the ship of state; nor that it pours oil upon troubled waters; but it does serve to keep humility in the crew."

In the last of those addresses, a few weeks after his overwhelming defeat by Roosevelt, wit was not excluded. "We had a good fight," he said of the campaign, "and when our opponents recover from the glow of victory and undertake to perform the sad rites of burying their dead promises, that will be another story."

Unavoidably I have resorted to published speeches in refuting the grotesque libel that the thirty-first President lacked the golden gift of laughter and the silver gift of satire. Those who know him at close range, in his relaxed moods, need none of the random proofs I have strung together in this chapter. To Hoover life is real and earnest, but it is life multifarious, as keenly aware of laughter as of tears.

CHAPTER VI

The Quaker Heritage

MEN RARELY OUTGROW THEIR CHILD-
hoods. Herbert Clark Hoover was born on August 10, 1874, in the
nearly all-Quaker hamlet of West Branch, Cedar County, Iowa,
the second son of the village blacksmith. The most vital elements
in shaping his character and his emotions are implicit in that
statement.

His life is rooted physically in the soil of the pioneer West of
the last decades of the last century and spiritually in the soil of
his God-fearing Quaker forebears. At no point did he feel impelled to rebel against his origins, as so many men must; or to
resent the rigid disciplines they imposed upon him. He grew
sturdily and whole, without lacerating inner conflicts.

Because he was poor and early orphaned, he had many homes.
But they were always Western homes, always Quaker homes, and
never lacking in human warmth. Hardships and sorrows were
part of his lot as a child, but not loneliness. He was continually
in the bosom of a large and affectionate family, and part of a
religious community in which friendship was not only a central
precept, but a normal practice. He is one of those fortunate people
who "belong" in a country and a family and a tradition, and draw
strength from their wholeness.

Not until he was twenty-three, and on his way to take full
command of a mature man's job in a distant land, did he set foot
east of the Mississippi. In the busy, fast-moving years that followed

he was destined to plumb this planet—its breadth in ceaseless travels, its depth in ceaseless mining operations. But before that crucial crossing of the Mississippi, in his most pliant years, he knew only a childhood on the Iowa prairie, a boyhood in rugged Oregon, and a young manhood under the California suns.

In short, he was of the West, born and bred. Its great horizons, its venturesomeness, its liberalism and tolerance were his by natural right. Even his physique—tall, tough, equal to the most punishing exertions—bespeaks the pioneer West. So does his love of the outdoors, his facility for camp life and roughing it.

The epic era of the opening of the West was tapering off at the time Hoover was born. The last free land in his native state gave out in 1875, a year after his birth. But the men and the moods of that era were still everywhere around him. Already the covered wagon had romantic associations; even the stagecoach was beginning to fade out. But most of the elderly Hoovers in the village of West Branch and surrounding farms had come there by prairie schooner only twenty-one years before his birth, and their talk was full of that audacity. His mother's family, the Minthorns, had come in the same fashion from far-off Canada seven years later. A Hoover uncle drove the stage between Davenport and Iowa City. From his own kin and others he heard fabulous accounts of the westward trek bristling with Indian skirmishes.

The social democracy of the West into which Hoover was born was not a condescending theory. It was a living fact, inherent in a new continent where men perforce relied on their own strength, met common dangers by pooling those strengths, and were not divided by inherited rank or privilege. The West nurtured a new people open to new ideas, in which the individual had physical and social elbow room for development.

The Rebecca Hoover who was Herbert's great-grandmother was born at the turn of the century and lived until very near its close. When she died in 1895 Herbert was going on eleven. To him, as to the rest of her numerous progeny, she seemed a wonderful living link with the beginnings of the American adventure in empire building. From all accounts she was the pioneer matriarch of tradition in the flesh, humorous but stern, strong and energetic and wise in the lore of the open spaces. The kind of great-grandmother, one might say, whom a typical American boy would have chosen enthusiastically as progenitress.

But Rebecca was more than that—a personification of the future President's dual heritage—for she was also the traditional Quaker matriarch, pious herself and strict in monitoring the piety of her offspring. She held herself responsible for the mundane morals and the immortal souls of three generations of her seed.

Of Rebecca it is reported, perhaps in exaggeration, that she opposed the screening of windows against insects as somehow a defiance of the Lord's intentions. She inveighed against worldliness even in its mildest forms, such as noisy play or immodest deportment, let alone its satanic expressions in greed or selfishness or tardy charity.

One may surmise that her grandson Jesse, Herbert's father, named for her own husband of blessed memory, gave the matriarch some unquiet moments. Though deeply religious, he was a lusty and life-loving sort, a good mixer with an ear for gossip. A mechanical bent had induced him to abandon farming for a smithy, to which in his last years he added a stock of new agricultural machinery.

But Herbert's mother, Huldah Minthorn, no doubt evened the family score in Rebecca's aging eyes. Huldah had attended a Quaker finishing school and taught school briefly and was rich in book learning for her time. The people of her faith held education in great esteem, whether for men or women, ranking it among the primary virtues. More important, Huldah was thrice blessed as one close to God, whom the spirit moved often and beautifully in Meeting.

Her shy spirituality made her the butt of her more worldly husband's affectionate chaffing. After his untimely death she became almost wholly the instrument of her spirit, and much in demand in Quaker communities throughout Iowa for the beauty of her preaching.

Through his mother Hoover inherited a strain of French Huguenot blood. For the rest, his ancestors on both sides were of the Society of Friends, as the Quaker faith is officially called, as far back as they could be traced with assurance. Andrew Hoover, a Marylander who moved his brood to North Carolina about a century before Herbert's birth, seems to be his first authenticated forebear. It was Andrew's son John who with his family and neighbors struck out for the Western Reserve in 1802, breaking ground near Miami, Ohio.

Half a century later, in 1854, Jesse Hoover and his wife Rebecca, then the heads of the family, made the journey by wagon to Iowa to carve out farms for a flock of tall sons. Nearly always the Friends migrated in large groups, since their religion requires a community of the faithful for its fullest expression. A considerable part of the population of Cedar County was made up of Hoovers and the multitude of their relations by marriage.

They wore the Quaker gray and spoke the plain speech filled with "thees" and "thys," and their days and years were centered around the meetinghouse. To all of them life was serious, without margins for frivolity and self-indulgence; and "doing good" was its main justification. In the Quaker view man is born pure, though the world corrupts him, and therefore even the wicked must be cherished and succored. The Quaker code enjoins service to others not as a duty or a sacrifice but as a God-given privilege; in it charity ranks above prayer and is, indeed, a sort of communion with God—with the "God" part in all mortal men.

Theirs is a faith that has neither fixed creed nor rigid sacraments. Its religious imperatives are of the moral rather than the theological order. Founded in England by George Fox in 1652, the Society of Friends took its name from the scriptural injunction, "Ye are my friends if ye do the things which I command." And of the things He commanded the Friends regarded one as supreme: "This is my commandment, that ye love one another."

Friendship, goodness, help to the helpless, a clean life filled with noble thoughts and deeds—these come closest to defining the Quaker ideal. From which it is apparent that this faith puts more store by good works in this life than eternal bliss in the next.

For the true Quaker there is no sharp break between things secular and things sacred; no interval between hardheaded business, let us say, and soft-hearted religion. Worship is not a Sunday soothing syrup for consciences snaggled by weekday necessities. Honest weight and fair dealing figure in Quaker sermons and traditional maxims alongside more abstract principles. It was George Fox, the founder, who explained that his Quakers prospered in business because "people came to have experience of Friends' honesty and faithfulness, and found that their yea was yea and their nay was nay; that they kept to a word in their dealings, and that they would not cozen or cheat them." He exhorted the members of his society to live like Christians—"so a child shall trade with you as a man because of the equity, and people shall not be afraid of one cheating the other, or destroying one another."

Though it arose as a protest against formalized religion and the pomp of hierarchy, Quakerism in time built a formalism of its own out of its renunciations. Its detestation of ceremonial found expression in ceremonials of simplicity in clothes, demeanor, speech, and worship. But the order remained a church without churchmen, a flock without professional shepherds. Since every human being partakes of the Godhead through his own better self, he needs no mortal intermediary for communion with the Almighty.

2

Worship in the unadorned meetinghouse is silent meditation among loved neighbors, interrupted only when some Friend is moved to speak on matters earthly or divine. The individual man or woman with the greatest moral insight and the God-given eloquence to communicate it becomes a minister in effect, without acquiring titles or a privileged position vis-a-vis God. Long silences are as much a part of the worship as the eloquent preachments and discussions.

In his whimsical fashion Hoover in his maturity recalled that this mode of worship was hard on children, from whom it demanded self-control beyond their fidgety years. "All this may not have been recreation," he attested, "but it was strong training in patience."

Charles Lamb once gave a description of Quaker worship which is as apt today as it was on the day he set down the words:

Reader, wouldst thou know what true peace and quiet mean; wouldst thou find a refuge from the noises and clamors of the multitude; wouldst thou enjoy at once solitude and society; wouldst thou possess the depth of thine own spirit in stillness, without being shut out from the consolatory faces of thy species; wouldst thou be alone, and yet accompanied; solitary, yet not desolate; singular, yet not without some to keep thee in countenance;—a unit in aggregate; a simple in composite;—come with me into a Quakers' Meeting.

The ethical principles of the Friends are not presented as divine commands surrounded by threats but in the guise of questions; of "queries" appealing to the Christian conscience and implying their own answers. For example:

Are the necessities of the poor, and the circumstances of those who may appear likely to require aid, inspected and relieved? Are they advised and assisted in such employments as they are capable of; and is due care taken to promote the school-education of their children?

Are Friends careful to live within the bounds of their circumstances, and to avoid involving themselves in business beyond their ability to manage; or in hazardous or speculative trade? Are they just in their dealings, and punctual in complying with their contracts and engagements; and in paying their debts seasonably? And where any give reasonable grounds for fear in these respects, is due care extended to them?

There again we can note the blending of the practical and the moral calculated to make the Quaker integral: religious in his living, and living in his religion. He is not provided with arbitrary answers but is expected to assume responsibility for his own spiritual bookkeeping. His faith is a personal experience, a direct relationship with Deity as interpreted by his own conscience.

Quakerism thus nurtures self-respect and self-reliance. It demands a sense of individual obligation and in turn provides scope for individual talent, for freedom of thought and conscience within the framework of Christian morals. Its individualism, however—and this is significant in comprehending the one American President shaped by Quaker mores—rests not on self-interest but on usefulness to others. It is an individualism suffused by compassion, and consequently at the antipodes from survival-of-the-fittest ruggedness. The Quaker ideal aims at the utmost development of the person not only as an end in itself but as a contribution to the greatest good of the community.

Professor Rufus M. Jones was able to write that in the task of world betterment "there is no sane and efficient program which does not include the old-fashioned Quaker faith (not sectarian) in the personal worth of the individual, a faith that a man is more precious than the gold of Ophir, a vision of the potential child of God in the submerged toiler, and, with that faith and that vision, the readiness to identify ourselves as friend with those who need us, the bestowal of personal care and sympathy, the sharing of the self as well as the sharing of money, the cultivation of the spirit of consecration to the tasks and needs of the neighborhood group in which we live."

The same thought was emphasized by a Quaker educator, Dr. Henry T. Hodgkin, in addressing other educators:

"The reverent spirit finds its object not only in nature but in our neighbors. . . . Nothing is more distinctive of the Quaker view of life than its persistent conviction of the worth of every man, the determination to see and honor 'that of God' in him. . . . It must be the distinctive task of Quaker educators to send forth persons who have no inner barriers and who approach all men of whatever race, creed, class, or nation with an open heart and deep respect."

I make no apology for these quotations in an essay on Herbert Hoover. The spirit that informs them shines through so much that the Quaker boy grown to manhood and eminence has had to say. Who can doubt the Quaker quality, for instance, in these words addressed by the thirty-first American President to members of the American Red Cross on April 12, 1930:

"It is, indeed, the spiritual in the individual and the nation which looks out with keen interest on the well-being of others, forgetful of ourselves, beyond our own preoccupation with our own selfish interests, and gives us a sense of belonging to the great company of mankind, sharing in the great plan of the universe and the definite order which pervades it."

Sentiments, these, redolent of the meetinghouse. Hoover has often pointed to the remarkable fact that, so far as he was aware, there were no Quakers on relief. Each community of Friends as a matter of course takes care of its own, and the immense charitable enterprises of the Society all over the world are proof enough that the solicitude is not limited to its members.

Speaking at a Quaker college in 1922, Hoover referred to the rescue work that has been carried on by the Friends from the great plague in London to the latest plague of world war.

"There must be something more here than accident," he declared, "that out of a body of perhaps two hundred and fifty or three hundred thousand people of all the world, there should have been contributed to humanity during all these centuries that sense of service. . . . It is perhaps unseemly for me or for you to speak of our own, but it is well to remind ourselves for our inspiration and the inspiration of our children that there is here a tradition, there is here the motivation of some great aspiration that follows through generation after generation of our people."

I am indebted to the fine book by Walter Friar Dexter, *Herbert Hoover and American Individualism,* for much of the material in this chapter. He has pointed out, among other things, that the Quakers were the first American Abolitionists. By the end of the eighteenth century there was no Friend in good standing owning chattel slaves; full ninety years before Hoover was born the Friends of Virginia directed that all those who failed to liberate their slaves be disowned by their local meetings.

It was, indeed, their abhorrence of slavery which drove most of the Quakers in our South, among them Hoover's ancestors, into the Western Reserve. The candidacy of Abraham Lincoln received almost unanimous Quaker support. Hoover's profound admiration for Lincoln, which he has evidenced in a thousand ways, is more than a personal predilection; it is intimately related to his religious background.

Herbert was only six when his father died and barely recalls him. But before his mother passed away he was nearly ten, so that her sweetness and humility remained with him forever. In the years of her widowhood Huldah Hoover supported her three children—Theodore the eldest, Herbert, and May the youngest—by taking in sewing. But her real vocation was preaching.

In any other denomination she would have become an ordained pastor, but among the Quakers she had no title or parish or remuneration, except in the love of those whom she exhorted and instructed. Increasingly she did receive free-will offerings to relieve her of the drudgery of the needle so that she might speak the word of God. Co-religionists all over Iowa and even beyond came to know her soft, unstudied eloquence.

Herbert remembers few of her words, but their purport, which was love and charity, colored his mind and feelings forever. When he declared, in accepting his nomination for President, "I come of Quaker stock," it was not a casual bit of biographical information. He was offering a key to his moral essence. David Hinshaw underlined that essence when he wrote:

Hoover the Quaker, given to reticence, distinctly modest, quick in sympathy for the oppressed, with great strength and instinctive gentleness and with astounding audacity of the spirit, is full of the manners and methods of his peculiar people. He does not represent Quakerism in its rigid interpretation, but the indelible impressions of childhood have matured into a manhood concerned with things of the spirit, and the fiber of that spirit makes it pliable but unbreakable.

In the course of his long, active life Hoover shed more and more of the externals of his fathers' faith. For the sake of the girl who was to become his wife and share his life's work, he learned to dance during his college years. He learned to take an occasional drink with congenial company, and to enjoy movies, theaters, and other recreations which the matriach Rebecca and his mother would have considered abominations. As a child he was chastised for fishing on Sunday; as a grownup he has fished on hundreds of Sundays without a twinge of conscience.

But he never shed any of the deep spiritual precepts implanted in his heart and mind in the formative years. In studying his career and his words, as I have done in some measure, one becomes more and more conscious of special qualities—a compulsive concern for the sufferings of others, especially children; a faith in the basic goodness of individual man; a distaste for ceremony and display—that are clearly in the Quaker tradition.

The fact is that Hoover, when he gave up business to head the Belgian rescue work at forty, did not go into politics. The suggestion would have appalled him. He went into public service, which is, alas, quite another thing. That is why the usual political yardsticks fail to give his true measure.

There is ground for dispute as to the degree in which he succeeded in the dedication that derived from a childhood in the meetinghouse; there can be no dispute as to the motives that inspired him. They were no sudden impulses but the flowering of seeds firmly and tenderly planted in his mind and heart.

There is a pattern in the Hoover story and its basic design is mercy. Neither the ravages of time nor the corrosions of political malignities have blurred its outlines. The sweet-faced, soft-voiced woman preacher of the Friends' settlement in West Branch, though she died early, did not live in vain.

CHAPTER VII

A Western Childhood

MOST AMERICANS SEEM TO HAVE FOR-
gotten how humble were Hoover's beginnings. A new generation,
in particular, as I have already suggested, is a bit nonplused to
learn that he came up from poverty and knew the ache of hard
work for pay when he was still a toddler; it upsets their mental
picture of him.

The public amnesia on this matter is owing in part to the fact
that he succeeded in business early and spectacularly. But chiefly
it is the result of the pounding propagandas of later years link-
ing him, with calculated malice, to such symbols of iniquity unlimited as Wall Street.

Among the birthplaces of American Presidents only Lincoln's
log cabin was a shade more humble than the cottage where Hoover was ushered into the world. The actual room in which he
was delivered with the skillful help of his aunt Ellen, volunteer
midwife to most of West Branch, was about seven feet by thirteen. It was part of a primitive but immaculately clean three-
room one-story house across the alley from Jesse Hoover's blacksmith shop.

Later, when it passed into other hands, this birthplace was
obscured by a two-story extension across the front. After Hoover
became President, it was fixed up as a hot-dog stand and profited
on the curiosity of tourists. Hoover's two sons bought the property
in 1934; their mother supervised the removal of additions and
restoration of the original cottage, which they deeded to the

village. It is now preserved as a national shrine by the state of
Iowa.

An engaging echo of the night of his arrival is available in a
letter from another aunt. "I had spent the day with Huldah, visiting and sewing," she recalled. "Next morning early Jesse came
and tapped on my window and said, 'Well, we have another
General Grant at our house. Huldah would like to see thee.' So I
went. . . . Herbert was a sweet baby that first day, round and
plump, and looked about very cordial."

General Grant was then President, of course. There was surely
no edge of premonition in Jesse Hoover's boast. Millions of
American fathers have announced the advent of millions of sons
with that same half-earnest pleasantry.

Herbert found a three-year-old brother—Theodore, known
far into maturity as Tad—waiting for him. A sister, May, joined
them in a couple of years. As Jesse's farm implement agency
prospered, they moved into a more commodious house which is
no longer extant. It was a warm, happy little family, with flocks
of uncles, aunts, and cousins for miles around. Of worldly goods
they had little and wanted little.

Few memories of his first years remain with Herbert. Neither
in this respect nor in any other was he a precocious child. The
clearest of these memories was literally burned into his flesh
when he stepped on a red-hot chip of iron while playing in the
smithy; he still carries the scar.

Another incident is sharp in his mind if only for the whipping
it earned him. The punishment may be set down as his first
sacrifice for scientific research. Watching a caldron of boiling tar
outside his father's shop, he fell to wondering whether the oily
bubbles would burn and what species of tar-colored flames they
would produce. From wondering to action was an easy step, as
easy as plunging a burning faggot into the tar. He had his answer
instantly in terrifying billows of smoke which brought neighbors,
and in due time the volunteer fire brigade, running to the rescue.
To this day, Hoover says, the sight of a picture of a volcanic
eruption revives a little of that terror in his heart.

Because of Jesse's illness, Huldah once packed her children
off to Uncle Benajah's farm. But they were soon hauled back in

mysterious gloom. At home they found their grief-stricken mother and a bevy of mourning relations around their father's corpse. He had been carried off by typhoid fever. Herbert had just passed his sixth birthday.

Luckily sorrows fade swiftly in childhood. Jesse left a thousand-dollar life-insurance policy. Not until years later did Tad and Herbie comprehend the self-denying solicitude with which their mother safeguarded this tiny hoard as a nest egg for their education. It was her fondest hope that the boys would go to college. She sewed deep into the night to nourish their bodies and read the Bible with them to nourish their souls. When summoned to preach away from home, she entrusted her children to one or another of the Hoover or Minthorn households.

One of the most impressive experiences of Herbert's childhood came to him about a year after his father's death. In part to relieve Huldah of one mouth to feed, he was taken for eight or nine months to Pawhuska, Oklahoma, to live with his cousins, the children of Major Laban Miles, United States Indian Agent to the Osage Nation.

He and his Miles cousins were the only white children in the agency school. With the half-tamed braves they explored the forests and streams, learned how to make and use bows and arrows, how to fish Indian fashion, and build a fire in the open in the economical Indian way. Much of Hoover's great love for the outdoors derives from those crowded Osage months. His quiet pride in the efficacious building of a campfire and in outdoor cookery is a measure of the zest he brought to that long-ago Indian interlude.

A triviality has stuck in his memory. A visiting missionary demanded to know the subject of that day's religious lesson. The little Indians told him promptly: "Ananias set fire to his wife," which perhaps was close enough to "Ananias and Sapphira, his wife."

When he was old enough to know anything, Herbert knew the value of money and the importance of frugality. In his seventh summer he earned more than five dollars picking strawberries; it was an immense sum, well worth the backache and sunburn. With his brother and cousins he collected old iron for the pennies it brought. Before and after school hours at the West Branch Free School he did the chores around the house—or on the farm when he lived with relatives—considered proper for young boys, and they were not light chores.

He was going on ten when pneumonia carried off his mother. He recalls vividly the family council of Hoovers and Minthorns, in which a few neighbors joined. The problem, he says, was "not as to who should undertake the duty of raising the three orphans, but who should have the joy of adding them to their own broods."

Even his schoolteacher, Mollie Brown (later Mrs. Curran), put in a bid for Herbert. As an unmarried lady, however, she was not considered equal to the responsibility. In the end Grandmother Minthorn took in May, who was little more than a baby; the Aunt Ellen who had helped bring him into the world and her husband, Uncle Allan, acquired Herbert; and Tad went to live with another uncle.

Allan and Ellen lived on a farm about two miles out of West Branch. For nearly two years Herbert's life was therefore adjusted to the routine of a typical farm of the period. Nearly fifty years later, speaking in Iowa in the course of a campaign swing through the country, he alluded to the extent to which those pioneer farms had been self-contained:

"We ground our own wheat and corn on toll at the mill," he said. "We slaughtered our hogs for meat; we wove at least a part of our own clothing; we repaired our own machinery; we got our own fuel from the woods; we erected our own buildings; we made our own soap; we preserved our own fruit and grew our own vegetables.

"Only a small part of the family living came by purchase from outside. Perhaps 20 per cent of the products were sold in the market to purchase the small margin of necessities which we could not ourselves produce, and to pay interest on the mortgage."

Having contrasted that mode of life with the modern farm with its specialization, its new comforts, its growing dependence on the total economy of the nation, he added:

"I do not suggest a return to the greater security which agriculture enjoyed in its earlier days, because with security were lower standards of living, greater toil, less opportunity for leisure and recreation, less of the comforts of home, less of the joy of living."

In any case, there was no dearth of tough work for a vigorous, intelligent boy on the farm of old. Its economic system, he has said with a touch of whimsy, "avoided class conflicts, labor boards, and arbitration. It absolutely denied collective bargaining to little boys. The prevailing rate for picking potato bugs was one cent a hundred, and if you wanted firecrackers on the Fourth of July you took it or left it."

The chubbiness of his childhood was giving way to the tall, muscular leanness of his boyhood. The babyish diminutive of Herbie was giving way to the more manly appellation of Bert. Except for the accent of special affection, as if he were the favored child, he was as completely the son of the house as any of his cousins there. In 1907 Hoover was to express his abiding love for this Uncle Allan by naming his second son for him.

When Herbert was eleven, no doubt after another family conference, he was told gently, "Thee is going to Oregon." That meant a painful separation from his whole West Branch world— but it also meant a thrilling journey to a new land, to join the most respected of his uncles, Dr. Henry John Minthorn, physician, missionary, teacher, Civil War veteran. The tears that came to the boy's eyes connoted not only the sorrow of parting but the joy of anticipation.

2

Outwardly the first eleven years of Hoover's life would appear restrained and even cheerless. Twice he was orphaned and passed from relative to relative. The Quaker way of life was not too conducive to the high spirits of a healthy growing boy. His early love of reading had to be indulged half in secret, for even *Robinson Crusoe* and the tales of Fenimore Cooper were too secular for the taste of his peculiar people. Comforts were scarce, money scarcer, and hard work—milking, weeding, currying the horses, gathering fuel, even dishwashing—a matter of course for all youngsters.

But we make a mistake to look on the life of a child with

grown-up eyes. "I prefer to think of Iowa as I saw it through the eyes of a ten-year-old boy," Hoover said some forty years later. From that vantage point the view is clearer and vastly more cheerful. It appears, indeed, as a happy, thrilling boyhood, "filled with the wonders of Iowa's streams and woods, of the mystery of growing crops . . . filled with adventure and great undertakings, with participation in good and comforting things."

These wonders were not the mirage of middle age. Hoover had been back to check his memories and had found them exceedingly good. The sites of his childhood were not much changed, and each of them stirred remembrance of all-suffusing joys and high moments of discovery.

There was, for instance, Cook's Hill—"that great long hill where, on winter nights, we slid down at terrific speeds, with our tummies tight to homemade sleds." There was the shallow swimming hole under the willows down by the railroad bridge from which one returned caked with "clean and healthy mud."

"And there were the woods down the Burlington track," he reminisced. "The denudation of our forest hasn't reached them even yet, and I know there are rabbits still being trapped in cracker boxes held open by a figure four at the behest of small boys at this very time. . . .

"One of the bitterest days of my life was in connection with a rabbit. Rabbits fresh from a figure-four trap early on a cold morning are wiggly rabbits, and in the lore of boys of my time it is better to bring them home alive. My brother, being older, had surreptitiously behind the blacksmith shop read in *Youth's Companion* full directions for rendering live rabbits secure. I say 'surreptitiously,' for mine was a Quaker family unwilling in those days to have youth corrupted with stronger reading than the Bible, the encyclopedia, or those great novels where the hero overcomes the demon rum."

Can it be that the magazine prescription was at fault? Or was the wiggly rabbit too wiggly for frozen thumbs to manage? However that may be, Herbie fumbled his share of the proceedings and the slippery piece of fur got away. The loss of a presidential election would seem a minor disappointment compared with this major humiliation. For forty years at least brother Tad and his own conscience held him culpable. "I never see rabbit tracks across the snowy fields that I do not have painful recollections of it," Hoover confesses.

There were pigeons in the woods and prairie chickens in the hedges for young hunters, and above all there was the fishing.

"We were still," he recalls, "in that rude but highly social condition of using a willow pole with a butcher-string line and hooks ten for a dime. Our compelling lure was a segment of angleworm, and our incantation was to spit on the bait. We lived in a time when the fish used to bite instead of strike, and we knew it bit when the cork bobbed. And, moreover, we ate the fish."

His earliest awareness of the stir of national events was a torch parade in the Garfield campaign. There were only two or three Democrats in West Branch—one of them conveniently a drunk and therefore a living reproof to the Democratic party. It must have been ritual rather than vote getting, therefore, that accounted for the parade. In Hoover's mind it looms larger and brighter than any of the thousand parades he was fated to suffer as a man.

No, it was decidedly not an unhappy childhood. Maybe it should have been, for he was an orphan and poor in a backwoods village. But it wasn't, any more than Huckleberry Finn's or Tom Sawyer's. Bereavements and sorrows, big and small, were blotted out by the "glories of snowy winter, the joining of the neighbors to harvest, the gathering of apples, the pilgrimage to the river woods for the annual fuel and nuts," and a thousand other momentous, epoch-making doings.

The Burlington track seemed to young Hoover a fascinating treasure trove. By industrious searching "you discovered gems of agate and fossil coral which could with infinite backaches be polished on the grindstone. Their fine points came out wonderfully when wet, and you had to lick them with your tongue before each exhibit."

Because we know the answers at the back of the book, the temptation is to detect the mining engineer of the future in the lad sorting stones on the railroad track. Then one recalls that his playmates were no less engrossed in the game but did not grow up to be miners. The temptation is even greater when we learn a further fact from the indefatigable Earl Reeves, who heard it from the eighty-six-year-old Dr. William Walker himself in the 1920s.

Dr. Walker was the village dentist, even as Jesse Hoover was the village blacksmith. When Secretary of Commerce Hoover visited West Branch he did not fail to call on Dr. Walker and— proving the absent-mindedness of cabinet officials—forgot two fifty-dollar notes on the old man's mantelpiece. The point about Dr. Walker, however, is not his dentistry but his collection of geological specimens.

"Many an hour," he told Reeves, "Herbert spent in my office poring over specimens while other children played. And gradually there was born in the boy the determination to win an education. For so often I would have to say, 'I don't know' in answer to his questions. That never satisfied him."

One suspects that the good dentist assigned a role to his geological display not uninfluenced by later knowledge. But it is undoubtedly a fact that Herbert hankered for learning, especially the kind one picked up outside of schoolrooms. He took after his mother in his hunger for knowledge and his idealistic urges, even as he took after the father whom he did not remember in his humor and his mechanical bents.

One thing is sure. There was in Hoover no trace of self-pity when he contemplated his childhood in Iowa—and in Oregon after that—in later years. There is none today. He did not feel that fate owed him any debts. In all sincerity he regarded his childhood as fortunate for all the sorrows that punctuated it. He came out of his first eleven years with a strong body, an alert mind, and a spirit richer than he could himself suspect.

On taking inventory of his enduring memories and his earliest influences, he was able to state without reservations, "It is the entry to life which I could wish for every American boy and girl."

3

Dr. Minthorn had practically demanded that his sister's boy be surrendered to him. His only son had just died and it seemed to him right that one of Huldah's orphans fill that place in his home and heart. And he had another powerful argument on his side, one that carried immense weight with a Quaker family. He had just been put in charge of a new school, the Friends Pacific Academy, forerunner of today's Pacific College, so that Herbert could continue schooling without digging into the tiny estate left by his mother.

And so, loaded down with blessings, sound spiritual counsel, and a huge hamper of provisions, in the care of a family going in the same direction, the boy made the seven-day journey by rail to Portland. En route he wrote long letters to Miss Brown, his beloved schoolteacher, describing the Rockies and his fellow passengers.

In Portland he was collected by a taciturn uncle in the familiar Quaker garb and conveyed to the new Friends' settlement called Newberg on the river Willamette, about twenty-two miles south of Portland. Aunt Laura and her three daughters, his cousins, were boiling pear butter for the winter when their kin from "the East" arrived and graciously invited him to eat all the pears he wished. Never having tasted that fruit before, he proceeded to gorge himself, with the result that he could not look a pear in the face again without wincing.

There was plenty of work and to spare for a husky lad in a family of girls. He became valet to the doctor's team of ponies and frankly hated the task; he milked the cow, split the firewood, helped Dr. Minthorn to clear tracts of fir forest. With school, long religious services, his letter writing to Iowa, he was busy enough. One of his first summers in Newberg he took a job weeding onions in the great bottom lands north of the town at fifty cents a day and board; the thirty dollars he brought back and conserved made him feel rich and almost independent.

He found ample compensations for the hard labors. There were the great wheatfields he loved to watch; the forest; the rivers swarming with fish; he wondered whether he would ever explore this new, more rugged land to his heart's content. In time he did, for a boy's hours are many times as long as a man's hours. Somehow he found leisure to play baseball with new friends, to build dams, hunt for grouse, and fish for trout.

Above all, there was Uncle John himself, a university man who had driven teams for the "Underground Railway" in Iowa as a boy, who had run away from home to enlist in the Union Army and taken part in the Battle of Shiloh. In his nephew's eyes he was a romantic character right out of the pages of a forbidden book. Besides doctoring, Uncle John superintended the new academy, where he taught the history and literature courses, took a leading part in the affairs of the Friends, and of course cared for his homestead.

Sometimes the boy accompanied him on visits to patients, which in that place and time meant jogging along rough and often hub-deep mud roads for hours. They would take turns at driving the teams. And though the doctor was sparing in words, he had a steep sense of duty which demanded that these intervals be used to instruct his nephew.

Herbert thus learned a lot about physiology in health and in sickness. He learned even more about Indian history; Dr. Minthorn had set up Indian schools in his time and, in fact, first came to Oregon as United States Indian Agent. Many of those jogging hours were also devoted to American history, with special reference to its central event, which was the Battle of Shiloh.

Not all Quakers are pacifists and certainly Dr. Minthorn was not one. "Turn your other cheek once," he instructed the boy, "but if he smites you, then punch him." He had another favorite maxim of his own making which registered on Herbert's mind: "The meanest thing a man can do is to do nothing."

The boy had a will of his own which at times, as in all normal families, clashed with his uncle's. There was even a period when Herbert stalked out in anger and boarded with other relatives. It could not have been serious, for when the Minthorns moved to Salem, the capital, he went with them.

4

The doctor had gone into the land-settlement business with Charles Moore, Ben Cook, and other Quaker friends. Salem was already a thriving city of eight thousand. The entrepreneurs had purchased several square miles of fat land and were parcelling it out as orchard plots to new settlers. They drew up truthful but enticing descriptions which were spread throughout the country, and their salesmen met new arrivals at Portland to explain the fruit-raising opportunities near Salem.

Herbert was fifteen at this time. He acquired the post of office boy for the Oregon Land Company, as the real estate development venture was called; his salary was fifteen dollars a month, and in time it was raised to twenty. Except for a short break, during which he drove one of the first horsecars in Salem, he remained office boy until he left for college, which was in two years.

The title made him in effect a general utility man. From the man who kept the books he learned the rudiments of bookkeeping. Briefly, indeed, he considered that as a career, rather than driving locomotives which was the preceding ambition; but the exemplar of the profession closest at hand was a dour and unhappy Scotsman, and that served to dissuade him. From a lady stenographer he learned how to type passably well. He took a hand also in drafting advertisements and blueprinting roadways and plottings.

One night a creditors' meeting was taking place at the company offices. It grew stormy and was getting nowhere. Suddenly the lights went out and the gathering perforce disbanded. Uncle John was locking up when he caught sight of his nephew, a guilty grin on his face.

"Did thee turn out the lights?" he asked in sudden comprehension.

"Yes," Bert admitted. "They were only running up the gas bill. There was no use in that kind of talk."

Another time Bert took a private flier in business, in partnership with the office boy of another firm. A sewing-machine agent had his shop on their street. Since he accepted old machines as part of the purchase price of new ones, and wrecked them as thoroughly as possible, he had a dump of smashed metal in his back yard. The boys paid him twenty dollars for the junk, after which they labored for weeks sorting parts and rebuilding machines. But even at one dollar a piece they could find no buyers for the resurrected goods. They lost their twenty dollars but, as Hoover now puts it, they "learned a powerful lot about the insides of sewing machines."

Ben Cook, one of his employers, was more than willing to discuss his office boy when Hoover had become a great figure in the great world. It was Cook, along with other Salemites who knew him "when," who launched a Hoover-for-President committee in Oregon thirty years later. Young Bert, he told inquirers, impressed them especially with his phenomenal memory. They came to refer to him as their "walking encyclopedia," for he knew the status of all deals, the contents of all letters, and the whereabouts of all documents.

"He was on the jump when there was anything to do," Cook testified, "but the moment he was through, out would come his geometry or algebra or history, and he'd sit, shoulders hunched over the little table in the corner, preparing for college."

Others, too, remembered him primarily in that studious posture. He was at the age, between fifteen and seventeen, when reading can become an absorbing passion for some boys. A Miss Jane Gray—he remembers her name to this day gratefully—made the spreading of good books among Salem boys her mission. It was she who introduced him to Dickens and Scott and other classics, and before long there were few books in Salem libraries which he had not read.

He had made up his mind to go to college. More than that, to a college of his own choice. Catalogues from dozens of institutions were delivered to his address. He knew that Dr. Minthorn could wangle a scholarship in some Quaker college, but his mind was increasingly fixed on science and engineering, departments in which Quaker schools were not interested.

When a business school was opened in Salem, he promptly enrolled for night classes. Fortunately one of the teachers was deeply interested in mathematics and delighted to discover that the Hoover youngster had a natural aptitude for it. Thus he was guided through elementary algebra and geometry at odd hours and at no cost except time.

In conversations with his associates Hoover has recalled how the dream of engineering was brought to the surface of his thought:

"An engineer from the East—a Mr. Robert Brown—drifted into the office on some mission and made the acquaintance of the office boy. In the course of our talks he discussed the advantages of college training for a profession. He spoke much of engineering.

"For a year I mulled over it, talking to all who would listen. I haunted the little foundry and sawmill and the repair shops of the town. I collected catalogues and information on engineering universities. I was determined to become an engineer. My leanings had been initially to the mechanical side. But I had visited a mining prospect in the Cascades with a mining engineer who persuaded me that his branch of the profession offered more choice. His study of the geology of the mines and his conclusions therefrom that the mine was no good excited my imagination."

About the same time reports began to appear about the new university being founded at Palo Alto, on the southern shore of San Francisco Bay, by the wealthy Senator Leland Stanford, as a memorial to his only son who had just died at the age of sixteen. It was to be a progressive institution, with the stress on technical and scientific knowledge and "usefulness" as its guiding ideal. A young scientist and educator who had already made a name for himself, Dr. David Starr Jordan, had been secured as president and was mobilizing a faculty of broad-minded teachers not yet set in rigid academic molds.

Herbert, having received the advance literature of this projected university, put away all the other catalogues, for he knew where he was going. At the same time his heart was filled with despair: the requirements for entry seemed beyond his capacity. He studied harder than ever, on the chance that he might crash through.

His lack of preparation was only half the tragedy. The other half was the opposition of Grandmother Minthorn, who had come to live in Oregon, of Uncle John, and others to a secular institution and one, moreover, without background. This once they realized that Huldah's son, though pliant and co-operative in other matters, could be obstinate on essentials. Happily the announcement of the entrance examinations to be held in Portland indicated that they would be conducted by a well-known mathematics professor, Joseph Swain—and Dr. Swain happened to be a prominent Quaker. A college with which he was connected could not be iniquitous, so the family opposition crumbled.

The opening of the new university was scheduled for the very month when Herbert would turn seventeen, August 1891. That spring he went to Portland and presented himself to Dr. Swain. He did not pretend that he was prepared for higher education. Though he failed, he impressed the Quaker educator with his proficiency in mathematics, at least as far as he had gone, and with his eagerness and intelligence. In his fumbling efforts Dr. Swain discerned solid abilities and a robust spirit.

He talked to the boy. In fact, he accepted an invitation to visit the Minthorns and other admiring Quakers in Salem. It seemed clear that Herbert could not afford several years of preparatory school, and that he should retake the examinations in Palo Alto. In the meantime he would cram the subjects on which he was weakest, and by coming to California a little earlier he could get some coaching from faculty people. Thus it was decided.

It was a worried, immature, gangling boy who set out for California that June. He was nearly six feet tall, lean and strong, toughened by pioneer life; the round, serious face under a mop of light hair was tanned and handsome and his jaws set in determination. He carried all his earthly goods with him: two suits of clothes, a bicycle, and about two hundred dollars. He could count on a little more from the remnants of his mother's legacy, spread thin over four years. Another Salem boy, the son of the local banker, was his traveling companion; the banker had insisted on paying Herbert's fare in consideration of some tutoring in mathematics for his son.

In the morgue of a Portland newspaper there is a yellowing clipping which tells—accurately, I can but hope—about Hoover's departure:

Finally, when the time came to leave Oregon friends for the big university, Grandmother Minthorn went down to the depot at Salem with her boy.

"I think thy mother would like to see thee now," she said, when

Bert stooped to kiss her soft withered cheek. "Thee has always been a good boy, Bertie. I shall always pray that thee does a conscientious work."

"Thee will have cause to be proud of me someday," Bert promised, with a smile whimsical enough to cloak his emotions.

CHAPTER VIII

College Years in California

PALO ALTO AT THE TIME WAS NOT
even a railroad stop. The two Salem boys alighted at Menlo Park
and found a hack to take them to the rambling country house on
the outskirts of the university grounds where early arrivals,
faculty and students, were put up. They naturally hastened to inspect "Stanford farm," as the campus was irreverently nicknamed
for some time; the mission-style quadrangle of buildings and the
accessory structures had been planted on what used to be a hay-
field.

They found buildings unfinished, dormitories draped in scaf-
folding, and throngs of workmen rushing the job in anticipation
of hordes of students. The sawing and hammering and swishing
of paintbrushes said "Hurry, hurry!" The freshness of the university, as if it were being made ready especially for them, thrilled
the more sensitive students. It was at the greatest possible remove
from the sense of hoary age with which a Harvard or a Yale is
invested.

About two weeks before the school doors opened Hoover
moved into Encina Hall, Room 38, and tradition has it that he
was the first person to sleep under its roof. With the help of Dr.
Swain, and by virtue of his experience as an office boy, he got a
job in the university office, where he helped to register the swarm
of boys and girls from all over America, but mostly the pioneer
West.

He had, of course, passed the entrance tests this time, with a few "conditions"; one of them, English, was to plague him through all the four years. Discovering that he was short one subject for the minimum entry requirements, he analyzed the electives and decided to stake his fate on elementary physiology. Fortified by the reading of two textbooks on the subject in two nights, he took the examination and passed—a demonstration of his exceptional memory and a dividend on those long rides with his country doctor uncle.

The truth is that Dr. Jordan and his associates were not too hard on applicants for matriculation in that first period. They were less concerned with academic records than with the student's appetite and potential for learning. The misfits could be weeded out later, as indeed they were, wholesale.

Hoover was the youngest student in that first class. For a boy reared in tiny towns and on farms, with little scope for his vigorous but largely unawakened intelligence, the life at Leland Stanford was endlessly stimulating and colorful. The university had drawn to itself a unique and highly varied aggregation of students and teachers.

The faculty was made up for the most part of men and women eager to break the traces of academic orthodoxy, devoted to the slogans of "usefulness" which then had the ring of a bold modernity. The student body counted young people from every layer of American society. Many of them, like Hoover, had only a sketchy kind of education picked up between chores, on the run; probably they would have been sent home for finishing courses by the older established institutions. Others were well-to-do young intellectuals attracted by the progressive aura around the new venture. There were many, too, who came because Senator Stanford had made provisions for good students in bad circumstances; more than one had reached California by "riding the rods."

Here were wider human horizons than Hoover had as yet glimpsed; exciting mental contacts; startling political and religious ideas, each of them personalized in some classmate. From all reports he said little and listened a lot; there was a wordless eagerness about him. But when he did offer an opinion it was curiously to the point, so that his presence among them registered—not dramatically, as in the case of the extroverts—but slowly, like an unfoldment.

The formal opening ceremonies took place on October 1, 1891, with the Stanford family and leading Californians in attendance. An aroma of paint and fresh lumber hovered over the oratory. Something about the newness of the place, the Santa Cruz foothills in the background, the noise and enthusiasm, so different from the traditionally hushed university atmosphere, gave the occasion a "gold-rush" feeling; and some of the big, rawboned students in the audience fitted perfectly into that fancy.

"Our university," Dr. Jordan said in his opening address, "has no history to fall back upon; no memories of great teachers haunt its corridors; in none of its rooms appear the traces to show where a great man has lived or worked. No tender associations cling ivy-like to its fresh new walls.

"It is hallowed by no traditions. It is hampered by none. Its finger posts all point forward."

Hoover recalls that he was mightily impressed. Stanford was to become the physical and intellectual focus of his life. He was fortunate: among the men he met there, classmates and teachers, he found an exceptional number who were peculiarly congenial to his type of mind and ideals. They were to figure among his dearest friends and most trusted co-workers in business, in social work, in public service. Within the precincts of Stanford he was to meet the woman whose devoted love and superb intellect were his greatest possession forever after.

The need to make a living would never be far from his mind. In partnership with two other students he organized a newspaper route. Then he started a laundry agency. Each Monday morning he collected bundles of soiled clothes, each Saturday afternoon he distributed the clean parcels. After a while he was able to hire helpers and leave himself free for other work; in his third year he sold the agency for the munificent sum of forty dollars. At the suggestion of a new friend, they started a co-operative residence for students in Palo Alto, but this he soon dropped because it took him away from campus interests.

Despite these multifarious activities, he made the freshman baseball team as shortstop. Alas, he stopped one a bit too short, spraining a finger so badly that he had to drop out. That was the end of his athletic career; except, as we shall see, as organizer and co-ordinator of all athletic and other student enterprises.

Dr. John Branner, the head of the department of geology and mining, was delayed until early in 1892. With his arrival, Hoover's real vocation began. Luckily for him there were only eleven students in that first geology class, so that he had the kind of personal attention which reached deeply.

He was a remarkable educator and human being, this Dr. Branner, besides being among the foremost geologists in this country. From the first he recognized in the immature-looking Quaker boy an aptitude for his specialty that had in it elements of genius. In need of a part-time secretary, and learning that Hoover could type, he engaged him forthwith. When summer vacation came along, moreover, he obtained for his favorite student an assignment with the Geological Survey of Arkansas. Hoover returned from the Ozarks "lean as a greyhound, as hard as nails, and as brown as a berry"—and about two hundred dollars ahead for his sophomore year.

As was perhaps to be expected, two or three other students griped about Hoover's "pull" with the geologist. Overhearing this talk, Dr. Branner explained patiently that it wasn't pull or luck that served Hoover but character. After indicating the way most men fumbled a job at hand, he said:

"But I can tell Hoover to do a thing and never think of it again. If I told him to start to Kamchatka tomorrow to bring me back a walrus tooth, I'd never hear of it again until he came back with the tooth. And then I'd ask him how he had done it."

2

At Stanford, as in most universities, there was a snob element, the Greek-letter crowd. As if to compensate for the lack of campus traditions and the presence of a lot of backwoods boys and girls, the fraternity and sorority groups put an extra polish on their exclusiveness and refinement.

The tall, reserved boy who delivered papers, collected laundry, and worked in a professor's office could hardly rate with that element. Besides, Hoover naturally fell in with the original thinkers, the radicals, the doers among his classmates. In what was partly a social and partly a political alignment, he gradually assumed a share of leadership on the "progressive" and "populist" side.

The Greek-letter minority had taken most of the control of student activities into its hands. It was in the sophomore year that a prophet appropriately named Zion raised the banner of revolt. He was more generally known as "Sosh" from the initial syllable of the sobriquet "socialist" thrown at him, and "Sosh" he remained even when he was a conservative businessman in San Francisco decades later. The great war between the Frats and Barbs—short for barbarians—was under way. It raged for two years and smoldered for many years thereafter.

The most barbarous of the Barbs were the students so poor that they lived in the "camp," a row of rough workers' shacks left over from the time the university was being constructed. Though Hoover could afford to live in Encina Hall and had some "swells" among his friends, the camp dwellers looked on him as morally if not physically their own.

To Hoover therefore Zion assigned the job of "delivering" the "camp" vote. This Herbert duly accomplished in a series of bull sessions in the shacks. Personable Barbs were assigned to work among the girls and apparently with excellent results. The outstanding freshman of the year joined lustily in the fight and guaranteed the votes of his class. His name was Ray Lyman Wilbur, known then as Rex Wilbur; many years later as Prex Wilbur, when he became president of Stanford; and still later as Secretary of Interior Wilbur in the Hoover cabinet.

The campaign was so hot that the faculty was a bit alarmed. Dr. Jordan wondered aloud whether he was nurturing "a little Tammany Hall" in his university. When the votes were counted, the Barbs had won virtually all the offices, and Hoover, for all his anxiety to remain in the background, was given large credit for the outcome.

During his second summer vacation, in 1893, and again thanks to Dr. Branner's recommendation, Hoover was employed by the United States Geographical Survey, as cub assistant to Dr. Waldemar Lindgren. It was the luckiest of his breaks. Dr. Lindgren was a top-shelf geologist; three months by his side, ranging the rough Sierras, tracing mineral strains over a vast area, were the equivalent of a dozen years in a school laboratory. As always when he worked with men, Hoover and Dr. Lindgren were to remain lifelong associates.

The problems of the university campus bothered Hoover. He thought of them constantly during that vacation. The many campus activities were run haphazardly; some of them had been monopolized for the profit of special groups; most of them suffered from chronic deficits. By the time he returned for his junior year a detailed plan had taken shape in his mind. He presented it to Wilbur, Hinsdale, Zion, and other Barb leaders.

The result of their conferences was a campus constitution, written by Hoover. With only slight changes it is still the basic student charter of the university. It proposed a better articulated student organization, with responsibility and full accountability for all campus activities, whether intellectual, artistic, or athletic. Its key official would be a paid treasurer, whose job it would be to make activities pay off and to present regular audited statements of receipts and expenditures. By thus organizing the finances—and this was characteristic of Hoover's special blend of idealism and practicality—it would be possible to help deserving students in distress.

When the caucus was ready to announce the plan, it insisted that Hoover run for treasurer under the new arrangement. He refused. Since it was a paid office, the opposition might charge that he had elaborated the project to make himself a job, he pleaded. Only the argument that the Barb ticket could not hope to win without Hoover finally swayed him—but on the condition that, constitution or no constitution, he would not accept a salary. To this condition he adhered after his election, though the enormous work the office involved cut into his other earnings.

The Barbs won overwhelmingly this time and the Hoover charter became campus law. To his laundry route, his work for Dr. Branner, his heavy study schedule to make up conditions, he now added responsibility for the "gates" at all university activities, from theatrical shows to football games. His was the principal headache when the till was empty; when sickness or some other trouble afflicted a worthy student; when funds were needed to send a team to play on the challenger's campus.

The fact that he prospered under the staggering load must be credited first to his unusual physical stamina; secondly to his natural gift for organizing time, for doing one thing intensively then turning to the next with equal concentration; and finally to that amazing mental grasp which enabled him to soak up effortlessly the knowledge for which others had to slave and sweat.

The Stanford athletic field was not fenced in at the time. Students were told off to collect entrance fees—usually a quarter—from all comers. At a baseball game one day Hoover observed that a bearded old gentleman had been allowed to enter free. The collectors had simply lacked the nerve to demand a quarter from that eminent guest.

Hoover did not relish the job either; but the team's finances were in a bad way, duty was duty. Benjamin Harrison proved that he was no gate-crasher when the blushing Hoover made his stammering demand. In recalling the episode he declares, "Justice must occasionally be done even to ex-Presidents and I here record that he took two more tickets."

An embarrassing moment of the same order occurred on a subsequent occasion, with Andrew Carnegie in the culprit's seat and Hoover again doing the dirty work.

A combination lecture and concert forum was being operated by an enterprising student as his private business and private risk. On leaving college he willed the business to Hoover, to whom the compound of culture, enlightenment, and money-making appealed strongly. And thus he found himself also in the role of impresario.

He did not do too badly in that role, though he came a few croppers. One of his more unprofitable "attractions" was a young congressman who, being virtually unknown, failed to draw a crowd. Two years later his name would have jammed the largest auditorium in California, for it was William Jennings Bryan.

And once Hoover bit off more than he could chew. With an associate he sponsored a concert in San Jose for a high-priced foreign pianist, one Ignace Paderewski. Admission prices were of necessity stepped up, to cover the artist's minimum fee of two thousand dollars. The famous musician found himself facing infamous voids in the concert hall, and the impresarios found themselves four hundred dollars short for the settlement. Hoover offered his personal note, based on nothing but good faith of course. But the Polish guest graciously canceled the obligation and everything ended happily, except that Hoover was left penniless.

Twenty-five years later, at a great public reception for Hoover in the city of Lodz, the same Paderewski, as President of Poland, thanked the American for having saved tens of thousands of Polish lives. In his response, Hoover recalled the San Jose incident and his host's graciousness. Thunderous applause testified the general conviction that the four-hundred-dollar debt had been repaid in full.

3

When the last summer vacation arrived, between the junior and senior years, there was some uncertainty whether a geologic survey post would be open for him. With several classmates equally anxious to make a few honest dollars Hoover therefore went into the sign-painting business, of all things. They obtained commissions from San Francisco businesses to paint and erect "eyesores" announcing their wares in the Yosemite Valley.

The boys had no more than reached the valley when a telegram overtook them. It notified Hoover to report immediately to the survey party. Upon turning their pockets and wallets inside out they confirmed the sad truth that all together they did not have enough cash on them to pay his stage fare to the railroad. Hoover set out on foot. He walked eighty miles in three days, arriving in time.

That summer's expedition through the High Sierras, again under Dr. Lindgren's command, saw the cub geologist blossom into a real assistant. It was exacting but invigorating work, on horseback most of the day, under the open skies most nights. When the maps of the survey were published by the Government Office, Hoover's name appeared beside Dr. Lindgren's in the credit lines. That was the first public recognition to come to

Hoover in his chosen field of endeavor—an unsolicited compliment by a man at the top of the profession to a youngster on its lowest rung. Among the multitude of honors that were to descend on him through the years, Hoover would rank this one in a class by itself.

As the youngest member in the expedition, he was made disbursing officer, which made him responsible to Washington for every penny spent. That burdensome distinction netted him an amusing story for his fat repertoire of personal experiences, though it was not in the least amusing at the time.

On awaking one morning the party discovered that one of the pack mules was dead. It devolved upon Hoover and two witnesses to report the loss and all attendant circumstances. As disbursing officer he was responsible for the full value, which was sixty dollars. An autopsy revealed that the mule, which had been tethered to a tree, had scratched his head with his hind foot, which got tangled in the halter rope; in trying to jerk out of the dilemma he had evidently broken his neck.

The report that in time reached the proper officials in Washington set forth these lugubrious facts. Two months later Hoover was duly and officially advised that mules do not scratch their heads with their hind feet, and that sixty dollars therefore had been deducted from his salary! Dr. Lindgren absorbed the loss, vowing that he would collect it from some "damned bureaucrat" when he returned to the capital.

The geologist, however, did not know the stuff of which bureaucrats are made. Some years later Hoover engaged him for consultation work in Australia. Dr. Lindgren's first words when they met at Melbourne were:

"Do you know that that damned bureaucrat never would pay me the sixty bucks! And do you know that I have since seen a hundred mules scratch their heads with their hind feet!"

Hoover later found and bought a statuette of a mule contemplatively caressing his head with a hind foot, but Washington never restored the deducted money. Showing that there are mules of various breeds.

How did the twenty-year-old Hoover look to his classmates? Fortunately we have an expert answer from a specialist in observing his fellow men. Will Irwin came to Stanford in 1894. He wrote:

Entering as a freshman, my first impression of Hoover, our most eminent senior, resembled that of some great impersonal force. Jack Reynolds and Jule Frankenheimer, the uncheckable halfback; Phat Downing, the mighty football captain; Charlie Field and Edward Maslin Hulme, the university poets; Bledsoe and Magee, the statesmanlike intercollegiate debators—them one cheered or joked from the bleachers.

But Hoover, while he walked humanly among us, was a kind of legend too; a supernally able personage. We both lived in Encina dormitory, so I must have seen him constantly at meals. I was playing football, so I must have beheld him conferring with Walter Camp, who coached us that year. I knew that he was a great man just by common report. Yet I have no concrete memory of him until that day when, playing center on the freshman team, I broke my ankle. . . .

Among those who came to visit him was Hoover.

I have carried for more than thirty years the picture of him as he stood framed by the yellow door of my dormitory room. He was tall—just under six feet—broad-shouldered, lean of figure. He wore one of those double-breasted blue suits which have since become almost a uniform with him. He had a slight stoop which, you felt, came rather from excess muscular development of the shoulders than from the midnight oil.

As he contemplated the damaged member, he carried his head a trifle to one side—another trick of attitude which marks him to this day. He had mouse-colored hair, as stubbornly straight as an Indian's, and hazel eyes so contemplative that they seemed dreamy. His round but powerful face had not a straight line in it. That oddity, I have noticed since, often characterizes the physiognomies of extremely able men—O. Henry and Lord Northcliffe, for example. He stood with one foot thrust forward, jingling the keys in his trousers pocket; a little nervous trick which he has never overcome.

Others present expressed sympathy for the wounded football player. But Hoover went into action, unobtrusively. He consulted the nurse about needs and the cost of an operation. He wrote a telegram to a San Francisco physician and sent one of the boys to file it. He was, in short, in quiet and efficient control.

Irwin recalled:

He did not say a word of sympathy for me—in pain and forever out of football—but I felt it nevertheless. Then at the door he turned for an instant and jerked out: "I'm sorry." Just that; but it was as though another man had burst into maudlin tears. The crown of that personality was shyness.

Then and there, I suppose, I put myself under his leadership. That kind of thing was always happening at Stanford. Even men who opposed him in the "great frat-barb war," coming afterward into association with him, began to lean on his sane and unruffled judgment. The whimsies of life have permitted some of us to follow him since in affairs and struggles whose actors were kings, principalities and powers, dynasties and armies, violences of which the nineteenth century never dreamed, incredible human sacrifices, Godlike benevolences. But the game was the same. . . .

Stanford was a co-educational university and we may safely suppose that girls were the principal scholastic interest of the boy students, or in any event second only to football. Dozens of those boys have reminisced about the future President who walked in their midst. But I find no reference to any "heart interests" credited to Hoover. Except one, and that one became his mate for life.

Since young Herbert was normal and good-looking and prominent, we must again rely on his shyness and his earnestness to explain that hiatus. It seems clear that he had neither the time nor the talent for frivolous flirtations. He did not learn to dance until his senior year—and that only so that he could squire the one and only "heart interest" to the proms.

This was in the pre-Hollywood century and the word "glamorous" was not yet in common circulation. But it would have fitted Lou Henry, the daughter of a small-town banker in Monterey, California. Her looks and her horsemanship aroused about equal admiration when she enrolled as a freshman during Hoover's senior year. Lou was tall, slim, blue-eyed, beautiful rather than pretty, with a mass of brown hair over a high forehead. She was the outdoor type, strong and supple. As a matter of course she was installed in one of the swankier sorority houses.

And, amazingly for a girl in those days, she had elected to major in geology. She had heard Dr. Branner lecture and her intelligence, which was of high order, had been aroused by the fascination of this planet's structure. For Hoover the amazement was raised to a dimension of the miraculous when he learned that she had been born, of all places, in Iowa, and only four months after his own birth.

From the first day, as she subsequently informed him, she had heard of Hoover. He seemed the key man in every extracurricular activity, and his geological prowess had become legendary. She imagined him as a mature, probably bearded, giant. One afternoon, in his laboratory, Dr. Branner was showing the tall freshman girl a unique pre-carboniferous specimen. Lou Henry paid no attention to the sun-tanned, immature-looking boy who stood near by; she was too familiar with that stare of fascinated admiration on his face to pay much attention.

Then Dr. Branner addressed him by name. "What is your opinion, Hoover?" He never got an answer. Hoover was tongue-tied and turning color. Whatever his opinion of the pre-carboniferous specimen, which he had himself brought from the last Lindgren expedition, there was no doubt about his opinion of the contemporary specimen of womanhood.

One story, solemnly recorded in a book, is that Lou Henry's sorority sisters objected to the social visits of a student whom, for all his great reputation, they still remembered as their laundry collector. Lou is supposed to have packed her things and moved out in anger. Whether the story is true deponent sayeth not. Suffice that the pre-carboniferous acquaintance flourished into an enduring and flawless human partnership.

Herbert Clark Hoover received his sheepskin in May 1895, with the first graduating class of the new university. He was within three months of his twenty-first birthday. Though he did not know it—less attention was paid to these economic crises in that period—the Pacific coast was in the midst of a depression. He had worked his way through those four years with exactly forty dollars to spare as basic capital for starting a man's life and work.

CHAPTER IX

Adventure in Mining

THE MOST EMINENT ALUMNUS OF LE-
land Stanford, class of 1895, was making the commencement
address to the graduating class of 1935. The country was still deep
in the mire of depression. He had no illusions about the kind of
economic world those boys and girls, clutching their diplomas,
were setting out to conquer. But it was not in his nature to counsel defeatism or flaccid reliance on "youth projects." He believed
profoundly that American opportunity, though comatose, was not
dead. His mind reached back across the chasm of four decades.

"Some years ago," he said, "I marched up, as you do, to receive
the diploma of this university. For me, as for some of you here
present, the occasion was somewhat distracted by the sinking
realization of a shortage of cash working capital and the necessity
of finding an immediate job.

"Put into economic terms, I was earnestly wishing some person
with a profit motive would allow me to try to earn him a profit.
At the risk of seeming counterrevolutionary or a defender of evil,
I am going to suggest that this test for a job has some advantages.
As Will Payne has aptly observed, it does not require qualifica-
tions as to ancestry, religion, good looks, or ability to get votes.

"I did not immediately succeed in impressing any of the profit-
and-loss takers with the potentialities of my diploma. The white-
collar possibilities having been eliminated, my first serious entrance
into the economic world was by manual labor. But somehow,

both in the stage of manual labor and in professional work, I missed the discovery that I was a wage slave."

He did discover the wretchedness of unemployment as his last dollars melted away. Between jobs at manual labor, he was to record afterward, he learned to know "the bottom levels of despair . . . the ceaseless tramping and the ceaseless refusals" at employment offices.

He headed, naturally, for the Sierras where he had ranged with government surveying gangs, in the mining areas of Grass Valley and Nevada City. His engineering degree netted him only pitying smiles; hard-boiled "practical" mine officials did not quite trust the effete diploma-bearing animal. It was best, he found, to dress rough, postpone shaving, and mangle your grammar.

Both his money and his credit at a shabby hotel were about exhausted before he got a job at the Reward mine. The name evidently did not apply to him. His reward for pushing a car at the lower levels on the ten-hour night shift was two dollars a day. In a couple of months, however, he was promoted to helper on a drill and achieved the social status of a miner. Then, after an interval of that "ceaseless tramping," he found work at full miner's wages at the Mayflower pits.

Most of the miners in that district were Cornishmen, speaking their ancestral dialect, which was colorful enough, whether in sacred disputation on religion or profane intervals of cussing. The college graduate in their midst was something of a curiosity, but they took him to their grimy bosoms. Some thirty-three years later those of his fellow workers who survived organized a Hoover committee and carried every Cornish vote in the valley for the Republican ticket. Always, as miner or mine manager, he left a trail of friends.

His brother Theodore had been forced to leave school in order that their sister May might continue in school. They were living in Berkeley, where Theodore worked as a linotyper. Having saved a hundred dollars and learned invaluable lessons about mining and miners, Herbert joined them. For the first time since her death, Huldah's three children kept house together. Harriet Miles, one of the cousins who had sat with him in the Indian school in Pawhuska, came to live with them.

Just as soon as Hoover began to earn money, he insisted that Theodore resume his college course; after a successful engineering career the elder brother returned to their common alma mater as dean of the Engineering School.

Over in San Francisco the reigning mining figure was an American of French birth named Louis Janin. Though he was too big-hearted and easy-going to be the richest mining man in the West, he was recognized as the ablest. Wherever men picked the bones of this crusty old planet for mineral wealth, there Janin's reputation extended. Hoover took his courage in tow and called on the gentleman.

Janin was a stout, garrulous, and amiable fellow. Fledgling engineers by the dozen came to him for work, any work; it meant a lot to have the Janin imprimatur on your career. He let them down gently. He took the boyish Hoover, for instance, to lunch in his club and ordered wine and spent more on the repast than his guest possessed in all the world. Not only was there no opening, he explained, but there was a long waiting line of experienced and well-recommended men.

Just to emphasize how hopeless the situation was, he remarked that the only job vacant in his organization was that of copyist. Which was Janin's blunder—or, as it turned out, his good fortune.

"That's fine," Hoover said in effect, "I can typewrite and I have a good handwriting. When do I report for work?"

The jovial Janin roared with laughter. He was cornered. As Hoover had guessed, a copyist close to the throne was more strategically located than an engineer on a waiting list. Within a few weeks Janin assigned the boy to a chore of research in northern Colorado. He was so well impressed with the report that copying went by the board.

That was the last time Hoover ever applied for a job; thereafter the jobs applied for Hoover.

As Janin's respect for the young man's abilities mounted, the assignments became more important. One of these took him to Steeple Rock, New Mexico, as assistant to the mine manager. He had sampled some tough camps by that time, but this was the toughest yet, a frontier "set" of the sort Hollywood Westerns would one day immortalize; a place, in his own words, that "practiced a good deal of original sin, especially after paydays."

It was one of the jobs that helped temper the steel under his shy exterior. He went about his duties among assorted desperadoes with a six-shooter on his hip and a rifle in his saddle guard. There was no jail in the camp, but a deep, abandoned shaft did as a substitute. The sheriff just lowered malefactors into the pit and threw the rope after them.

A mine is not merely a hole in the ground. It is a complex problem in machinery, supplies, transport, power, water, and a thousand other elements. It is a problem in choosing and weeding men, improvising quick answers to sudden technical questions. Hoover was being paid more with every passing month, but the education he garnered could not be calculated in dollars and cents. His gift for detail and organization and judging men, and that sixth sense about metals and fuels which is inborn, came to the surface almost from the start.

After a year or so in the field, Janin decided he needed him in the home office. The firm had been engaged as expert counsel in a great mining litigation in Grass Valley. The briefs had been prepared by Judge Curtis Lindley, tops in his profession. But Hoover had one advantage over the judge—he had worked in Grass Valley pits and knew every acre of the sites involved. So he tore the briefs apart, steered Lindley in the right directions, helped win the case, and made life-long friends in the process.

By that time Janin knew that he had a "gold mine" in Hoover. It must be set down as proof of his Gallic gallantry, therefore, that he released the boy when an exciting opportunity showed up.

A gold rush was under way in Central West Australia. "The City" in London was the money center of the world. Through its counting houses millions of pounds were being funneled into the new developments. And the City had a healthy respect for American gold-mining methods and American engineers. In October 1897 Louis Janin received a cabled inquiry from Bewick, Moreing, and Company, the best-known and most highly esteemed firm of mining consultants in England.

They had been retained by clients as agents on ten Australian gold mines, as well as an array of prospecting sites. Huge investments were at stake. They needed a young man, for the job would be strenuous in the extreme—but not too young, for it required thorough experience; say a man of thirty-five.

Janin reported afterward that Hoover stared in speechless awe when he was offered the post. Six hundred dollars a month sounded like sudden wealth, but what mattered more than money were the horizons for expansion, the headlong plunge into the very center of the profession. Though Janin did not conceal his candidate's relative lack of experience, he gave the kind of answer that clinched the appointment. In indicating that his protege was not yet thirty-five, he was well within the truth—by twelve years, in fact.

And so the Iowa lad said farewell to Lou Henry, now a junior; they were not exactly engaged but there was what was called in that age "an understanding." He took leave of his family and friends. He was off on an adventure that would make him as familiar with Australia and China and India, with South Africa and the interior of Russia, as he was with Newberg or West Branch. On his way eastward he paused at West Branch, where assorted Minthorns and Hoovers marveled at his rapid rise to man's work, for they remembered him as a very average little boy.

Then he crossed the Mississippi for the first time, headed for New York, for London, for Australia. for the world.

2

Between California and London he grew a beard to mask his boyishness. If Mr. Moreing, who was the big boss in the firm, and other dignitaries were astonished by his youth, they were too well bred to comment on the crime. Besides, they went immediately into a detailed discussion of the Australian job with him and realized that there was nothing boyish about his mind and temper.

A week end at Mr. Moreing's elegant country estate for the final consultations turned up one minor terror for which even the New Mexican experience had not prepared him. His name was Buttons and he sniffed audibly at the scantiness of the American's wardrobe; worse, he insisted on helping a bearded man dress!

It was a long journey to Australia—by way of France, Italy, Egypt, India—and at the end of it, smallpox having developed on board the vessel, came ten tedious days of quarantine in a western Australian port. The newly built narrow-gauge railway took Hoover three hundred miles inland to the railhead at Coolgardie.

Americans, knowing the feel of California in '49 from their literature, can more readily visualize Coolgardie, Kalgoorlie, Leonora, and the other mushrooming towns on the Australian desert. It was a flat and desolate land of vast distances covered with low, bristly sagebrush, where the mercury rarely dropped below one hundred even at night; a land in which water was almost as valuable and more rare than the gold for which thousands of men were hunting feverishly. Only the "Persian carpet of immortelles," as Hoover described it, spread once a year after the brief rainy season, broke the yearlong monotony of the parched and cracked landscape.

It was a sultry, dusty, insect-ridden world of clapboard and corrugated-iron houses, unlicked men, vile liquor, and soaring hopes that too often petered out in sordidness. No one has recorded what the mine managers and engineers, many of them grizzled veterans, thought of the boy sent to lead them. What is known is that almost from the first day he became "the Chief" to his men; and that "the Chief" he remained to those associated with him in all the years that followed.

Hoover inspected the mines, discounted those that seemed to him uneconomic, and focused his energies tenaciously on the few that showed promise. He brought in specialists from many parts of the world, but particularly from California. He laid out plants, ordered American equipment, introduced processes that were new to Australia, and sometimes just new. Rapidly he carved islands of order out of a turbulent sea of chaos; for the first time certain financiers began to see a profit on their investments.

Because of the water situation, ragged Afghan camels served better than horses. To this day the sight of the animal makes Hoover seasick. In instalments of thirty or forty miles a day, he journeyed with the nauseous caravans from one of his mines to another; or on the trail of rumors that sometimes made millionaires in London and New York and more often fizzled out in disappointments. And all the time he "panned" for dependable men as eagerly as the lone prospectors panned for gold. When he found them they usually remained "Hoover men" to the end of their days.

The life was every bit as strenuous as the Londoners had promised. Of nights, when the rest of Kalgoorie or Leonora was loud with payday guzzling and fighting, Hoover was in his sweltering corrugated offices, working and planning. He seemed detached, above the fevers of that place and time, a cool mind clicking away in the swirling excitements.

Now he had plenty to report to the blue-eyed girl still at Stanford. Some of the things he described she could understand perfectly, being a geologist herself; the new filter press he had introduced, for instance, which was in time to be copied by the whole industry. And there were bits of humor to transmit too. The burro who ate wax matches, starting an internal blaze that had to be put out with water through a funnel. The vegetable garden he tried to coax into being in defiance of parched soil and salty water, netting two pathetic cabbages at a cost of only $250 a head. The eccentric characters who gravitated to a boom region.

Once the high-born Briton who was Governor General of Australia visited the district and was conducted by the reception committee to a mine which Hoover managed. In his usual garb when on the job, a pair of overalls, he conducted his guest personally down the shaft. When they came up on the surface the Governor graciously thanked the nice young man—and gave him a five-shilling tip.

On one of his camel treks into the interior Hoover camped overnight near a prospect which the owners, a group of Welshmen, called "Sons of Gwalia." They took him through their primitive mill and "showings." Others had seen the place—it was one of dozens of hopefuls—and moved on. Hoover, with that sixth sense to guide him, stopped short. He knew at once that this was "it," and took an option.

It required a special kind of courage for a man of twenty-four to urge, on his own judgment, an investment of half a million dollars; $250,000 for a two-thirds interest in the property and $250,000 more for working capital. London followed his hunch and voted him a small interest in the enterprise. As of 1940 the Gwalia mines produced a total of $45,000,000 in gold and paid out $8,000,000 in dividends.

Hoover worked too hard to be lonely. He found tag ends of time, moreover, to indulge his great hunger for reading; not only the English and French classics, economics and technological tomes, but the classics of antiquity became part of his mental armory. And despite the normal quota of failures, he had the deep satisfaction of achievement. Recalcitrant mines began to hum and pay off. Areas which did not even have a name a year earlier were turning swiftly into populous and prosperous communities. The Gwalia workings, to which he now gave his major time, were yielding the yellow metal beyond his high expectations. He was able to send money home to his family and toward the support of needy friends.

In retrospect he was to write of this period: "To feel great works growing under one's feet and to have constantly more men getting good jobs is to be master of contentment."

His name was beginning to appear in the mining journals and even on the financial pages of London papers. Melbourne and Sidney publications respectfully solicited his views on this and that. In Australia, miners talked of him as "Boy Hoover" with an intonation that meant "boy wonder." There were some who dubbed him "Hail Columbia" Hoover—H. C. being conveniently his initials—because of the fervor with which he pushed American machinery and men.

All the same, homesickness was beginning to gnaw at his nerves after nearly two years of the desert. A girl in Monterey (Lou Henry had now graduated with honors and was back home with her family) certainly had something to do with his condition. He was thinking of going home when a cable reached him which settled the immediate future neatly. It came from Peking, China, and was signed by Mr. Moreing.

China was then in the throes of the short-lived "reform and progress" movement under the so-called Young Emperor, Kwang Hsu. The Celestial Empire seemed ready for westernizing influence to unlock its sealed-up natural riches. The principal European nations shoved and intrigued for privileged positions in the process.

The Chinese-owned Chinese Engineering and Mining Company was floating a large bond issue in England, France, Belgium, and Germany, and it was in this connection that Mr. Moreing had gone to Peking. The company owned coal mines and cement plants and was raising the capital in part to construct a coal-loading port at Chinwangtao on the Gulf of Chihli.

The nominal Chinese manager of this company was a former stable groom risen to wealth by devious routes, one Chang Yen-mao, whom the Young Emperor had also put at the head of a newly established ministry, the Bureau of Mines. He was seeking a foreign specialist as his right-hand man in the bureau. The European nations, snarled in a great knot of partnerships and rivalries, each hoping for a juicier bite of roasted China, coveted that post under Minister Chang.

Mr. Moreing wisely counseled Chang to choose an American and bypass the whole pack of diplomatic intriguers. Chang agreed, Moreing produced the man. An offer was cabled to Australia. It involved a dual responsibility: manager of the coal-and-cement corporation and director of all Celestial Mines, known and especially unknown, under the Young Emperor's new Minister. It carried a combined salary of $20,000 and all expenses.

Two messages went forward simultaneously over Hoover's signature, one to Peking and the other to Monterey, California. The first was an emphatic Yes. The second was an affectionate request for a Yes, which arrived with record speed.

3

Hoover journeyed to the second stage of his great adventure, China, by way of England and California. When he reached London in January 1899 he needed no beard or other disguise. He had proved himself and justified Janin's trust. No one cared any longer whether the man who activated the limping Australian properties and developed the fabulous Sons of Gwalia was twenty or eighty.

From Mr. Moreing, now back home, he got a fill-in on his coming tasks. The coal-and-cement end was clear enough; it meant building railroads and an ice-free port, organizing production and transport—practical work for a practical man. The Chinese Government end was exalted but nebulous and shadowed by palace intrigues. It was to remain nebulous to the end; even before Hoover reached China several months later, the Young Emperor had been dethroned and imprisoned by the Empress Dowager, his mother. The "Westernizing" plans, mining included, were left in midair.

Lou Henry became Mrs. Herbert Hoover in her parental home in the picturesque mission town of Monterey on February 10. The Henrys were Episcopalians, though Mrs. Hoover later joined the Society of Friends. A Catholic priest who was a friend of the family, Father Ramon Mestres, officiated, but it was a civil ceremony; he was acting in the capacity of civil magistrate. On February 11 the newlyweds sailed from San Francisco, loaded down with all the books on Chinese life, history, and customs they could corral.

A month's voyage across the Pacific was their honeymoon, a rented house in the foreign compound of Peking Lou's bridal home. While Hoover threw himself into the complex affairs of his dual job, Mrs. Hoover turned the house into a home. For this she had a unique talent which eased their lives in a dozen foreign settings for twenty years to come. She commanded the usual battalion of Chinese servants and began the study of the Chinese language, with excellent results.

Anyone who has lived in a foreign colony in the East knows the elaborate structure of social life and protocol that prevails there. Both his business and official positions entitled Hoover and his wife to top-shelf social positions. But the multi-lingual colony found them disappointing and even alarming in their choice of friends, native and foreign, on the basis of personal predilections and without regard to social lines. The Hoovers had no patience for the rigmarole of "society."

It was a comparatively simple matter to import a few of his Australian associates and get work going for the Chinese Engineering and Mining. The harbor of Chinwangtao was cleared and port construction speeded; rails were laid; the 25,000 Chinese in the coal mines were kept busy. But the Ministry of Mines was another matter, for here politics and intrigue, rather than engineering, set the pace.

Logic dictated intensive research on coal, iron, steel, lead, zinc, copper. These were the things readiest to hand and the things the Chinese people most needed. But Minister Chang operated on a devious political logic of his own. He was hoping to dazzle the Empress, fortify his official status, and incidentally get his hands on treasure at government expense by locating gold. Hoover pleaded for permission to dig for coal and iron where they existed, but was shunted to prospecting for gold where it might or might not exist.

It was primarily on the search for the yellow metal that Hoover and several of his assistants journeyed thousands of miles, endured hardships, on occasion fought off bandits. The most distressing of those hardships was the magnificent style in which, as plenipotentiaries of a self-important Minister with public funds to burn, they were obliged to move.

The first of these expeditions was typical, both in its scale and its futility. It was into Jehol, to a site about one hundred and fifty miles from the railroad. Hoover had his first taste of Chinese pomp and inefficiency, of magnificence tempered by bedbugs. He needed only a few specialists, a cook and interpreter, a few good ponies and pack mules. But Minister Chang was building "face"; only the most ponderously showy setup would do for his Director of Mines in the Celestial Empire traveling on affairs of state.

On the railroad leg of the trip Hoover met one of the truly patriotic leaders of China. Tong Shao-yi, a graduate of Columbia University, was the director of the Northern Railways of China and the largest Chinese stockholder in the coal-and-cement corporation which Hoover was managing. In years to come Tong would twice serve as Prime Minister of China. The friendship of the two men was to last for many decades, as long as the Chinese statesman lived.

At the railway destination Hoover and his companion, geologist George Wilson, found the personnel of their expedition awaiting them in noisy and panoplied grandeur. Twenty officers commanded a hundred cavalrymen; there were flocks of graded officials, servants, grooms, coolies, some two hundred animals, and mountains of luggage. The cavalcade, when finally it began to roll, was slow-moving and uncomfortable but vastly impressive, with banners flying, advance heralds, and rear guards.

For all of Hoover's impatient pushing, the monstrous magnificence rarely made more than twenty-five miles a day. Nights were spent in bug-infested inns. Meals were a lengthy, many-coursed ritual. In the end he adjusted himself with a sigh to the Chinese tempo and caught up on his reading. Finally the cavalcade reached the gold-mining interior of Jehol.

The advance heralds had done their work all too well. Thousands from miles around awaited the "foreign mandarin" who, the story went, had magic "green eyes" that saw through earth and solid rock to the gold below. He was trailed by fascinated men, women, and children who spied on his every magical move.

The reports of gold in Jehol were true enough. The site was being worked now, as in past centuries, by the crudest methods. But Hoover and Wilson noted that the best veins had been exhausted long before. The current workings were thin and would not justify exploitation with modern machinery. Their most memorable find was a foreman who had once worked in California and greeted them solemnly with all the English he had retained: "Hello, boss!"

The interpreter assigned to Hoover had some trouble translating his Chinese emotions. Things that were bad he described as "damn" and things that were disastrous (which were a lot more frequent) as "really damn." No doubt he had a name, but to Hoover and the mining staff he was known only as Really Damn.

Local expectations of magic gold discoveries by the green-eyed one reached a pitch where a harsh announcement of failure might have precipitated a riot. Really Damn therefore explained with elaborate apologies that the foreign mandarin's findings could not be disclosed except to a most exalted personage in Peking. The exalted personage, His Excellency Minister Chang, was disappointed by the report but not discouraged in the great search.

The mining industries of China were in fantastic confusion. Foreigners were grabbing concessions with the connivance of grafting officials. Freebooters of a dozen nationalities were schem-

ing deals and compounding overlapping contracts. Great dignitaries were selling huge properties that did not belong to them.
There were no laws, or too many laws, and no trace of a national
policy to guide officialdom.

The best thing that Minister Chang could do, supposing he was
concerned for the obligations of his office, was to impose some
order on this confusion. Such was the burden of Hoover's advice.
In line with it Hoover made a study of Chinese mining legislation, of existing and projected concessions, and then drafted a
decree regularizing the rules of the game.

Its fundamental aim was to safeguard the Chinese people's
ownership of their natural resources and to guarantee proper
royalties for the government and decent conditions for Chinese
labor. It was one of the first attempts to protect China against
the encroachments of foreign exploiters and native grafters. A
few high-minded men, such as Tong, fought for it. Chang and
his brood of foreign advisers sabotaged the project. Perhaps they
knew better than the idealistic young Californian that no logical
order made sense in the face of the cyclone of violence just then
being brewed in the palace and beyond.

Hoover did bludgeon Chang into authorizing an investigation
of coal deposits west of Peking. The field outlined by the American engineers contained more anthracite coal than all the known
deposits in the world combined. It was to become the primary
objective of Japanese imperialism, then of Russian imperialism,
in the coming half century.

The gold hunt went forward in flea-bitten splendor. Always the
journeys were gummed up by grandeur. They followed the rain-
bow paths of rumor to Shantung, Shansi and Shensi, Manchuria,
and the Gobi Desert. Mrs. Hoover went with her husband on
some of them. Coolies trotted alongside with empty but gaudy
sedan chairs to prove that it was not poverty but eccentricity
which forced the foreign pair to ride horseback like commoners.
At provincial capitals there would be elaborate receptions and
exchanges of gifts with local overlords; among them they found
a few men of great wisdom, culture, and charm.

No high-powered Americans could crash through the thousand-
year layers of ceremony and seemliness. If they found no gold,

they found food for thought and matter for a lifetime of reminiscence. There were also episodes of danger to add spice to the futilities.

Perhaps the most memorable of these expeditions was the one that took Hoover as far as Urga, the Mongol capital of Tibet in the Gobi Desert. The thirty-nine days were largely wasted as mining research but highly rewarding as cultural experience. Hoover made a state call on the Dalai Lama or Living Buddha. He found the deity paddling a bicycle in great glee around the inner court of the lamasery and was entertained with gramophone records; these Western marvels to relieve the tedium of godhood were the gifts of the local Russian Consul.

The wanderings under banners and military escort took Hoover to Kalgan at the Great Wall of China and to remote regions where American missionaries sometimes greeted him; to points on the Yellow River and a dozen other rivers. They netted reports in which he pleaded for the abandonment of the search and indicated by-product discoveries of vast deposits of less glamorous metals. He came to know more about the underground treasures of China than any other man of his time.

Meanwhile rumblings of violence echoed through China. Sporadic attacks on foreigners were flowing into a torrential explosion. A society that called itself I Ho Tuan—the Mailed Fist —and which Europeans called "the Boxers" was rolling up massive force. It was an amalgam of political fury and religious fanaticism, pledged to drive all foreign devils into the sea and destroy all Chinese who had trafficked with the foreign deviltry. Whether the Empress Dowager backed the movement was not clear, but clearly it was a reaction against the Young Emperor's reform efforts.

Returning to Peking from a wearing trip, Mrs. Hoover developed sinus trouble. Since the physician they most trusted was in Tientsin, they decided to move their headquarters to that city. By May more and more stories of missionaries murdered, their women tortured, Chinese "collaborationists" (to borrow a word from the future) hacked to death began to filter through. Hoover decided to call all his men in from the field—a decision that undoubtedly saved many lives.

By the end of May the foreign settlements in Peking and other cities were beleaguered. About eleven hundred sailors and marines of half-a-dozen nationalities arrived in Tientsin from the warships anchored at Taku. Unhappily they brought only one cannon and a few machine guns. Some optimism was sustained, however, because a local imperial army of 25,000 under foreign officers and with foreign equipment was deployed in the Tientsin area. It was generally considered dependable.

4

The foreign compound of Tientsin was an elongated area of several parallel streets, in all about a mile long and a quarter of a mile deep, with the river on one side, a thickly populated and odoriferous Chinese suburb on the other. On June 13, 1900, the storm broke. The "dependable" army turned its guns on the foreign officers, killing a few while the others fled to the compound. It was war, with the chances of survival seemingly remote.

Herbert Hoover, as the foremost civilian, thus found himself at twenty-six the commander in chief in an unequal struggle. The ranking naval officer, a Russian colonel named Wogack, assumed military command. To Hoover fell the technical responsibilities and, no less important, the organization and husbanding of food supplies and water. This was his first experience as food controller.

The foreign colony numbered about three hundred, some eighty of them Americans. More than a thousand Chinese, most of them Christians, also sought refuge in the settlement. In addition, Chang Yen-mao and Tong Shao-yi, with their families and retinues and subordinate officials—in all about six hundred souls—crowded into the area and became Hoover's personal responsibility.

Having discovered a providential supply of sacked rice, sugar, and other products in warehouses, Hoover soon had more than a thousand terrified Chinese and all the able-bodied foreigners at work building barricades with these sacks. Overnight the settlement was shielded on its three land sides, with troops stationed at dangerously wide intervals.

That the ill-armed naval contingents and civilian volunteers held off the swarms of attackers for more than a month seemed in retrospect almost incredible. What they had in their favor was compactness of strategic position, discipline, and intelligence. Had the Boxers and Chinese soldiers had a plan, any plan—had they attacked from three sides at once, for instance—the defense probably would have collapsed.

Every man, woman, and child had specific duties to perform on a twenty-four-hour schedule. The waterworks, unfortunately, were outside the barricades. Squads of daring men, Hoover often among them, stole out night after night, worked the pumps and boilers, and returned before dawn with supplies of safe water. A herd of cattle was salvaged and, under Mrs. Hoover's direction, provided milk and some meat.

It was estimated that 60,000 shells were fired into the settlement during the month which seemed years long. Casualties were heavy. Only two doctors and one trained nurse were on hand to care for the wounded; hospitals were set up and Mrs. Hoover made their smooth functioning her chief duty. "There were no pacifists in that settlement," Hoover had cause to explain years later. Enemy artillery ignited fires faster than the harried defenders could put them out.

There was a terrible night when hysteria got the upper hand. Some stray bullets started the dangerous rumor that the refugee Chinese within the compound were sniping. Messengers rushed into Hoover's home with the news that an undisciplined British bully, a Captain Bailey, had aroused a mob and rounded up the six hundred Chinese under Hoover's care. Drumhead trials were under way, with mass lynchings to come.

When Hoover, on a bicycle, hurried to the scene he found that Chang and Tong and other outstanding persons had already been "found guilty." Bailey only laughed at his protests and threats. Hoover rushed to Colonel Wogack's headquarters and in a few minutes returned with enough military force to disperse the mob and rescue all the Chinese.

There was a day when a shell burst through Tong's roof, killing his wife and a baby daughter. Hoover, who lived across the street, rushed into the burning house and carried another of Tong's little daughters to safety through a hail of bullets.

About eighteen years later, when he was American Food Administrator in Washington, the Chinese Ambassador, Wellington Koo, invited the Hoovers to dinner. At one point Mrs. Koo said smilingly, "Mr. Hoover, we have met before. I am Tong Shao-yi's daughter, whom you carried across the street during the siege of Tientsin!"

About forty-six years later Hoover was in Shanghai in the course of his globe-girdling mission for President Truman. Two Chinese ladies, married to important local men, asked separately for an appointment. Each of them came on an identical errand: to thank him for saving her life. They had been among the children he had protected against the lynching mob.

Toward the end of the siege the joyous news came that fifteen hundred American Marines and Welsh Fusiliers were on their way from Taku. The following day they arrived, with marine buglers at their head. Of all the music he has ever heard, Hoover likes to tell, there was none so beautiful as "There'll Be a Hot Time in the Old Town Tonight" as rendered by the approaching buglers. Women and children were evacuated, though Mrs. Hoover and several others on their own insistence remained at their posts.

The reinforcements were too small to assure safety. The fighting continued and there were many dark moments. But they had brought artillery and machine guns. With them came, also, a few American correspondents. One of them was Frederick Palmer. Another was the aging California poet, Joaquin Miller, representing the Hearst press. Miller became something of a problem. Having gotten his fill of Tientsin color stories, the old gentleman made arrangements to start out for Peking by rickshaw. The chances of his getting through alive were not one in a hundred, but he would not listen to reason. In the end Mrs. Hoover bribed the rickshaw boy to desert him, stranding an unhappy bard in relative security.

About the middle of July the danger was ended. The Boxer uprising had been crushed. The siege of Tientsin was far more costly in blood and more desperate than the one in Peking, but it got less than its share of fame. The Boer War in South Africa was underway at the time; the beleaguerments of Kimberley,

Mafeking, and Ladysmith are celebrated episodes, yet all three together suffered fewer casualties than Tientsin.

5

With the end of danger came the end of solidarity among the foreign military contingents. A wild grab for Chinese wealth began, and the properties under Hoover's management did not escape. The Russians seized the coal mines; Cossacks carted off carloads of machinery into Manchuria; the British grabbed the harbor works; the Americans helped themselves to the company's fleet of transport vessels. The local Chinese, too, dug into what remained, in particular carrying off the railroad tracks.

To salvage the bondholding interests, the company was reorganized as a British corporation—this on Minister Chang's own suggestion. The deed of property was in Mr. Moreing's name. Certain rights were reserved, of course, for the Chinese owners, but the control shifted from China to Europe—a fact which very nearly cost Chang his conniving old head.

The Hoovers returned to London, where the reorganization was approved and additional capital raised. Agreement having been reached, Hoover was sent back as general manager on increased salary; he was voted, besides, a minor stock interest. Early in 1901, after leaving his wife in Japan for the rest she badly needed, he returned to Chinwangtao.

The Bureau of Mines having expired somewhere in the melee, he now had only one job on his hands, but it was an amazingly complicated one. To reassemble the pieces of the Chinese Engineering and Mining Company, the engineer had to turn diplomat. Delicate negotiations and not so delicate big-stick threats were needed to extract the various grabs from the various grabbers and to appease conflicting foreign and Chinese interests. A young Belgian diplomat, Chevalier De Wouters, was designated by the home office to help him.

In the end the company assets were more or less restored and in time the enterprise began to function. Even the rails came back, through the simple expedient of advertising a reward and immunity to the Chinese who would bring them back. As for the purloined machinery in Manchuria, the Czar's government agreed to its return—after which it had to be ransomed from his army officers.

Productivity expanded swiftly and with it the original Chinese stock rose 500 per cent in the new issues in the stock markets of the world. On his authority from the foreign owners, De Wouters negotiated a settlement with Chang and his group of Chinese interests, assuring them certain functions and a bloc of stock. Hoover, being a technical and not a financial agent, had no direct authority in the negotiations. But he approved the arrangement as just to all concerned. A memorandum embodying the terms was signed.

In the autumn of 1901 Hoover was informed that a Belgian syndicate had quietly bought up enough stock to assume control of the company. Soon thereafter the Belgian representative, Emil Francqui, arrived to take over. One of his first acts—over the urgent protests of Hoover—was to repudiate the De Wouters-Chang memorandum, alleging fraud on Chang's part.

This repudiation was to have completely absurd repercussions for Hoover when he found himself neck deep in American politics. Though he had scant respect and less affection for the intriguing Chang, the ex-Minister of Mines, Hoover felt that the Chinese had both moral and legal justice on their side. He took their part against the Belgians and, failing to win his point, refused to remain on as general manager despite Francqui's urging.

Chang, now discredited at the palace in Peking, saved his head only by promising to obtain justice in the courts of England. The litigation lasted nearly six years. Hoover was not personally involved; he was not a defendant or a party to the controversy. But he did testify, and his evidence was wholly pro-Chinese. It was the most influential element in ultimately giving the Chinese a substantial victory. He had simply told the truth as he saw it in line with his Quaker conscience. But he won the gratitude of Chinese leaders.

From 1920 forward, however, political foes in America, having obtained a cockeyed version of the story, tried to use it as a smear brush on Hoover's character. Amazingly, incredibly, they turned the facts inside out to accuse him of having "exploited" the Chinese! More than a quarter of a century after the events, wholly unable to decipher the intricacies of the business, they sought to present his friendly help to the Chinese as its very opposite. The Chang litigation still shows up, in a vague and confused fashion, in anti-Hoover talk.

But that is running ahead of our story. Hoover was winding up his affairs when he received a cabled offer of a junior partnership from Bewick, Moreing and Company. He accepted. These four and a half years in the field had made him indispensable to the London organization. Already his name loomed large in the mining world.

With Mrs. Hoover he returned to California and after a brief vacation they proceeded to London. He was just over twenty-seven, but professionally a veteran, knowledgeable and tempered by four years surcharged with experience. He had a little money laid aside and profitable interests in Australian and Chinese mines. He had magnificent health, a matured mind, a well-founded record of leadership and organization under the most difficult circumstances.

From his Chinese adventure he emerged with a genuine feeling of respect for the Chinese people as a whole. "The impression I have held of them," he was to write long afterward, "is one of abiding admiration. Here 90 per cent of a huge mass live so close to the starvation line that someone falls below it in nearly every village every year. Yet they live with patience and tolerance. They have the deepest fidelities to family ties and the fullest affection for their children. They work harder and more hours than any race in the world. True, they are superstitious beyond belief, but they have a vivid sense of humor. They are courageous, as witness the armies they have created. They are highly acquisitive, and one need have little fear that this great mass will ever be Communists for long."

CHAPTER X

The Great Engineer

POLITICAL PROPAGANDA SUCCEEDED
to some extent, years after he had retired from the profession, in
putting an accent of irony into the phrase. But Herbert Hoover
was in sober and literal fact the Great Engineer.

In all the history of mining industries there have not been
a dozen men in a class with him for scope and comprehensiveness
of accomplishment. This is not my opinion, of course. It was the
considered opinion of the mine-engineering fraternity, a clannish
and hard-boiled group without inhibitions in appraising its own
practitioners.

They attested their judgment continually through the years by
loading him with all the honors, titles, offices, and medals he was
willing to carry. To them Herbert Hoover was an incandescent
name long before the world at large heard of it. In his early thirties
he was widely regarded in his profession as the world's outstanding mining engineer; by the time he was forty this regard was
unanimous.

There were greater experts in this or that specialized branch of
the field—geologists, metallurgists, power engineers, chemists,
construction engineers. These were often the specialists whom
he employed, deployed, and directed on thirty or forty great
enterprises in all parts of the world at once. But there were few,
if any, who could compare with Hoover for all-around proficiency; for his extraordinary blend of technical knowledge,
mechanical know-how, organizing ability, and business acumen.

As our industrial twentieth century went into stride, it was insatiably hungry for metals and minerals. Never had so much of the stuff of a mechanical civilization been turned up in so many places; and nearly everywhere the sure mind of Hoover directed much of the exploring, digging, smelting, and transportation of this stuff. In the course of his engineering career an aggregate of at least a million workers were employed in undertakings where he played a decisive role. At the moment he quit, at the outbreak of the Great War in 1914, more than 150,000 were drawing their pay from mining works with which he was connected.

In the thirteen years after he left China he girdled the globe eight or ten times. During the first half of that period, for about seven years, he operated as part of the century-old firm of Bewick, Moreing and Company, the following six years as a free-lance engineer.

With the London firm he served primarily as "outside" man, the practical engineering executive in the field. It was a field that stretched from Colorado, California, Canada to Europe, the Near East, Australia, South Africa, and India. In his free-lancing period he had dozens of the top men in the profession under his command, not exactly as partners but as associates; he fitted the man to the job as required. The geography of his career expanded to take in Russia and Egypt, Latin America and Abyssinia, Scotland and Korea—names which indicate the breadth of the activity without defining it in full.

Hoover had modest offices in San Francisco, New York, London, Paris, St. Petersburg, Mandalay, and at times a dozen other cities. But his real offices were the ships and trains that rushed him from one vast project to another; his principal filing system was that phenomenal brain of his, that "card-index memory." It became a commonplace in his life to hasten from 30 degrees below zero in Siberia or Korea to 100 degrees in the shade in the Malay Straits or the Levant.

Despite the extent and worldwide dispersal of his labors, he managed to keep abreast of books and ideas and political trends. He found the leisure to read and to study; to write endless technical papers and to publish a textbook; to translate, with Mrs. Hoover, a medieval classic that had stymied the classicists; to lecture in universities and assume a growing amount of responsibility for the affairs of Stanford University.

Political currents had direct repercussions on so many of his enterprises that he was necessarily concerned with the intricate drama of world events. But professional interests aside, he was forever observing, comparing, making inner judgments. He had started with a heritage of American and Western and Quaker precepts and preferences. Now he was testing these in the fires of global reality. He was hammering out his philosophy of life, his social and economic views, on the anvil of direct experience. Few Americans destined for public leadership have been so close to the multitudinous world, its dizzying patterns and contrasts, its variety of peoples, customs, and ideas.

A telescoped recital of his career conveys an impression of hurry, crowding, excitement. A lesser man would have been an ulcerous nervous wreck under the strain. But Hoover had the blessed ability to carry towering loads with a genuine nonchalance. He remained unhurried and unexcited. He knew how to dismiss the trivial and secondary, to focus on essentials. He had that rare talent of keeping jobs apart in his emotions, so that the griefs of one did not intrude to color and dampen another.

In only one of those thirteen years did he fail to spend some time in his own country. Mrs. Hoover was by his side in nearly all of his earlier wanderings; in the latter part of this period, the education of their two boys kept her more and more in California.

I have read somewhere that one of these sons traveled around the world twice in his first year. Be that as it may, it is a fact that Herbert, Jr., born in London in 1903, set off for Australia in his fifth week; and that his brother Allan, born in 1907, likewise in London, went promptly on a journey to Burma, likewise at the advanced age of five weeks.

I find Hoover asserting in his notes that "traveling with babies is easier than with most grownups." Whether his wife concurred in that opinion is open to serious doubt. But she toted her baby boys in baskets to the most outlandish segments of the world map under the most trying conditions; she toted them on horseback and camelback; she shielded them against Arctic cold and tropic heat, against mosquitoes and sandstorms and polluted water.

For Lou Henry knew that her husband, paradoxical as it may sound, was at heart a homebody who abhorred hotels and was deeply attached to familiar things, to his own house and furniture and flocks of pets. No matter where the tom-tom of professional duty summoned them, California, and specifically Palo Alto, spelled home. It was the fixed point of their compass of hopes and plans. There they built their permanent family seat.

In London, where the Hoovers spent more time than in any other spot except California, they acquired a rambling old place near Kensington Gardens, known for generations as the Red House. It had a spacious garden and was shaded by a spreading oak tree. Vernon Kellogg, who knew its hospitality well, described it as a "bit of transplanted America, and, in particular, a bit of transplanted California." Hundreds of Americans learned to value its homey flavor. They came to know the dog Rags, and the Persian and Siamese cats which were so often on Hoover's lap, the pigeons in the garden, and the boys' menagerie in the upper rooms.

Men and women with famous names and gilded titles came there, but only because the Hoovers judged them interesting and genuine. The Hoovers steered clear of Society with a capital S. They were homespun in their tastes. An evening's guests might count a top-shelf statesman or financier, but it was likely to include also a prospector fresh from the Klondike, a writer or painter, a railroad man from India, a Quaker acquaintance from back home.

But always there were people, always there was lively talk and the friction of clashing views. Though a renowned specialist, Hoover was universal in his mental interests and his avocations.

2

Since I am not writing a biography, I am under no obligation to record even the peak moments of those years or to respect chronology. I have indicated only as much of his childhood and early manhood as may help give the "feel" of his personality. I am being even more summary in dealing with his major engineering period; a sampling to suggest its magnitude and its special Hooveresque quality must do.

Bewick-Moreing managed properties or served as technical advisers on a fee basis plus a percentage on profits. As a junior partner Hoover received an agreed percentage of these earnings. The firm's deed of partnership specifically forbade any member to engage in stock-market speculation. They made money, but never by manipulating pieces of paper or "mining" too-eager investors.

On the contrary, their special function was to restrain speculation by revealing the hard facts under glittering promotions. Their most valuable stock in trade was rigid honesty and dependability. It was on competence, on stepped-up production, on reduced costs, that their income depended.

As the youngest and newest member of the firm, Hoover was therefore well within organization policy in warning the industry and the public on numerous occasions against the speculative fevers associated with mine financing. The technical journals of those years contain interviews and statements in which he assailed high-powered promoters and satirized the gullibles who let themselves be snared by promises baited with big figures.

He set himself boldly against the gaudy promotional side of his industry in a more concrete fashion also. He dared to deprecate bonanzas. The health of the mining business, he argued, depended on hard work and rationalized production, not on sensational accidents. The greatest lure to investment dollars was the gold mine; people who thought twice before putting their savings into mere iron or zinc didn't think at all before sinking it in gold. But Hoover was convinced early that gold-mining was the toughest and least remunerative branch of the business.

For him the backbone of mining was the exploitation of large bodies of low-grade ores. He preferred always a stable and continuous business to the speculative flash in the pan. And he did not hesitate to make these views known as he went deeper and deeper into the industry. His spectacular victories were not in gold but in zinc and lead and coal; in transforming abandoned low-grade workings into steady profit makers.

In his opinions and methods he therefore represented the oppo-

site pole from what American journalese implies by the word
"promoter" pronounced with a grimace. This, however, did not
discourage the people who long afterward howled in many keys
that Hoover had been "a promoter, not an engineer."

He helped raise millions of dollars to finance old and new
projects, but only when he had investigated them personally;
only on the basis of a full and frank picture of the potentials
involved. Always his profits or losses were related to output and
cost of production, never to the ups and downs of investment
fevers. His name as a consultant or on a board of directors
became in the mining world a guarantee against speculative
promotions.

At the turn of the century the mining booms wrecked more
fortunes than they made. There had been plenty of self-delusion
and fraud. The get-rich-quick artists feared firms like Bewick-
Moreing. It was when the bubbles burst, when alarmed stock-
holders sought to salvage some of their millions, that honest tech-
nicians were called in. Not once but dozens of times Hoover took
over mismanaged, over-expanded, seemingly hopeless mines; in
a year or two or three he made them solvent and profitable. "We
were engineering doctors to sick concerns," he has phrased it
himself, speaking specifically of his free-lance period.

So many people had been brutally burned in the boom fevers by
the time Hoover joined the firm that there was a veritable epidemic of contrite honesty. Everyone seemed eager to press out the
water and establish his mines on a solid businesslike foundation.
This reaction against the boom, against false optimism, brought
more and more business to the organization.

In 1908, when he resigned from the company, the projects under
its management in Australia alone produced a million tons of
metal annually, valued at $18,000,000. This was essentially Hoover's
doing. Many of those properties had been losing millions when
he took charge; by 1908 he had reduced costs 40 per cent, while
raising wages and expanding employment all around. And Australia represented only a fraction of the firm's clients.

Toward the end of 1902, only a year after Hoover entered
Bewick-Moreing, the firm suffered a terrific body blow and
Hoover happened to be the one to take its full impact. Mr. Bewick,

who was no longer active in the business, was off hunting moose in Canada. Mr. Moreing was off hunting tigers in Manchuria. Hoover, who had been in London all told less than three months, faced the music virtually alone.

On reaching his office one morning he found a letter on his desk marked "private and confidential." It was a handwritten confession—by A. S. Rowe, chief accountant of the firm and a junior partner. Rowe was a middle-aged, conventional fellow of good repute; the last man who would have been suspected of the nerve and the imagination for large-scale peculations.

But there it was, the fantastic confession, ending in a hint of suicide. The very evils the firm was fighting had overwhelmed its own accountant. For a long time, Rowe revealed, he had been speculating in American railroad stocks. He had resorted to fraud to cover mounting losses. Now he was a million dollars in the hole—a million dollars which he had in part taken from the firm's cash and largely raised by issuing forged certificates of stock, forged checks, and using other thieving devices. It was defalcation on a breath-taking scale, with clients of the firm as the principal victims.

Failing to reach the senior partners by cable, Hoover summoned a few of London's leading financiers and mine specialists among his acquaintances. They sat openmouthed as he read them the confession. The one thing perfectly clear was that Bewick-Moreing was under no legal obligations whatsoever; they could not be held accountable for the forgeries.

One of the older men turned to Hoover. "Young man," he said, "you are new in this firm and new in English business. We would all like to help you. We would first like to know if you have any ideas as to what you would like to do."

Hoover answered promptly, "I would *like* to pay every dime over the counter, whether we are liable or not."

The tension was relieved when the questioner declared "tuppence" would be a better expression under the circumstances than "dime." The young partner did not need any more advice than that. On his own authority, at the risk of Mr. Moreing's later disapproval, Hoover issued a statement to the press. It announced the facts of the disaster, indicated that the firm was legally in the clear—then pledged that every tuppence would be made good to the victims notwithstanding.

This demonstration of honesty beyond the call of formal duty—a million dollars beyond it—made more of a sensation in London than the defalcations themselves. It was a week before the tiger-hunting senior got the shocking news. He instantly approved Hoover's policy and assumed 75 per cent of the obligations; 25 per cent was assumed by Hoover and another junior member.

In one swoop the young American's savings from five grueling years in Australia, China, and elsewhere were thus wiped out. The larger part of his surplus in the following three years, likewise, went to pay off the Rowe crimes. Eight years of his gigantic labors—nearly half of his total engineering life—went to the voluntary restitution of another man's, a stranger's, thefts.

Rowe did not commit suicide, but fled to Canada, leaving his wife and children destitute. He was caught and condemned to ten years in prison. Mrs. Hoover—and this is a fact London never knew—helped to care for Rowe's innocent family until he finished his sentence.

Hoover's personal standing as well as the reputation of Bewick-Moreing was immensely enhanced by this episode. It became one of the great legends of business probity. Their clientele grew enormously, so that in the long run the million dollars came back with interest in new business.

Surely it is one of the brightest pages in the book of any man's business record. But there are no limits to political legerdemain. Even this act of daring and honesty on Hoover's part would be "processed" in time into another smear on his character in anti-Hoover books.

3

In the summer of 1904 Hoover traveled to South Africa to inspect certain coal and gold sites. At this time the Rand mines had begun to employ Chinese coolie labor, imported seasonally as required. Hoover had no more to do with it than you or I. But to this day the absurd story that he "exploited coolie labor," launched by political press agents, still floats on the waves of folklore.

One of the jokes of the situation is that the Chinese laborers fought and schemed and even killed for the privilege of being exploited. A few months in the Transvaal earned them enough money to sustain their families for a year or more in China.

The greater joke is that Hoover was outspoken in opposition to this cheap labor. As a mine manager, not as a humanitarian, he contended that the cheapest labor is the most expensive, because it is the least productive. Speaking before the Chamber of Commerce in the Transvaal, he cited his lower costs per ton in Australia with labor that was paid decent wages and provided with decent conditions. Excerpts from that speech are on record in the London *Chronicle* of the time. And he enlarged on the idea in his lectures at Columbia and Stanford four years later, as well as in his book, *Principles of Mining*.

This is as good a place as any to note the remarkable fact that there were no strikes or lockouts in any of the mines under Hoover's management anywhere in the world, in years when similar mines were being racked by labor troubles. He was one of the few great industrial leaders in the first decade of our century to believe in peaceable labor unionization and to translate his belief into practice, sometimes over the objections of financial agents.

His formula for profitable operation was simple: higher wages, more labor-saving machinery, lower costs, and larger production. He found that honest labor organization fitted well into this formula. In reading words like the following from his book, *Principles of Mining,* bear in mind that he was talking to management, not to the public; and that this was 1908–09 when such views sounded radical and heretical to most businessmen:

As corporations have grown, so likewise have the labor unions. In general, they are normal and proper antidotes for unlimited capitalistic organization. . . . Given a union with leaders who can control the members, and who are disposed to approach differences in a business spirit, there are few sounder positions for the employer, for agreements honorably carried out dismiss the constant harassments of possible strikes. Such unions exist in dozens of trades in this country, and they are entitled to greater recognition. The time when the employer could ride roughshod over his labor is disappearing with the doctrine of *laissez faire* on which it was founded. The sooner the fact is recognized, the better for the employer.

In that passage on labor-capital relations he went on to quarrel with the orthodox economic assumption of the period that workers were a "commodity" and wages governed by laws of demand and supply. "In these days of international flow of labor, commodities, and capital," he wrote, "the real controlling factor in wages is efficiency." More efficient production, he urged, could be the common ground for co-operation between labor and capital. "No administrator," he remarked, "begrudges a division with his men of the increased profit arising from increased efficiency."

Not all of his enterprises panned out, of course. There was, for instance, the Lodder River System, a gold-bearing site in Victoria, Australia. By the processes of frenzied finance, six million dollars of investors' money had been sunk into the development and lost. Its chief promoter had ended his own life when his house of stock certificates tumbled around his head. The investors hired Hoover to study the picture.

He reported that there was only a marginal chance of making those mines yield; while there was gold, the geological conditions made its retrieval almost impossible. A subterranean river under lava deposits had to be overcome. In full awareness of the heavy odds against them, the investors decided to throw two million dollars more into a last desperate salvaging effort. Hoover thereupon undertook the greatest pumping operation in mining history, but finally the Lodder System had to be given up.

For contrast there was the famous Broken Hill operation, also in Australia. In that silver-lead district there were great mountains of tailings, the residue after silver had been extracted. They were regarded as waste; no one had succeeded in processing the zinc and other by-products out of this slag. Hoover acquired some five million tons of this waste for his group, as well as an array of low-grade mines which others had found uneconomical.

In the following years he had plenty of griefs at Broken Hill; experiment after experiment collapsed in futility. But in the end he found economic methods for extracting the zinc and for making the despised low-grade ores pay dividends. He worked out the so-called "flotation" process, which since then has become standard. Broken Hill became one of the world's richest sources of silver, lead, and zinc. Its production from Hoover's time to the early 1940s has been estimated at $400,000,000.

For every mine he considered worth developing there were a dozen or a score which he reported as unpromising. His explorations took him to Mt. Sinai for the Government of Egypt; the turquoise resources he uncovered evidently had been valuable in the days of the Pharaohs, but tastes in turquoise had changed in the passing millennia. His engineers made a survey of his country's mineral resources for the Abyssinian King of Kings and Conquering Lion of Judah. The results were completely discouraging; had Mussolini studied those reports he might have been dissuaded from his bloody Ethiopian aggression.

By all odds the most formidable, heartbreaking, and in the end profitable of Hoover's labors were in the inaccessible reaches of Burma, on the frontier between India and China. With Mandalay as his base of operations, he started his investigations there while still with Bewick-Moreing and continued them in his lone-wolf period—reversing the roles at that point by engaging Bewick-Moreing as technical managers.

It took him more than five years, as one of his biographers put it, "to transform some deserted works in the heart of a jungle into the foremost producer of its kind in all the world." He made a number of long sojourns at the site, with his family installed in a leased house in Mandalay, and it was to be the last of the properties in which he would retain ownership interest. Indeed, the Burma mines became the chief foundation of his personal fortune, which, however, was never remotely as great as common report claimed.

Hoover, like many other engineers in the business, had heard about the abandoned silver mines in the impoverished Shan State. It had been the fabled source of Ming silver. Worked as early as the year 1400, it seemed to have petered out by 1850 and was now being scratched on the surface in most primitive and profitless fashion. On the basis of reports by geologists whom he sent to the spot, Hoover late in 1904 decided to see for himself.

The site seemed to have been deliberately placed by a perverse nature behind mountain barriers and almost impassable jungles. But what he saw convinced Hoover that the building of roads, the laying of rails across two mountains, the throwing of bridges across dizzy gorges, were all justified. The Oxford-educated Shan Sultan mobilized 30,000 of his tribesmen, at good wages, to do the work. Hoover put most of his own savings, and more as he earned it, into the project and organized a financing group. Not merely as mining but as engineering the undertaking became one of the marvels of mining annals.

By 1908 the Burma mines yielded their first substantial hoards of metal, though major production was not reached until 1916. The Shan State, from one of the most miserable in the area, became the most prosperous. Tunnels, one of them two miles long, had to be dug to get at deep underground deposits. A huge smelter was erected on the grounds, as well as mills, hydroelectric plants, houses, towns, schools, hospitals. In thirty years the Burma property gave the world 1,500,000 tons of lead, 125,000,000 ounces of silver, zinc, and other products in proportion—to an aggregate value of over $350,000,000. It gave employment to some 100,-000 Chinese, Shans, and Indians, and is still accounted the world's number-one silver mine. Hoover sold out his interests in it in 1918.

The most notable of his enterprises after he cut loose from the London company and established his chief headquarters in San Francisco were in Russia. The Kyshtim estate, in the Urals, near Yekaterinburg, took in an area as large as a small European country. It had provided an extravagant living to a distant branch of the Romanoff family for many generations, but had been continually depleted. Some 100,000 workers and peasants dependent on its mines, forests, and accessory activities were sunk in poverty and ignorance.

Early in the century the current owner, a Baron Mellor Zakomelsky, turned to a Russian-born Briton, Leslie Urquhart, to refinance and activate his properties. Urquhart plowed under huge sums of investor money but the estate went from bad to worse. In 1909 he called in Hoover, the most famous "doctor of sick mines," to save the patient.

Hoover saw the latent possibilities of Kyshtim, and was assured a free hand in their exploitation. He brought in experienced engineers from Butte, Montana, where geological conditions were analogous. He built modern furnaces, provided economic transport facilities, erected factories to process some of the iron and steel into salable finished products.

Almost at once the estate began to show profits, this despite, or because of, the fact that the American management provided the highest wages in all Russia and raised standards of living and learning for 100,000 souls. The fame of Kyshtim as a model industrial area spread through the sprawling country, and Hoover was engaged to survey all the so-called "cabinet mines," personal properties of the Czar's family.

A curious side light: It was a book written by an American correspondent in 1891—*Siberia and the Exile System* by George Kennan, an uncle of the George Kennan who is at this writing Russian expert in the State Department—that gave Hoover the most valuable clews to possible mineral and mine deposits. The book had created a sensation as an exposure of terror and slave labor in Russia, so that Kennan became celebrated among liberals as a great friend of that country; nowadays, alas, those who expose worse terror, and greater slave labor, are indicated as "anti-Russian" and "reactionaries" by the new-fangled liberals of our muddled times.

In any case, Hoover read Kennan carefully and from his eye-witness accounts judged which of the "cabinet mines" might be worth surveying. The most promising, he found, were in the Altai Mountains in the southern reaches of Siberia. Again he conquered problems of inaccessibility to explore and begin development of what was probably the most extensive and richest body of ore ever discovered on this planet. Ten million dollars were raised to finance what became known as the Irtysh Mine.

By the time the Russian Revolution canceled out all his labors, the Kyshtim development in the Urals was earning a profit of $2,000,000 a year, and it was only in its first stage. When the Bolsheviks took over, the management was dismissed. Within a few months the whole enterprise was paralyzed and on the rocks. Theories of public ownership and management may be rhetorically heart-warming on paper. In practice they merely restored the old misery, hunger, and desolation.

What was lacking, as Hoover later put it, was the "tuned intelligence" which spells the difference between profitable and losing operations. One after another the furnaces broke down and there was not the "tuned intelligence" to revive them. By 1923, when Hoover's men were in the region on an errand of mercy—famine relief under the American Relief Administration—they found that little remained of the magnificent Kyshtim workings. Local people, recognizing one of the old American engineers among the relief workers, begged him to transmit a message signed by them which in time reached Hoover. It was a touching and pathetic message, imploring him to come and give them work again, promising that they would be "good and obedient."

These Russian developments demonstrated that wealth could be produced with free labor where slave labor failed. In due time conscienceless stories based on falsehoods were to be spread far and wide, especially by the Communists, alleging that Hoover's opposition to the Soviet regime was motivated by his hopes of retrieving those properties. Unfortunately for the myth-makers, he had disposed of his Russian holdings in 1915, before the Revolution.

Even if he were the sort of man to adjust his principles to prospects of profit, he stood to gain exactly nothing by an overthrow of the Soviet regime. Having seen their sufferings with his own eyes, Hoover had been always and outspokenly on the side of the Russian people against their tyrannical government; this even when he had an office and a home in the Romanoff capital. In opposing the Kremlin tyranny, he is still on the side of the Russian people.

4

The immensity of his professional interests, as I have already indicated, did not restrict Hoover's intellectual horizons. In the course of his travels he accumulated a remarkable library of technical and engineering books of all centuries and all countries. He was fascinated by the ancient cultures, human and technical, which still showed above ground, like the open ends of antique "workings," in the life of hundreds of millions of human beings.

One of the old books that intrigued him was the celebrated *De re metallica* published in 1556 by Agricola, the Latin pen name of a German scientist of that century. Though scholars had tried to translate it into French, English, and German in the intervening centuries, they had given up the task as hopeless.

To begin with, the book was written in a vulgarized Latin which scholars found insuperable. Second, it was a technological work, abounding in nomenclature and formulas which the Latinists could not decipher. Since there were no ancient words to describe medieval engineering processes, Agricola apparently had invented them or transliterated German and French expressions into a Latin of his own coinage.

On and off for years Hoover, and especially Mrs. Hoover who was the Latinist of the family, had played with the book, translating passages for the fun of it. The mining ideas of 1556 presented quite a problem to Stanford graduates. For instance, Agricola took into account the mischief-making of "gnomes" and how to propitiate them.

In 1907 the Hoovers decided to undertake a translation in all earnestness. They carted their notes and manuscripts with them all around the world half-a-dozen times. It became their principal "game" for spare time and during the long journeys. They found excuses for visiting the actual mine sites in the Alps and elsewhere which Agricola mentioned; and made researches in Saxony where he had written the volume.

Sentence by sentence, paragraph by paragraph, they read the three-hundred-and-fifty-year riddle. It was in effect a job of scientific detective work. They set up laboratories and worked out Agricola's formulas to check their intuitive translations. They deduced obscure meanings by dovetailing known facts. And in five years they were ready with the first accurate English rendition of the classic.

Some years before Hoover had helped put his friend Edgar Rickard into business in London as publisher of a mining journal dedicated to "selling" American methods, men, and machines. The magazine had prospered. It now sponsored the publication of Agricola in an elegant format, bound in white vellum like the medieval original edition, and reproducing the original woodcuts and initial letters. It is today a highly valued collector's item. The translation, of course, was signed jointly by Mrs. Hoover and her husband.

Repeatedly during these years Hoover contemplated retirement, which to him meant dedication to public service on a full-time schedule. Financial reverses and the appearance of challenging engineering offers interfered. But the dream was never far from his mind. It edged close to reality in 1908, about the time he severed relations with the London firm.

He accepted an invitation at that time to deliver a series of lectures to the engineering students of his alma mater and took under serious advisement its invitation to join the faculty. But the Burma and a few other huge ventures were "cooking" and could not be left on the fire without endangering other people's investments.

He repeated the lectures at Columbia University and they became the basis for his *Principles of Mining,* published in 1909. The book remained a standard college text for decades and is still widely used. In 1912 he joined the Board of Trustees of Stanford. Remembering his doughty struggle to co-ordinate student activities, he contributed the initial $100,000 for the building of a union hall where those activities are now centralized.

Because it seems to me to reflect the quintessence of Hooverism, I want to tell a little story which, so far as I can discover, has never before been told publicly. Though its principal characters were Jews—as in the first Noël story of all—it is in a sense a Christmas story. It began on the day after Christmas of 1913, when Hoover stepped into the Bank of California to cash a check and was buttonholed by the bank president, Frank Anderson, who told him a sad tale:

Two great California families, Sloss and Lilienthal, were on the edge of bankruptcy. They had over-extended their business operations and found themselves unable to meet a mountain of notes, mostly personally endorsed, falling due in the days ahead. The families were meeting at that very moment to wrestle with their troubles, involving ten first-rate companies and related enterprises, $60,000,000 in various securities, some four hundred banks. The bankruptcy would deliver a terrible blow to the whole state.

What they needed, Mr. Anderson thought, was a cool outside mind—a Hoover mind—to help them. Would he consent to talk to them? He did, immediately. They took him fully into confidence. He judged it another case of mismanagement and tangled finance, for the Lilienthals and the Slosses were people of sterling honesty. Thankfully they accepted his advice to fight it out and placed themselves under his monitorship.

For ninety days and nights, Saturdays and Sundays included, while his multifarious personal affairs waited, Hoover worked with these people, their lawyers, their bankers. The details are too ample and too complex. He staved off creditors at times by sheer force of his reputation for probity. He reorganized some companies, merged others, and carefully husbanded every resource to prop up a leaning tower of finance.

He got wind, for instance, of the fact that Sloss, Sr., at his death had left $2,000,000 for his wife, now ninety years old. Her sons, even in their extremity, did not wish to alarm the matriarch whom they adored. Hoover took it on himself to visit her. The grand old lady understood at once. She said that fifty or a hundred thousand dollars would be more than enough to keep her for such years as remained to her. The rest was at his disposal. Hoover insisted on leaving her half a million and covering the rest with securities in her sons' businesses. The $1,500,000 was crucial in paying interest and saving the Sloss-Lilienthal empire.

What would his fee be for salvaging $60,000,000? The grateful families were ready to pay, eager to pay, anything he asked. He got the full amount he asked for, though over their violent protests; namely, nothing. He had not injected himself for profit, he explained, and therefore could accept no fees. Another contingent of Hoover cultists was born in those tense three months.

I do not wish to imply that this abbreviated account begins to do justice to his record as the Great Engineer; one might as well try to pack the contents of a department store into an overnight bag. New facets of that career are uncovered each time you read another book touching the subject or talk to another person acquainted with that stretch in the man's biography.

Only another engineer, one associate of his explained to me, can comprehend fully the quality of Hoover as a creative miner:

the fertility of his technical devices, the daring of his concepts. The greater the obstacles, it seemed, the keener his enthusiasm. He used camels to haul timbers one hundred and seventy-five miles through mountain country. He based vast smelting and manufacturing ventures on wood fuel, "extracting the last by-product of charcoal as part of an interlocking conservation scheme." He recovered ores in our own West with entirely new methods of underwater dredging. In his field he was distinctly the innovator, the revolutionary.

At the end of his professional life, on the threshold of a second and greater career, as humanitarian and social servant, the forty-year-old Hoover was a man seasoned by unique experiences; with a great surgeon's sureness of touch in handling practical affairs; with a mind not only vast in expanse but rich in depths, like the most generously endowed of his many gold and silver mines.

Completely unknown to the public at large, he was the most famous of all in his own field. To hundreds of men who had worked with him and under him he was "the Chief." They were not merely Hoover men but Hoover zealots. The best of this human crop was to follow him into his new career as devotedly as they had followed him from Australia to China, from China to Russia and back again.

Though he had lived so much abroad, he was profoundly American, having been in effect the self-chosen apostle of American technology to the technical heathens of the globe. The so-briquet "Hail Columbia" had stuck, and with good reason. He was American in a more significant sense. Having sampled every living and moribund civilization extant, he had developed an ever-deepening and ultimately a passionate patriotism for his homeland. America seemed to him, with all its faults and all its crudities, not simply an extension of European civilization but a new civilization, unique and integral, and rooted in concepts of human freedom. To him "democracy" was more than a convenient political catchword; it was a reality to be cherished and defended and expanded.

As an Iowa Quaker he had been, one might say, born a Republican. And it was the Republicanism of Iowa Quakers—populist, liberal, grass roots in its essence—that meant anything to him. He registered as a Republican when he was old enough, in Berkeley, though he was off on his life's work before he could vote. In 1912 he supported Theodore Roosevelt's bull-moose movement against the regular Republicans.

Hoover was in London when the fatal shot was fired at Sarajevo on June 28, 1914. Among other things it shattered a piece of delicate diplomatic negotiation on which he was engaged for his adopted state of California. European nations had shown themselves reluctant to take part in the Panama-Pacific Exposition scheduled in San Francisco and Hoover, as an extracurricular assignment, had agreed to do something about it. Already he had succeeded in getting Germany, France, and England to reverse previous decisions not to participate, and he was working on other governments.

His wife and sons joined him immediately after schools closed for the summer vacation. It would enable them to enjoy another of those rare intervals of normal family life. Little did they dream that normal life, for them and for most of mankind, would seem a bright memory and a forlorn hope in the months and years ahead.

The Hoover whose fortieth birthday was celebrated by his little family and a few intimate friends on August 10 at the spacious Red House was a "self-made" man in the finest American tradition, an authentic Alger hero. The West Branch blacksmith's son stood at the pinnacle of his chosen career, well to do, respected, rich in friends. Yet it was a somber celebration. For Germany had declared war on France exactly a week earlier. The modern scourge of total war had begun to engulf the blundering human race for the first but, alas, not the last time.

CHAPTER XI

The Relief of Belgium

THE OUTBREAK OF WAR IN 1914 stranded nearly two hundred thousand Americans, among them some thirty thousand school teachers, amid the dislocations and hysterias of Europe. Tens of thousands of them were piling into London, frightened and without funds. Banks had ceased to honor American checks and other paper. Our consulates, legations, and embassies on the continent were besieged by hordes of these refugees. Frontiers were being closed without warning. Ships were scarce and growing scarcer. It was a tangle of confusions touched by panic.

On Monday afternoon, August 3, a bank holiday, American Consul General Skinner telephoned Herbert Hoover. He was in a mess, he announced. Hundreds of tourists, morose, anxious, indignant, horror-stricken, were milling around his consulate, demanding help. What could Mr. Hoover suggest?

"I did not realize it at the moment," Hoover subsequently declared, "but on this Monday my engineering career was over. I was on the slippery road of public life."

He met the immediate crisis in the consulate by scraping up a few hundred pounds in cash and setting up an exchange-and-loan office. The clamorous Americans were lined up before desks manned by Hoover and other engineers. Those who had dollars received some English currency in exchange; the rest received ten-shilling loans against IOU's. That would tide them over until a sensible repatriation plan could be worked out.

A worse crisis, however, had overwhelmed the Embassy the same day. It was beleaguered not by hundreds but by thousands. They insisted that Uncle Sam, in the person of Ambassador Walter Hines Page, "do something" forthwith. They were citizens and taxpayers, weren't they? Uncle Sam was momentarily as flustered as his nephew Skinner. And learning that this fellow Hoover had taken over in the consulate, he hastened to dump the whole muddled emergency in his lap.

Hoover's own house was not exactly in order. The war had deranged his mining empire seriously, at some points disastrously. Markets and transport arrangements were in chaotic transition stages; valuable cargoes on the high seas had to be diverted to new destinations; large numbers of men and women who looked to him for orders and succor were caught behind suddenly closed borders. But the bigger problem unloaded on him by Uncle Sam took priority.

Within twenty-four hours an American committee, mostly composed of his own friends and business associates, was functioning in a stratum of calm above the storm of confusions. At his initiative similar committees were formed in other European centers. Mrs. Hoover organized a women's division to care for unaccompanied women and children.

In a few days the improvised refugee rescue mission was operating with reasonable speed if not altogether smoothly. It had the attributes of a bank, shipping company, diplomatic agency, and tourist bureau, with charity and social-service functions thrown in for good measure. Vast numbers of Americans were evacuated from difficult zones, cared for at points of concentration, and in time shipped home. It was all done so quietly, so expeditiously, with so little ballyhoo, that only a few realized they were witnessing a miracle of organization and efficiency. Somehow Hoover found the staff, the cash, the food, the clothes, and above all the passenger ships, so that by the time Congress appropriated a million dollars for the job of repatriation, much of it had already been done.

This was the first time Americans outside the mining and financial worlds became aware of the man Hoover. And American correspondents had their first taste of a public figure who seemed strangely determined to keep himself out of the public light.

In six weeks the Hoover committee handled about 120,000 Americans in varying degrees of distress. Over and above the crucial banking service for those with money, it raised and distributed substantial sums on a charity basis. The volunteer personnel worked day and night; though they could not guess it, this was for many of them a dress rehearsal for the big show of rescue work on an unprecedented scale to begin in the near future and to last nearly nine years.

Along with the efficiency there was great faith. With a few friends whom he drew into the gamble, Hoover induced an American bank in London to cash any kind of American paper, on their personal pledge to make good the losses. Obviously there was neither the time nor the machinery for checking credit ratings. Before the exodus was completed, $1,500,000 had been cashed—that was the extent of the gamble. But faith was vindicated: less than $400 was lost in the huge transaction.

In the avalanche of work and worry there were nuggets of diversion. Hoover recalls, for example, the old lady who would not board a ship without his written guarantee that there would be no U-boat attacks. Under the circumstances even Great-grandma Rebecca would have tolerated the little deception as Herbert obliged with a document. Then there was the woman, being repatriated at public expense, who declared a hunger strike for better accommodations than steerage. She was maneuvered into a seat in the committee lunchroom, where the aromas of edibles broke her resistance in a few hours.

Hoover likes to recount also the complex woes of a rich man's daughter from Lansing, Michigan, who had lost her ten trunks, including a trousseau, before she reached London from the mainland. Papa came through with money to replace the trousseau. Having bought the best that London had to offer, for safety's sake the girl consigned the packages in care of the committee at the Savoy. That was her error, for the committee had an Old Clothes Department to which all clothes were delivered as a matter of routine. The women in charge were astonished but mighty pleased by the landfall of finery, and some of the humble recipients found themselves more elegantly dressed than ever before in their lives. The blunder was not discovered until Miss Lansing came for her packages a week later. Papa threatened to sue but thought better of it.

Then there was the American Wild West show which descended on the Savoy in full Indian and cowboy regalia. It had traveled a long way, from far-off Poland in fact. The troupers had lost or sold their animals and orthodox clothes as they proceeded, saving only the costumes on their backs; so London had something to stare at while they waited to be transported to the United States.

So little suspicion did Hoover have of what history was preparing for him that he made reservations to sail with his family for America. After several postponements, Mrs. Hoover and the boys went alone, expecting him to follow in a few weeks. Announcement of their safe arrival took the jocular form of a cable from Herbert, Jr., reporting conquest over seasickness and the consumption of seven cream puffs in one Atlantic day. The English censor was never quite convinced that it was not a code and mumbled pointedly about the penalties for espionage.

Hoover's passage was booked for October 25. With his stranded countrymen under smooth control, he was organizing his private affairs with a view to a long sojourn in California. The fates that preside over such ironies looked on and smiled in knowing amusement.

2

Let us turn back for a moment to 1907. Hoover came up from his desert diggings to greet Dr. David Starr Jordan, in Melbourne on vacation. After he had caught up with the Stanford news and gossip, he was willing enough to answer his old "prexy's" questions about his work and plans.

"I have run through my profession," Dr. Jordan remembered him saying. "It holds nothing more, except money, of which I have enough already. . . . When I return to London, I think I shall resign, and after a while go back to America to see if there is not some form of executive position in which I can serve my country."

He resigned, but as we have seen, he did not retire. Five years later Will Irwin, waiting for his ship in a European port, ran into Hoover on his way back from Russia. They picked up the threads of their old campus friendship and talked, as boyhood acquaintances will, of their hopes for the future.

As Irwin recalled their conversations, Hoover thought he was getting closer to the financial independence mark when he could give up business without being unfair to his dependents. "What then?" Irwin wanted to know. Hoover did not have a precise answer. The nearest he came to formulating that persistent inner nudging was to declare that he was "interested in some job of public service—at home, of course."

Other friends of this period recall similar allusions to public service. As one who has had no personal experience in either field, I have sometimes thought that money-making is a little like drink to the addict; he resolves to quit when he has had "enough" but never recognizes the "enough" point.

It is probably a fact that for Hoover wealth was never an end in itself but the means to an end: the self-sufficiency that would allow him to serve his fellow men. It was not a dream of self-abnegation but of self-fulfillment. He talked of doing something for humanity and his country in the way other rising young men talk of achieving yachts and estates. He simply had a gnawing hunger of the spirit and promised himself to indulge it as soon as he could afford it.

In accepting a trusteeship at his alma mater, in consenting to represent the Panama-Pacific International Exposition abroad, he was edging closer to that reserve vocation. Yet, had it not been for the war, he might have been held in the groove of international engineering by the inertia of business triumphs and the magnetism of ever-larger mining problems. The great cataclysm of 1914 forced the decision.

He was packing for the journey to America when an engineer whom he knew only slightly, Millard Shaler, came to see him. Shaler had just arrived from Brussels, the captive capital of a conquered nation, and was full of the horror of that tragedy.

Belgium imported at least 75 per cent of its breadstuffs and 50 per cent of other foods. The invaders had requisitioned local supplies, so that stocks were dangerously low. The seven million inhabitants were helpless prisoners, ringed by German bayonets on land and by Allied blockade on the coast. A terrifying catastrophe was clearly in the making unless help from the outside came quickly. "In two weeks the civil population of Belgium, already in misery, will face starvation," Brand Whitlock, the American Minister in Brussels, had just reported to President Wilson.

Hoover steered Shaler to Ambassador Page, who had the plight of the Belgians close to his heart. Meanwhile the Secretary of our Brussels Legation, a brilliant young diplomat named Hugh Gibson, as well as a number of eminent Belgians, had arrived to press the relief agency. And all of them when they talked relief spelled it Hoover.

Now there is a curious counterpoint in the music of Hoover's life. Repeatedly the episodes and personalities of one phase show up dramatically in another, like recurrent themes. It was a Belgian group, back in 1901, which had precipitated his withdrawal from China; now it was the travail of Belgium that was holding him in Europe. The Belgian financier with whose policies he had disagreed at the time, whom his testimony helped defeat in an English court in the notorious Chang litigation, was Emil Francqui. At the head of the Belgian group now in London pleading for swift aid to a cornered and famished nation was the self-same Francqui.

The problem was continually under discussion in the Embassy. At one point the Belgian rose impulsively and approached his old adversary.

"Mr. Hoover, I owe you an apology," Francqui said. "You proved right in that Chinese matter. We in Belgium are today faced with the life and death of our people. There is only one man in the world who can organize the job. He must be an American. You are the man."

The Ambassador, Shaler, Gibson, everyone else joined in this plea. They all recognized the size of the sacrifice they were urging upon him.

War conditions had endangered Hoover's far-flung business interests; these required his personal attention more compellingly than ever. At least a dozen major and twice as many minor undertakings were involved. Consulting fees netting him at least $100,000 annually were involved. Moreover, he was in an ideal position to make himself one of the world's richest men if he chose. He happened to have the inside track in the race for base metals, especially zinc and lead, at the start of a long war in which these products would be worth their weight in gold. A large slice of available war metals was directly or indirectly under Hoover's control, and there were few people alive with such intimate knowledge of untapped sources of supply.

He asked the Americans and the Belgians for a few days to make up his mind. For a relatively young man with a deep sense of obligation to his family, it was not an easy decision he faced. Though rich, he was still far from the goal he had set for himself as the measure of independence.

For some future playwright with the insight to dramatize the Hoover story there is a superb scene ready-made—the scene in which a forty-year-old American must choose between incalculable wealth and the arduous, thankless career of public service.

There was never any doubt that he would accept the challenge of human misery. From the first day he took the lead in planning the effort. One evening, as the need to mobilize food without delay was being outlined by the Ambassador, Hoover was seen to glance at his watch then leave the room briskly. A few minutes later he returned and resumed his place. Later Mr. Page asked him why he had absented himself so abruptly. Hoover explained that he wanted to catch the New York market before it closed for the day; he had cabled an order for several million bushels of wheat earmarked for Belgium.

Clearly he was already committed to the relief undertaking. His only problem was whether to retain his business interests or to renounce private ambitions entirely. For three nights he wrestled with the crucial decision. Will Irwin, then a war correspondent, was stopping at the Red House and has recorded that he heard his host pacing his room during those nights. On the fourth morning, when Hoover came down for breakfast, he seemed unusually serene.

"Well," he said to Irwin, sensing perhaps that his guest had followed the inner struggle, "let fortune go to hell."

He said it as casually as if he were canceling a week-end vacation, rather than giving up the near certainty of immense wealth. Recalling that moment, Irwin wrote afterward: "I felt then, I know now, that I had witnessed a significant moment in history."

It was a decision destined to affect the lives of literally hundreds of millions of human beings. From that moment the story of Hoover became the substance of world history. Never had a great business career been so sharply renounced for a greater career of social service.

"The business is in your hands," he announced simply to his associates. He apologized for leaving them on their own at a trying juncture and made himself available for advice should critical situations arise. But they understood, as he wished them to understand, that he was through with mining and active money-making forever. He transferred all the lush fee contracts and resigned from a score or more directorates, retaining only a nominal and inactive place on the board of the Burma Land Mines.

From that day until this Hoover has not accepted for his private use a dollar in remuneration for any of his manifold public services. From the first hour of his Belgian job to the last of his recent mission for President Truman, he has even paid his own travel and out-of-pocket expenses. His salaries as Secretary of Commerce, then as President, went into a special fund for disbursement in full for charitable causes, to raise the wages of aides who needed it, or to pay for expert personnel not provided by the official budgets. Money that came to him for writing or speaking went likewise to private and public causes.

Associates on his new course, from 1914 forward, if in a position to do so, have followed his example in refusing remuneration and in paying their own expenses. More than that, they have contributed money to enable others, who had no means of their own, to work with Hoover on projects of benevolence. No Quakers themselves, merely out of affection for the Chief or through conviction, they have lived by his Quaker dictum that public service is a God-given privilege, not a business. Besides, they recognized the force of his familiar adage that people in public life must have "glass pockets."

These are just a few of the myriad things about their ex-President that Americans know only vaguely if at all.

3

The bibliography of books, pamphlets, and articles about the Belgian Relief runs to several closely printed pages. Its major facts and incidents might be crammed into a large volume, its human drama can never be compassed by words. In the few pages that follow I can only hope to suggest the vastness of the enterprise, the uniqueness of the problems it posed, the single-minded devotion of the man who carried it through successfully.

It was not only a new kind of undertaking for Hoover, remote from his life's experience, but a new phenomenon in the experience of the human race. In solving its piled-up problems and resolving its never-ending crises there were no precedents to offer guidance.

Hoover and his staff had to break down the opposition and remove the distrust of all belligerents; to find food for seven million people (ten million before long, as the French-occupied areas were added); to raise the money to pay for it and the ships to transport it; to deliver the food through hostile armies and navies; to distribute it equitably and assure that none of it was diverted to military uses.

"The knowledge that we would have to go on for four years," Hoover later declared, "to find a billion dollars, to transport five million tons of concentrated food, to administer rationing, price controls, agricultural production, was mercifully hidden from us. I did not know it but this was to be not only a great charity to the destitute, but the first food administration of a whole nation in history."

To an English critic of some phase of the work he once said that the undertaking was "like trying to feed a hungry kitten by means of a forty-foot bamboo pole, said kitten confined in a barred cage occupied by two hungry lions."

One of those lions was the helmeted Germany, the other was the Allies. It is not generally understood that bitter opposition to feeding the Belgians and constant interference with the job did not come solely from the Germans. British and French leaders, too, had to be sold on the idea, and to the very end powerful groups in both countries were loud and sometimes effective in blocking the work. The most intense hostility to feeding the occupied sector of France, for instance, came from Frenchmen.

The military minds on both sides were in control. As the struggle resolved into a stalemate of bloody attrition, of mutual bloodletting, the human element was utterly forgotten. It was Hoover's task to make the voice of crying children heard above the roar of battle, and he had only neutral sentiment to use as a megaphone.

The strategy of blockade became increasingly important in Allied thinking. Fear that some of the food funneled into Belgium might be used by the Germans outweighed sympathy for the captive populations. "Let the Huns provision the territories they have overrun," many top Allied leaders thundered. "If they cannot or will not do it, the blood of the victims will be on *their* heads, not ours. Let the world see the bottomless brutality of these beasts, even if a few million innocent lives are lost."

The Germans at their end demanded the lifting of the blockade. "Stop your naval war on civilians," they howled, "and there will be no relief problems. Why should we let you feed Belgians and Frenchmen while you are starving our German folk? Feed all or none! Besides, this is total war, not a parlor game. We can't have a lot of neutrals in our operational zones spying on us and lying about us." It was a point of view that became more insistent as the extreme jingo mood and Junker control deepened.

Moral and humane appeals were so much thistledown in the fierce winds of hatred. Hoover had to rely on more solid arguments, the kind that were veiled threats. Persistently, until the day America entered the war, he forced the belligerents to recognize that neutral public opinion—and primarily American opinion—would be horrified by the mass starvation of ten million non-combatants. The surest way to drive America into the Allied ranks, he convinced the Germans, was to starve Belgium. The surest way to alienate America, he convinced the Allies, was to block the relief of Belgium.

President Wilson and the entire American diplomatic corps sided with Hoover. But there was a vocal minority at home, with Senator Henry Cabot Lodge at its head, attacking his efforts as pernicious "entanglement" in foreign wars. His relief activities and his later support of the League of Nations made Hoover an unpopular figure in their ranks so far as the dominant Republican leadership was concerned.

Though the job was 98 per cent American, Hoover wisely set up a façade of honorary chairmen that included all the key Spanish and Dutch diplomats. Thus he could talk to the fighting nations with the authority of three leading neutrals. American Ambassador James W. Gerard and his Spanish and Netherlands colleagues in Berlin, the corresponding diplomats in London and Paris, fought continuous battles to keep the "forty-foot bamboo pole" from being knocked out of Hoover's hands.

At critical junctures, however, it was Hoover himself who rushed from one capital to another, and at times to the secret German headquarters at Charleville on the fighting front, to save the work from annihilation. Few of the ordinary Belgians and Frenchmen knew by how thin a margin they were saved again and again from the living death of slow starvation. "He is the best diplomat of us all," the Spanish Minister in Brussels told our relief workers there.

The majority of the British Cabinet were opposed to the whole American scheme for feeding Belgium. They attached high hopes to the blockade; they had more urgent uses for food and shipping; they resented the injection of humanitarian considerations into a "realistic" struggle for survival. Hoover wore them down by the sheer logic of his position, reinforced by the threat of American indignation. Ambassador Page, of course, was a tower of strength for him in these long-drawn-out duels.

Lloyd George was not yet at the head of the government, but he held a key post and swung enormous weight in the Cabinet. He began a crucial conference with the American engineer in a frankly hostile spirit. Other leaders present let the little Welshman conduct the debate while they listened. Immunity for relief ships from Allied seizures, unhampered passage through blockade lines, British financial support for the Belgians—these were the great issues at stake.

At the end of a long afternoon Lloyd George announced, "I am convinced." He asked the American to prepare a statement embodying his arguments for presentation to the full Cabinet. When they met again, Lloyd George shook Hoover's hand warmly. "You've put up a great fight—and you've won," he told him. The British Government voted one million pounds a month for Belgian relief.

In Berlin the opposition seemed insuperable. The neutral diplomatic pressures had failed to move the military clique. It was a cold opposition, mechanical, impersonal, seemingly impervious to common sense, let alone common humanity. Hoover talked to political and military leaders, one by one and in groups; he talked for hours, for days. Because they had hopes of keeping America neutral, the Germans listened—and finally capitulated almost on his terms.

Berlin agreed to facilitate the feeding of conquered areas, under conditions which would provide absolute guarantees that not a morsel of the food reached German mouths. They allowed a large freedom of movement for relief workers and undertook to stop the requisitioning of Belgian food and cattle. In return Hoover pledged that his organization would abide loyally by its neutral obligations.

Unhappily few arrangements with governments at war settle anything clearly or for long. The proof of that pudding was literally in the eating—whether the Belgians and the occupied French, that is to say, would have enough to eat. There were conflicts of authority between central governments and local military and naval commanders to be adjusted. There were individual officials who refused to co-operate. Where delay of a consignment meant hunger for hundreds of thousands, red tape must be slashed and special privileges exacted by sheer nerve—Hoover always had enough of this in reserve. The British, fearful that the enemy might seize supplies without warning, insisted that no more than a week's imports be accumulated in Belgium at any time. This meant that the flow of food had to be constant, uninterrupted, accurately estimated.

The Commission for Relief in Belgium—C.R.B. as it came to be known—obtained immunity for its ships on seas swarming with submarines and paved with mines. At its peak it operated a fleet of sixty cargo vessels totaling nearly three hundred thousand tons under its own charter and flying its own flag—the initials C.R.B. in red on a field of white—as well as four hundred barges plying between Rotterdam and Belgian harbors.

"In time," Hoover was able to record, "we won the confidence of both belligerent sides and became a sort of neutral state of our own. We in effect issued our own passports and visas. We flew our own flags on our ships."

Hoover was the one man who moved freely across all frontiers and all military lines. He was head of a new Great Power, enjoying political and moral authority surpassing that of any existing nation. Its country and its capital were on no map, but they coincided with what remained in the world of human decency and Christian sympathy.

Juggling diplomatic relations to keep corridors of supply open was only the beginning of the unprecedented business. Immense amounts of money had to be found. Belgian resources abroad were exhausted in a few weeks. Appeals for private contributions yielded some funds and served to keep the memory of human brotherhood alive in a time of universal slaughter. They provided $52,000,000 in the four years—a great sum in itself but only a tiny fraction of the colossal finances needed.

One of Hoover's remarkable achievements, therefore, was his success in forcing the Allies to provide continuing subsidies, either in outright grants or in the form of loans to the Belgian Government. But the purchase and stockpiling and transportation of vast quantities of foodstuffs could not be interrupted while money was being raised. The C.R.B. continually assumed huge financial obligations without knowing precisely when and how it would make good. Referring to one difficult period, Hoover was to remark:

"In order to insure an increasing stream of food for the next few months I had incurred a debt of $10,000,000 over and above our assets. I had financed this purchase by personally accepting trade bills payable on arrival of the ships at Amsterdam. This money—amounting to many times any resources of my own—was not in sight and the vanguard of the ships was on its way."

The relief job was not, as most people assume, all charity. The great majority of the Belgians could afford to pay for what they received, provided it was made available. Hoover's most brilliant financial improvisation was in making the profits on sales to the solvent help cover the major cost of caring for the destitute. This involved procedures of incalculable complexity. The number of people dependent on straight charity naturally increased as the war dragged on; toward the end half the Belgian population and most of the French in the occupied area were on the charity side of the ledger. Some three million children were being fed by the C.R.B. directly, over and above the rationing mechanism.

So extraordinary was the "tuned intelligence" behind the gigantic enterprise, however, that when it was all over there was a balance of $33,000,000, which went into establishing a Belgian-American educational exchange that is still functioning.

The logic of the relief effort inevitably also placed responsibility for local food supplies upon the Hoover organization. Before long the Americans in Belgium and in the occupied part of France were administering a perfectly co-ordinated rationing system, to make sure that the richest and the poorest got no more than their just share of limited supplies. They ran the flour mills, bakeries, dairies, and a dozen other industries, and commanded the entire agriculture of the nation. In the "operational" zones of France, where Germans helped cultivate the land, it was Hoover's delicate and heartbreaking task to negotiate the apportioning of the crop between the armies and the population.

Nations at war competed for the food resources of the neutral world; nations not yet at war were building surpluses as insurance against involvement. It was in that kind of world market that Hoover found rice in Rangoon, corn in Argentina, beans in Manchuria, wheat and meat and fats in the United States—

one hundred thousand tons of food every month for nearly four years. Even keener and tighter was the competition for shipping tonnage, but in this, too, he succeeded.

An anecdote has come down from those days that tells more than figures. Hoover was pressing a British Admiralty official for a permit to export certain supplies. Of what use would the permit be, the official said in effect, when there isn't a single ship available? "We've got the ship," Hoover said quietly, "and it's already loaded."

In the early stage of the work one of Hoover's assistants remarked, "Someday some swine will rise up and say we either made a profit out of this business or that we stole the money." Hoover, too, had foreseen the possibility. In point of fact such "swine" did rise up now and then. From the outset, therefore, the leading firm of British accountants, headed by Sir John Plender, was drawn into the organization. It not merely audited the books, but did all the bookkeeping with its own staff, this without remuneration. Contributions of a few dollars or a few million dollars poured in, usually in checks made out simply to H. C. Hoover. Sometimes as much as fifty million dollars was deposited to his account. Not a dollar went astray.

The final auditing covered nearly a billion dollars. The internal food resources administered by the several score Americans on the spot amounted to roughly another billion. Because so many hundreds of Americans, so many thousands of Belgians, gave their time and unlimited energies without pay, *the overhead costs came to less than half of one per cent* (0.43%)—a record well-nigh miraculous; many efficient benevolences are pleased if they can keep overhead under 20 per cent; the administrative expenses of UNRRA after World War II came to about 20 per cent.

For Hoover, as he phrased it himself, it was "a gigantic trust executed in the name of the American people, the luster of which should be protected from defilement by any person in the future." In the perspective of time the luster remains undimmed and undefiled. It was an undertaking which, while it fed the body of Belgium, also fed the soul of America. It was the practical expression of our country's revulsion against man's inhumanity to man.

4

The roster of the C.R.B. as first established included the names of Millard Hunsiker, John B. White, Clarence Graff, Edgar Rickard, Hugh Gibson, Millard Shaler, Captain J. F. Lucey, W. L. Honnold, T. O. Connett. Except for Gibson, these were all engineers. Hundreds of others joined the great humanitarian effort, among them W. B. Poland, Perrin C. Galpin, Dr. Vernon Kellogg, Dr. Frank Angell, Ben S. Allen, Julius H. Barnes, Maurice Pate, Will Irwin, Warren Gregory, Walter Lyman Brown, Prentiss N. Gray—but the list is far too long to be given here. The whole contingent of American Rhodes scholars in England at the time, about twenty young men, volunteered their services. But long as the roster seems, it was amazingly small considering the magnitude of what these men accomplished.

That their work was so incredibly effective despite seemingly insuperable obstacles amid the passions and confusions of war, can be explained only by the personality of Hoover. This is the unanimous verdict of those closest to the effort, whether Americans or Europeans. Vernon Kellogg, who was one of them, wrote:

"Those of us who have lived through the difficult, the almost impossible days of Belgian relief . . . have come to an almost superstitious belief in his capacity to do anything possible to human power. . . . People sometimes ask me why Hoover has such a strong hold on his helpers. The men of the C.R.B. know."

Men and women with only a normal endowment of physical, mental, and spiritual stamina cannot survey the story of Belgian Relief without marveling how one man could have carried that load without breaking down. The historians of the undertaking can organize their materials, analyzing each of the major categories of problems separately. It is too easy to forget that Hoover had to solve them simultaneously.

"Whether internal distribution, care of the destitute, or shipping were relatively the worst problems I could never decide," he was to say in retrospect. "No day went by without a fight to keep part of the mechanism from breaking down."

It was a mechanism that had its wheels and pistons and fuel spread over half-a-dozen countries, most of them ringed with steel. At least once in five weeks, sometimes oftener, in the first three years Hoover traveled from London to Belgium and back; normally he included Paris, The Hague, and Rotterdam on the itinerary, but frequently it was widened to take in Berlin, Berne, Amsterdam, Charleville in the fighting zone.

In all, he crossed the North Sea forty times, in small Dutch vessels in constant danger of being blown to smithereens by floating mines or too-eager U-boats. It was on these sea journeys that he wrote the first volume of his life story for his sons; its placid, at points even humorous, style hardly suggests the conditions under which it was composed. I trust the American people will not see that book for a great many years to come, since the author seems determined not to have it published while he is alive.

Twice during the Belgian Relief period he crossed the Atlantic to America, to fortify the work at this critical terminal. American sentiment was, throughout, the motive power and the diplomatic leverage that kept the work going.

During the first of these visits, in 1915, Hoover learned that Senator Lodge was planning to have him cited for violation of a moldy criminal law against individual Americans dealing with belligerents. Hoover called on the senator to discuss the matter and got only angry denunciations for his pains. Personal bitterness is so rare in Hoover's notes that the few instances stand out starkly; his candid dislike of Lodge is one of these. Of course the senator never carried out the threat; the unqualified support of the press and the President for Belgian Relief curbed his enthusiasm.

One of the people who offered his full support during this visit was former President Theodore Roosevelt. The afternoon Hoover spent with him was a first meeting and the beginning of a cordial friendship that lasted as long as Roosevelt lived.

On his second American visit, in January 1917, Hoover accepted an invitation to address the New York Chamber of Commerce. This, he wrote afterward, was his "first public address of any pretension—and certainly the audience received it with patience." Which is a striking indication of the extent to which Hoover had escaped public appearances.

"He is a simple, modest, energetic man who began his career in California and will end it in Heaven; and he doesn't want anybody's thanks," Ambassador Page reported to Woodrow Wilson at the start of the Belgian undertaking. Hoover, incidentally, developed a towering esteem for the Ambassador, which was fully reciprocated. This is the more noteworthy because they did not see eye to eye on the issue of American entry into the war.

The first announcement of Belgian Relief had been made, on Hoover's insistence, in Millard Shaler's name. Thereafter Hoover could not keep his own name from skyrocketing without seeming to evade the full responsibilities of his difficult position. But he fought against personal publicity. Those most directly connected with the press and public-relations aspects of the job, men such as Will Irwin and Ben Allen, have attested (in pride mixed with annoyance) that the Chief hampered their work by rejecting endless openings for personal exploitation.

The American press, as always keen on the scent of personality stories, clamored for "human-interest stuff" about the head of the greatest relief effort in human history up to that time. The little they got was without the help, and usually in defiance, of Hoover himself. "Play up Belgian Relief," he kept instructing his press staff, "not Hoover."

He could not sidetrack the fame that was his destiny. It was a time of warriors and politicians of war, but slowly the name that symbolized benevolence and the code of mutual help moved forward in world consciousness until it led all the rest. Diplomatic pouches reaching Washington and private reports to the President bulged with praise for Hoover that had in it overtones of awe.

As was to be expected, various belligerent governments bid for his services, dangling titles and honors before his eyes. He was so horrified by those hints that they were not repeated. And private groups (as Mr. Page informed President Wilson in one communication) besieged him with fat offers if he would resign and go to work for them. Obviously they did not understand Hoover; like the politicos of a later day they mistook him for one of their own.

Not a word about the relief organization could appear in the German-censored Belgian press. Nevertheless Hoover's name was known and venerated. During his periodic visits in Brussels, sometimes accompanied by his wife, he strove to remain out of sight. His shyness in the face of acclamation came close to being a phobia. Besides, pro-American demonstrations in a conquered area would have alarmed the conquerors and hurt the work.

Yet word of his presence in their midst did spread through the Belgian capital now and then, and tens of thousands of simple people found their own way to express gratitude. On one occasion, for instance, people came to the legation door day after day—singly or in twos, to avoid the appearance of a demonstration—and left their "cards"; these ranged from elegantly embossed pasteboards to scraps of butcher paper with a name scrawled on it. Each day, as another huge pile of these tokens was unloaded on Hoover's desk, he fingered them pensively, sighed and returned to work.

Once, after Hoover had completed a conference with a Junker officer in Brussels, the German said, "Well, now, Herr Hoover, as man to man, what do you get out of all this? You are not doing all this for nothing, surely?" The American felt that it was futile to explain. For that matter, a few Americans had as much difficulty understanding or believing disinterested service as the German.

He did have to explain, in detail, when a question of the same order was put by the Minister of Foreign Affairs of Spain, where Hoover stopped on returning from his second visit to America. It was clear to him by then that the United States was soon to be in the war. Formal administration of the Belgian Relief had to be transferred to another neutral.

"What is your salary, Mr. Hoover?" the Foreign Minister in Madrid asked archly. "What do your assistants get? What salaries will our nationals receive?"

The expression in the Spanish politician's face showed that he did not quite believe his guest's assurances that neither he nor most of his top associates were being paid. Their Spanish successors proved quite generous in assigning themselves salaries.

We do not begin to sum up the Belgian Relief effort when

we record that 5,290,735 tons of food and clothing were transported, costing $927,681,485. Quantities do not convey the dimensions of the accomplishment. The major crises and the major victories—the million incidents and heartaches—do not show up in Sir John Plender's final accounting.

There were dread moments when the entire Relief seemed doomed to collapse, and other moments when Hoover threatened to call the whole thing off unless London or Berlin yielded to his demands. The episodes of stark tragedy and pathos and humor have filled books; those who took part in the work can talk of it fascinatingly for hours. And in all the stories the figure of an Iowa Quaker lad grown to manhood looms heroically, unforgettably. I confess to a feeling of inadequacy that I cannot reflect more than a minute fraction of the deep impression which a study of that historical undertaking has left on my senses.

A British journalist who worked for some time under Hoover in these years, F. A. Wray, subsequently tried to express his judgment of the man. I quote only a few sentences:

"An utter absence of 'side,' coupled with a very kindly and a completely unassuming manner, were the characteristics which struck one at the outset. Throughout the entire time he was running the biggest individual job in the world he put on no more airs than the simplest citizen. One could size up in a moment his terrific determination, his extraordinary grasp of detail, his tremendous efficiency.

"Very few men have drawn forth so great a degree of loyalty in associates. My own connection with the Belgian Relief was typical of Hoover methods. I received a telegram reading: 'Want you for Rotterdam tomorrow.' It was taken for granted I would go. Every preparation had been made, down to the last detail. I left London at 3 A.M. the next morning."

During the life of the C.R.B. and after it was dissolved Hoover evaded all honors so far as he could without giving offence. But grateful peoples named streets and squares for him and raised statues to him. When broached on the subject of decorations, he explained that it was against his democratic convictions to accept them. But, he sometimes added with a twinkle, his hard-working assistants collected "buttons" and ribbons. As a result, his associates in the Belgian and later relief work—men such as Edgar Rickard, Maurice Pate, Perrin C. Galpin, Admiral Lewis Strauss —have stacks of those "buttons."

"They're really for the Chief—I'm just the custodian," one of them told me.

The problem of how to express a nation's eternal appreciation must have bothered King Albert of the Belgians. He respected Hoover's feelings in the matter. But one day, when Hoover was visiting him after the armistice, he informed him that his government and parliament had created a new order to be bestowed upon only one person and to expire with that person. Then he solemnly bestowed the title of Friend of the Belgian People, carrying with it honorary citizenship, upon his guest. Hoover accepted.

Since the French Government was directly concerned with the relief undertaking, the auditors in 1919 submitted the tremendous accounting to Paris for its final examination and scrutiny. The French sent it all back untouched. "We have tasks more pressing and more fruitful," they said, "than questioning the integrity of Mr. Hoover."

CHAPTER XII

"Food Will Win the War!"

WHEN COLONEL EDWARD M. HOUSE came to Europe in 1915 and again in 1916 to explore the chances of a mediated peace for President Wilson, he consulted at length with Herbert Hoover. For Hoover was the one American in a position to see Armageddon whole, from all sides of no-man's land; from the vantage points of self-righteous leaders in Berlin, London, and Paris alike; through the eyes of generals who walked with death and little children who walked with hunger.

He could tell the shrewd little emissary and his friend in the White House why their "peace without bitterness" was a fantasy far removed from the blood-drenched earth of Europe. He could tell them that in this war, as in few before its advent, people hated their enemies more than they loved themselves. What they wanted was not peace but victory, not victory but vengeance, which left no room for the compromises implicit in a negotiated peace. Even those leaders in warring countries who were sickened by the prolonged slaughter dared not make an open move; they would have been crucified by their own people. Europe was pinioned by hate.

Rightly or wrongly, Hoover blamed this in large part on the fact that food had been turned into a weapon—a weapon which made the young, the aged, and the women its first and sometimes its only targets. The soldiers, munition-makers, and others who did war work would always be adequately fed; only the "useless" masses could be starved by blockades.

Wherefore he urged President Wilson to begin his crusade for a compromise peace with practical measures to reduce the prevailing temperatures of hatred. And that, he argued, could be done only by inducing all belligerents to rule out starvation of civilians as a war strategy. In short, he wanted the President to use his immense influence to cut enough holes in the surface and U-boat blockades to let through subsistence food for noncombatants.

It was a less showy program than the liberal and radical peace-now advocates in America at the time would have liked the head of Belgian Relief to recommend. But it was closer to the realities of the situation. An idealist to the core, Hoover would never be popular with the kind of idealists who require big daily helpings of soul-stirring but futile slogans to subsist. The practical ingredients in his make-up would never allow nebulous emotions, however noble, to drown out reason.

But he was at one with the liberal and socialist groups in America, at least in the first two years of the world conflict, in opposing American military participation. He often explained his reasons to Page, to House, and to the President. The fact that Hoover became a key figure in Wilson's "War Council" notwithstanding is token enough that the wartime President did not misunderstand those reasons.

Hoover was much too close to the war to invest it with any romantic glamor. Having dealt continually with both sides on rock-bottom questions of humanity, he could not agree that either side had a monopoly on justice or on wickedness. Beyond most men in public life he was aware of the thousand-year historical conditioning, the deep-rooted power politics, behind the struggle, and therefore doubted "our ability to change those forces and, in consequence, to make a lasting peace." Wilson's heartbreak at Versailles would prove how right he was.

Hoover was convinced, moreover, that America's moral, economic, and military might "would enable us to dominate the peacemaking more effectively" if it were not among the nations physically exhausted and emotionally implicated in the bloodletting. Whether he was justified we cannot know, except by the negative evidence provided when American idealism was defeated and humiliated.

The German declaration of unlimited submarine warfare early in 1917 helped to soften Hoover's opposition. It is likely that his conversion was hastened by the sinking of Belgian Relief ships in disregard of Berlin's pledges; the ten million lives in his care were for Hoover a direct and very personal responsibility. Also, the collapse of the Romanoff dynasty, giving the people of Russia a chance for liberation, seemed to him to take the smell of hypocrisy out of the "war-for-democracy" slogans.

On May 3, 1917, at the President's request, he returned to his native land. Before that he had quietly studied food and other war problems in conferences with top Allied people at Mr. Wilson's behest. "Food mobilization" had been accepted as a fundamental American obligation. The formation of a special war agency to handle every phase of it was the President's suggestion, and there is little doubt that the availability of Hoover stimulated that decision.

Better than any other observer, Hoover knew the seriousness of food shortages in Allied Europe. He was aware that in Allied military thinking bread rightly ranked with bullets in any inventory of immediate needs. The continuous and adequate flow of food, indeed, was second in importance only to military action in defeating the Kaiser. This is the task that Hoover took upon himself and carried through so brilliantly that neither soldiers nor civilians on our side went on short rations for a single day in the final nineteen months—the American months—of the war.

Hoover must therefore be acknowledged as one of the real architects of the victory. That was what General Pershing meant when he wrote a personal message to Hoover, "whose contribution to the success of the Allied cause can hardly be overestimated."

The prevailing system of food mobilization in European countries was on a rigidly dictatorial basis. One man controlled crops, rations, prices, everything, and enforced his orders by police methods. Rarely did these "dictators" last more than six months. Hoover had made up his mind even before he returned to the

United States that the system, undesirable per se, was particularly unsuitable for Americans. They could be led, he said, but not driven.

In accepting Wilson's invitation to take command of all food resources and their effective use, Hoover stipulated that he would receive no salary, not even the symbolic dollar a year. His whole plan of organization and operation was based on the principle of voluntary co-operation, and the American Food Administration probably offers the largest and most successful practical test of the principle in modern history.

At the armistice his staff rested on some eight thousand full-time and 750,000 part-time volunteers throughout the nation. The paid employees—1,500 in Washington and 6,500 in local offices—were almost entirely clerical.

The methods of the administration, too, were almost exclusively of the voluntary varieties. Some thirteen million housewives and heads of family "signed the pledge" of free-will conservation of food. A committee of volunteers without police power enforced conservation in public eating places. Special committees of the most respected experts in their fields made the rules and enforced them in specific branches of the overall job. There was no rationing; there were any number of requests and recommendations but few "orders."

In applying his theory of voluntarism Hoover looked on the saving of money as the least of its benefits. He believed then—as he did twelve or thirteen years later in setting up a nationwide relief organization during the depression—that a paid bureaucracy, tending to expand and perpetuate itself, is a blight on any such national undertaking.

Another phase of his food administration policy which was directly related to his concept of democratic life should be mentioned. That was his belief in local and state responsibility as against a politicalized federal control through arbitrary central "directives." This, however, did not remove the need for thinking and planning at the center; on the contrary, the plan could function effectively only on that assumption.

He put that view in one pregnant sentence in testifying before a senate committee on the Food Administration Bill. "My idea," he said, "is that we must centralize ideas but decentralize execution."

Therefore he favored one-man executives rather than the hydra-headed committees and bureaus which Wilson preferred. While in sympathy with the President's dread of putting excessive authority in any individual's hands, he argued that the cure of inefficiency was worse than the disease of single direction.

As far as the food setup was concerned, he overcame Wilson's opposition by proposing, in a stroke of semantic inspiration, an administrator to head up a food administration. These names, in fact, did help squelch the talk of a "food dictator." (In years to come Hoover would wince as he watched his verbal invention proliferate like a weed in endless New Deal administrations and administrators.) In time Wilson came to realize the need for one-man leadership, and dramatized the fact by putting Bernard Baruch in charge of munitions after various boards had bungled the job.

But having centralized ideas under a single director, Hoover then placed his emphasis on maximum decentralization in putting them into effect. Every state had its own food controller who in turn worked through city and county units of volunteers familiar with local resources, conditions, and psychology.

Hoover remained the nominal head and continued to carry the primary responsibility for the Belgian Relief even while he was administering American food. But the American staffs in Brussels and other German-held areas were of necessity released. Most of those, unsuited by age or other circumstances for military service, volunteered for the Food Administration.

Many of the names which figure in the Belgian story show up in the Washington story; Washington men appear again in the American Relief Administration after the war's end. Hoover was developing a body of specialists in the new science and art of provisioning entire nations. Having begun by caring for ten million, they continued by dealing with the food needs of two hundred million, and ended with administering the feeding of between four hundred and five hundred million on an entire continent.

In mentioning Ray Lyman Wilbur, Julius Barnes, Lewis

Strauss, Robert Taft, Dr. Alonzo Taylor, Ben Allen, Edward M. Flesh, Judge Curtis Lindley, Dr. Vernon Kellogg, Dr. Raymond Pearl, Edgar Rickard, Gertrude Lane, we are only touching names at random in a long and honorable list of Americans who share Hoover's laurels in the great food job of World War I.

Wartime agencies in Washington in 1917–18 were notoriously overloaded with retired military men and civilians in the gaudiest military regalia they could wangle. There was about them the noise, the excitement, and the chaos of a parade. The Food Administration was an exception. It was all civilian and businesslike in looks and in mood—"the only war agency," as Hoover later put it, "which wore no bells and costume jewelry."

A more impressive, and perhaps not unrelated, fact is that it emerged as the only major war agency that was not investigated by Congress after the shooting was over, or charged with misfeasance at any time. The shining fact gets an extra polish when we note in the record that the Grain Corporation alone, one branch of the enterprise, did a business of some nine billion dollars.

2

The very landscape of America shrieked the reminder, "Food Will Win the War!" and the American people responded magnificently. Every housewife became a soldier in the war on waste in the kitchen and in the dining room. Meatless and wheatless days, new dietary habits to release the fats and grain needed for the armies and export, the "clean-plate" ideal, and a hundred other devices depended for success on the willing co-operation of the average American.

The bill establishing Hoover's agency gave it important regulatory powers, through licensing of food manufacturers, jobbers, and wholesalers, as well as of retailers doing more than one hundred thousand dollars business a year. It provided no coercive controls on farmers, stock growers, and other primary producers, or on the immense army of retailers below the one hundred thousand dollar line, or on the ultimate consumer.

Even the power to withdraw licenses for violation of wartime regulations, however, was used sparingly. The spirit in which

Hoover dealt with business interests was clearly indicated in the statement he issued outlining the aims of the administration:

"The Food Administration is called into being to stabilize and not to disturb conditions and to defend honest enterprise against illegitimate competition. It has been devised to correct the abnormalities and abuses that have crept into trade by reason of the world disturbance and to restore business as far as may be to a reasonable basis.

"The businessmen of this country, I am convinced . . . realize their own patriotic obligation and the solemnity of the situation, and will fairly and generously co-operate in meeting the national emergency. I do not believe that drastic force need be applied. . . . But if there be those who expect to exploit this hour of sacrifice, if there are men or organizations scheming to increase the trials of this country, we shall not hesitate to apply to the full the drastic, coercive powers that Congress has conferred upon us in this instrument."

The fable that Hoover is a know-nothing supporter of laissez-faire capitalism, come hell or high water, looks pretty silly when matched with such a statement; or when matched, for that matter, with his far-reaching regulatory actions as President. But he did devote thought and effort to safeguarding normal economic processes. The whole complex of raising, processing, and distributing food remained less controlled, closer to normal, in the United States than in any other belligerent country. It was not his way to attempt to solve an emergency by wrecking the social patterns being saved, or by systematizing the emergency on a more or less permanent footing.

As Food Administrator he did not rely blindly on the good old law of supply and demand. He imposed a web of regulatory guards which enabled the law to operate without going haywire. Unrestricted price competition in a world at war, he said, would not curtail consumption by armies—costs did not matter in that domain—but would strike at consumption by the lowest-income groups. He did not hesitate to use abnormal methods for abnormal times—always with a frank admission that government interference was the least of an array of war evils and must be dispensed with at the earliest moment.

The control of wheat, the most vital single food item, he achieved through the United States Grain Corporation, which was the sole channel for military and export provisioning. It was capitalized at its peak at $500,000,000 and served as a stabilizing force for producer and consumer alike, given the war conditions. On dissolution at the end of the war it returned to the Treasury every dollar it had drawn, plus a reasonable interest for its use. The same was true of the Sugar Equalization Board. Its record stands out in sharp contrast with the vast losses wrapped in scandals suffered by other economic war agencies.

The price of wheat was fixed for the duration, largely to prevent suicidal bidding by desperate warring nations. It was not Hoover, however, who did the fixing. The price was set by a group representing all elements in the business and the public as well, appointed by President Wilson. The President disclosed at the time that "Mr. Hoover, at his express wish, has taken no part in the deliberations" nor even "intimated an opinion" on the figure finally agreed upon.

The American wheat crop of 1917 was a failure; a winter of exceptional harshness punched holes in the 1918 estimates. By the end of 1917 surpluses were close to the exhaustion point. Meanwhile Hoover's observers on the scene and Allied statesmen clamored for quantities far above those planned. In January the English Food Controller, Lord Rhondda, cabled:

"Unless you are able to send the Allies at least 75,000,000 bushels of wheat over and above what you have exported up to January first, and in addition to the total exportable surplus from Canada, I cannot take the responsibility of assuring our people that there will be food enough to win the war."

America, under the leadership of Hoover, came through. The principle of voluntarism was justified by results. Reporting to the President at the end of the initial year, Hoover could show exports not only of wheat but of all other essential foodstuffs between 35 and 50 per cent above the preceding year; this despite the demands of our own military establishment.

Inevitably there was some food profiteering which a more rigid police system of enforcement might have obviated; although the black-market evils in police states raise some questions on that score. Hoover showed scant patience with the leeches. It was he who in July 1918 proposed to the President that the nation's tax power be used to siphon off excess profits into the public coffers. At Wilson's request he put his proposal into a letter addressed to Senator Simmons. It stands on the record to confound those who have considered it politically expedient to bracket Hoover with Big Business.

Though his particular assignment was the crucial one of food mobilization and distribution, Hoover played an active role in the whole civilian strategy of victory as one of the outstanding members of the President's "War Council." His worldwide experience gave his voice a resonance that often made it decisive in formulating policies beyond his own vast department. No less often, of course, he fought for lost causes in the council room and the chambers of the Commander in Chief.

For instance, in the light of Hoover's personal knowledge of Russia and the Far East, the President asked his views on the proposed Japanese invasion of Siberia. Hoover counseled against this with all his energy. Whether the Japanese succeeded or failed, he insisted, the invasion would only serve to rally the Russian people behind the extremist regime; besides, if the Japanese succeeded in conquering any portion of the mainland they would insist on holding it as a reward. But Wilson, reluctantly it is true, submitted to Allied pressures and the invasion went forward with a token American force taking part.

The Food Administrator shocked Washington by proposing that we relax the blockade of the Central Powers enough to permit the feeding of enemy children and weaker women. He drew up a practical plan for providing such relief through neutral intermediaries, under airtight guarantees, essentially along the lines of the Belgian precedent. He argued that this would in no way affect the military equation, while building valuable good will for America in the mass of German people.

His arguments were cogent. He projected them to the forefront because mere appeals to decency and charity would be a waste of breath in a time of inflamed war sentiment. But under surface arguments was the fact that Hoover wept inwardly for the hungry ones in Austria or Germany as he did for those in

France or Belgium or Russia. His sympathies for Man Crucified were not a matter of policy and did not stop short at any geographical or racial line.

His proposals, of course, were brushed aside as visionary. In the perspective of time, who can be so sure that they were not the most practical of all? Hatred, like love, can become romantic beyond reason and logic.

"I did not myself believe in the blockade," Hoover wrote of World War I in the midst of the second. "I do not believe in starving women and children. I did not believe that it was the effective weapon of which the Allies were so confident. And, above all, *I did not believe that stunted bodies and deformed minds in the next generation were the foundation upon which to rebuild civilization*."

In the peace terms submitted by Wilson to the Germans toward the finish there was a clause committing the victors to the principle of helping feed the vanquished. It was Hoover who succeeded in injecting that clause, and after the armistice he fought like a lion to make good that humanitarian promise.

His eagerness to feed enemy children even while war was at its height needs to be underlined. It was not sufficiently recalled or stressed when in World War II, both before and after America was involved, Hoover pleaded for effective relief of the children of Greece, Poland, France, Norway, and other Hitler-held lands.

Obscene minds could see in that solicitude for the innocent victims of the holocaust only another "Hitler lover." From the proud perches of their self-righteous propaganda and official respectability they spat insults at Hoover, at anyone who dared remind them of simple human obligations. Cynics all, having renounced their Judeo-Christian inheritance, wandering without moral compass in their ideological jungles, they could no longer recognize human beings under political labels and classifications —not even in just-born babes.

But all that is a commentary not on Hoover but on his critics. Had the Hoover view prevailed in World War I, the chances of a Hitler emerging would surely have been reduced. It is certain, at least, that hordes of the Hitler recruits had minds deformed by near-starvation in their childhood.

While stimulating the production of food, combating waste, and promoting food abstinence, Hoover did not lose sight of the certainty that all Europe, winners and losers alike, would face shortage and in huge areas actual famine when the fighting ended. The reserve he built up helped to prevent the physical and moral crippling of millions on that continent. The administration of that great work of human salvage, too, fell in due time to Hoover. It was to be the greatest responsibility ever loaded on one pair of shoulders, a job terrifying in its magnitude. But Hoover, having accepted the responsibility for Belgium, had set himself on a road from which there could be no turning for a man of his background and native impulses.

It seems almost frivolous to have thus compressed the story of the Food Administration into a few disorganized pages. A bibliography listing only the more important books about that agency lies before me—there are twenty-two of them.

CHAPTER XIII

Salvaging a Continent

HERBERT HOOVER WAS NOT FORMALLY
a member of the Peace Mission in Paris, though he shared rooms
with the American delegates at the Crillon and remained in constant consultation with them and with President Wilson. In a
sense he was their most valuable liaison with the European actu-
ality, screened from their view in conference halls by competing
greeds and war-born delusions. The "Hoover organization," with
human tentacles in twenty-odd countries of the shell-shocked continent, was the main and often the sole reliable source of current
economic and political information.

The Big Four and their assorted experts lived in a wilderness
of committees and commissions dedicated to bamboozling each
other and especially successful in bamboozling themselves. But
the several thousand "Hoover men"—the term described them
more accurately than the variety of titles and sanctions under
which they worked—lived amid the rubble and depravities of
war's aftermath. They dealt in concrete detail, not in diplomatic
formulas, with famine and typhus, with transport and communications, with coal and iron, with the immediate human consequences of hatreds in eruption and hopes in collapse.

Hoover at the Peace Conference was concerned, as he phrases
it, "with the gaunt realities which prowled outside." These, unhappily, were not rated as primary concerns by the embattled
peace-makers. Later, looking back, they had reason to know (and
a few the grace to admit) that their sorry peace would have been

buried in an avalanche of death, with Bolshevism feasting on the putrefaction, had Hoover failed to deal as swiftly and wisely as he did with those "gaunt realities."

An English delegate, John Maynard Keynes (later Lord Keynes), wrote in retrospect:

"Mr. Hoover was the only man who emerged from the ordeal of Paris with an enhanced reputation. This complex personality . . . his eyes steadily fixed on the true and essential facts of the European situation, imported into the Councils of Paris, when he took part in them, precisely that atmosphere of reality, knowledge, magnanimity, and disinterestedness which, if they had been found in other quarters also, would have given us the Good Peace."

Within a fortnight after the last guns barked Hoover was back in Europe. He was there as the President's plenipotentiary on all matters of food and provisionment under the armistice; as representative of the American Food Administration (though no longer its administrator) and chairman of the Grain Corporation; as head of the continuing Commission for Relief in Belgium and of the American Relief Administration soon to emerge. Before long he was also Director General of Supplies and Relief under the Supreme War Council and, after that was dissolved at his own suggestion, head of a Supreme Economic Council of his own design which functioned to the end.

It was hard to know under which of these interlaced authorities Hoover and his staff did what they did. But it mattered not at all, for they did what they believed had to be done, in blithe contempt of formalities. Though it embraced a congeries of titles and functions (most of them conveniently vague), the Hoover organization was close-knit by loyalty to its chief and welded by a unifying intelligence. Here, as in Washington, the men on the job had almost limitless autonomy within the bounds of a set of "centralized ideas."

Once, when General Pershing was asked what precisely was Hoover's position, he replied, "Mr. Hoover is the food regulator of the world." If that was too broad in one respect, it was too narrow in a dozen respects. Relief, after all, is not just a matter of finding and handing out edibles. It involved demolition of towering diplomatic obstructions and imposing patterns of order on areas of anarchy. In every country and community the local leadership had to be found and organized and trained and supervised to guarantee fair, economical, effective distribution of supplies. It involved shipping, money and credit, harbors and railroads, fuel and power, and virtually all other economic factors.

Besides, what began as relief expanded unavoidably into large-scale rehabilitation. Hoover was by no means the "economic dictator" he was labeled in the press, but he was the economic activator in nearly all defeated and liberated nations. Out of abysmal chaos he helped conjure the minimum of order and subsistence which made a return to approximate normality possible.

Before his work was completed, his comrades in benevolence were operating telegraph lines, canals, ports, railroad networks, coal mines, hospitals, nurseries—this over and above the vast primary tasks of gathering food, paying for it, hauling it from overseas, then deploying it like divisions of a great liberating army to combat hunger, disease, and moral disintegration where these ruthless enemies were in occupation. Repeatedly cargoes being rushed to one destination had to be suddenly switched to some sector where danger was more urgent. A hundred times anarchy was headed off in the nick of time by the arrival of bread and medicines.

Will Irwin, who reported the spectacle as a foreign correspondent, would write: "I think of Hoover as a chess master, playing twenty games at once, and most of them blindfolded."

Victory over the Central Powers had created more problems than it solved. War is a discipline—its end spelled confusion. Civil conflicts were under way in Russia; territorial and dynastic conflicts were under way in the Baltic and Balkan countries and in the bleeding fragments of the Austro-Hungarian empire. Eastern Europe from Finland to the Levant was in economic collapse and political convulsions. Germany presented a bloody froth of violence on a great sea of lethargic miseries. Currencies were in hopeless disorder, and there was galloping inflation everywhere.

The great common hatred that had held the Allies together exploded into a lot of little hatreds that drove them apart.

Hoover was one of the few, along with Colonel House and Mr. Baruch, who had urged Wilson not to go to Europe. They believed that the President's voice would carry farther coming from the White House than face to face with the hagglers and bargain-hunters of European power politics. Soon after his arrival in Paris, Wilson asked Hoover what he thought of the general situation.

He got a frank answer that disturbed and perhaps exasperated him. As Hoover recalled the interview afterward, he painted for the President the picture of "greed, robbery, power, sadistic hate, and revenge" in individuals; "fevered nationalism, imperialism, militarism, reaction, determination to decimate and dominate" in nations. He said he found no tolerance, integrity, or generosity among the winners—not merely toward the losers but toward one another. Wilson demurred, insisting his friend was too harsh; but about two months later, recalling this conversation, he said to Hoover: "I have often agreed with you."

Over this landscape of riotous passion and deep despairs, trampled by War and Death, now rode the other two Horsemen of the Apocalypse, Famine and Pestilence. Hoover's first step was to send expert investigators into the stricken lands to chart the extent and character of the manifold disasters. On the basis of their careful reports he foretold "the worst famine since the Thirty Years' War," when a third of Europe's population perished, unless help could be brought without delay.

The investigators found a death rate as high as 30 per cent in some Baltic and Balkan cities; children with the bloated bellies of the last agonies of hunger in Germany, Hungary, Poland; cannibalism in Armenia and other places; women tearing the flesh off rotting horses with their bare hands; skeletonlike children and women scavenging in offal heaps everywhere.

Hoover could not wait for self-righteous statesmen to formulate decisions. While they argued, he acted. Just as he had bought wheat for Belgium before a relief organization was set up, just as he had started food conservation at home before Congress passed its enabling act, so now he set huge quantities of supplies in motion toward Europe and within Europe before he knew where the money was coming from and whether blockades would be lifted.

His field men were told in effect, "Feed the starving by any

means, only quickly." When necessary these men blustered and
bluffed through opposition to move cargoes to appointed destinations. Their credentials signed by Hoover were honored as passports in places where ordinary national passports only evoked
suspicion. Hoover men on their own in isolated places exercised
power that was as often assumed as assigned.

The thrilling story has come down of a lone doughboy accom-
panying a trainload of food destined for Vienna from an Adriatic
port. Somewhere in the Balkans the train was stopped by military
guards and ordered to unload its cargo. The American soldier
didn't quite grasp the politics of the situation, so he jumped on
the locomotive and commanded the engineer to put on full steam.
He covered the flabbergasted guards with an automatic and the
train pulled out. He "wasn't working for no kings or generals,"
he said in reporting the incident; he took orders only from the
Chief. It was typical of a thousand such incidents in a thousand
tight spots.

A disturbed American officer on his staff once came to see
Hoover in Paris. He wanted to make a clean breast of something,
and this is the story he told:

Civil war was raging in Dalmatia. The officer and two doughboys were caught in a crossfire on a mountain road above Cattaro.
On investigating they discovered that the entrenched armies, perhaps a thousand guerrillas in all, were willing to call the battle
off, but neither of the commanding generals cared to lose face by
crying "Uncle." Neither would surrender to the other.

That was simple, the officer pointed out—they could both surrender to America with their honor intact. In drawing up the
formal capitulation paper, however, he became alarmed about involving the United States of America in a foreign fracas, so he
wrote in "United States Food Administrator" instead. In a ceremony staged in the best movie tradition, he collected swords from
the two generals; after which he put members of their armies
to work reloading the trucks.

But he got to worrying whether he hadn't put the Chief on a
diplomatic spot by using his name, and here he was in Paris
explaining it all. Hoover, with a straight face, wanted to know
what happened to the swords. The officer still had them. In that

case, he ruled, if the officer would give him one and keep the other as mementoes of the Dalmatian peace, the episode would be considered liquidated. Later Hoover wrote him that he was "of the stuff that had made America a great country."

Multiply that little drama by ten thousand and you begin to feel the texture of that continent-wide crusade against hunger.

2

Men such as Robert Taft (later senator), Dr. Alonzo Taylor, Vernon Kellogg, Lewis Strauss (later admiral) from the Food Administration came to Paris with Hoover. They were joined by dozens of veterans of the Belgian job, among them some of the former Rhodes scholars. Hugh Gibson, by that time First Secretary of our London Embassy, was assigned to Hoover as diplomatic go-between with other governments. On General Pershing's orders several thousand able and seasoned army men were detached as Hoover needed them; the Navy and Marines, too, contributed personnel. About fifteen hundred American businessmen and engineers, technically still in the armed forces, were soon deployed through twenty-five nations as economic organizers and spark plugs. Many of these, and civilians as well, made themselves so indispensable that they were engaged by various governments to remain as advisers after the Hoover organization was dissolved. Like their chief, his top assistants who could afford it worked without salaries.

A white-and-gold house on Rue Lubeck in the Trocadero district, run as a co-operative boardinghouse, became home for the duration for Hoover himself, many of his assistants, and field men reporting in Paris. A building on Avenue Montaigne served as working headquarters.

There were fifty rooms full of men, mostly in army and navy uniform, the clatter of typewriters, adding machines, telegraph instruments, the voices of direction and instruction; the walls covered with ocean maps upon which every morning little flags showed where hundreds of ships were and where they were going; charts of twenty-five countries showing what their stocks of food were and what they would need in the next month. There were no photographs of starving children, no evidences that all this machinery had to do with human suffering, the hopes of freedom, the future of nations, and the prayer of peace.

The work in the flesh-and-blood countries mirrored on those charts was the opposite of inhuman and mechanical. The very news that the Hoover of Belgian fame was back on the job in Europe, having spread from the Atlantic to the frontiers of Russia, "acted like magic in restoring hopes to these despairing millions," Vernon Kellogg attested from direct observation. He added: "It was owing more to Hoover and his work than to any other single influence that utter anarchy and chaos and complete Bolshevik domination of eastern Europe were averted."

There was a domestic American aspect of this gigantic enterprise that should not be overlooked. By the summer of 1918 there were ample grounds for hoping that the German armies would soon be routed. But those responsible for an uninterrupted and even stepped-up flow of food across the Atlantic could not gear their efforts to a hope. They dared not relax the building of safe surpluses; commanders in the field warned them not to discount the possibility of years of fighting still to come.

America at the armistice was therefore caught with huge stocks of provisions, some of them perishable, and immense new farm productive capacity. Agriculture had expanded to the tune of 15,000,000 tons of exports as against a prewar 5,000,000 tons. Unless Europe, weeping and begging for food, could receive it quickly, collapse of farm prices and a far-reaching economic debacle seemed inevitable.

In fighting for the right to rescue Europe, including the vanquished peoples, from famine, Hoover was at the same time fighting to safeguard the farm and food industries of the United States. It was a case of economic imperatives at home and humanitarian imperatives abroad coinciding—with Allied suspicions, continuing blockades, and appetites for vengeance sitting stubbornly athwart the roads to both sets of goals.

Hoover was successful in clearing the roads, but not without blood, sweat, and tears. The very congressmen and editors who assailed him for trying to "feed the Huns" were giving him hell at the same time for the dangerous food surpluses. On the latter score his critics did not know the half of it. Not until peace had been signed did the public learn about the decisive Battle of the Pork which he had fought almost single-handed in behalf of the farmers, packers, and a dozen related economic groups in the United States.

Surplus breadstuffs could be bought and stored by the Grain Corporation, but pork products were perishable. All the Allies had placed huge orders, and America had extended itself to meet these demands. But with the war's end those orders were abruptly canceled. Hoover argued and pressed and threatened until practically every pound of that pork was taken up—by England, France, the Belgian Relief, and the American armed forces. I tell it in one sentence, but it sums up scores of conferences, months of labor, endless negotiations.

Hoover held the line on pork prices. Those whose economic lives he saved never realized how near they were to misfortune. American doughboys in those months had cause to grouse about their monotonous diet of ham and bacon; they could not guess that they were eating for the safety of farms and jobs at home.

In his armistice address to Congress, President Wilson had repeated assurances that we would "relieve distressing want" in the conquered countries. "Hunger," he said, "does not breed reform; it breeds madness and all the ugly distempers that make an ordered life impossible." He was speaking words drafted for him by Hoover.

Like most of the other noble Wilsonian promises, this one ran headlong into the calculated callousness of power politics. It took Hoover many anguished weeks to crack the blockades around neutral countries; nearly four anguished months to break through the blockade around Germany. The Allies, and in particular France, were bitterly opposed to letting food reach the starving, disease-ridden, disarmed Germans. In the effulgence of their triumphs, Clemenceau and Foch seemed impervious to reason. "There are 20,000,000 Germans too many anyhow," the Tiger told the press. Had the official French view prevailed, had the blockade continued until the signing of a treaty, millions would have perished, additional millions of children would have been crippled in body and mind.

The four months of unrelieved hunger after the cessation of hostilities seemed to Hoover not only a human scandal but "a crime of statesmanship." He caught France red-handed selling textiles to the Germans despite the blockade and the Italians selling arms for gold to Béla Kun's communist agents in Hungary— and exposed them all before the Supreme War Council.

At one of the endless meetings on the issue, General Plumer, head of British occupation troops in Germany, showed up. He told the stubborn statesmen that his soldiers were sickened by the horror; they could no longer bear the sight of bloated children rummaging in the garbage like famished dogs. At another meeting Hoover exclaimed:

"The uses to which the blockade of foodstuffs is being put are absolutely immoral. I do not feel that we can with any sense of national honor or dignity longer continue to endure this situation. . . . I wish to solemnly warn the Conference as to impending results in total collapse of the social system in Europe."

Scathingly he countered American criticism of his supposed tenderness toward the enemy. "We do not kick a man in the stomach when we have licked him," he said in a public statement; "we must write now into history such acts as will stand credibly in the minds of our grandchildren." But Congress, in voting $100,000,000 for European relief, specified that no penny of it must reach former enemies, old or young.

The American delegation, however, backed Hoover. The Italians and the British fell into line. On March 7, 1919, Hoover again faced Lloyd George, as he had faced him nearly five years earlier on the Belgian issue. He accused the British of sabotaging the relief of distressed millions while mouthing philanthropic phrases. After hearing the ungarnished indictment, Lloyd George again declared himself convinced.

And the following day he came through brilliantly in backing Hoover before the War Council. His blast against French intransigeance on feeding Germany was said to have been one of the most eloquent of his lifetime. He heaped hot coals on Clemenceau, despite the fact—more likely because of the fact—that the British were almost equally to blame. Hoover won; the blockade, so far as food and clothes and medicines were concerned, was lifted.

"You may start your shipments," one of the French delegates said smilingly, in acknowledgment of defeat.

"They started weeks ago," Hoover replied grimly.

In which he was merely telling a remarkable truth. The moral courage of the man showed up repeatedly in the way he started relief shipments for the stricken areas on his own authority long before the diplomatic opposition had been removed—often long before the physical road blocks of wrecked transport had been removed.

The food administration, as I have already indicated, became a railroad and harbor administration, a coal administration, a hygienic administration. The succession states in Central Europe had purloined one another's rolling stock and cut the Austro-Hungarian railway system into five national segments. Hoover's men succeeded in crashing through impassioned nationalisms to reopen those roads. To move their millions of tons of lifesaving supplies they restored canals, put harbors into condition, mobilized rolling stock, and supervised thousands of miles of railways. Then it became apparent that the near-collapse of the Silesian and Polish coal industries was hampering reconstruction in half the continent, and Hoover was obliged to take over in that domain. Colonel Anson C. Goodyear, selected for the post by General Pershing, and his American staff doubled coal output in a few months.

The work of benevolence could not go on without speedy communications. It fell to Hoover, therefore, to open up a continent-wide telegraphic network, which in that period was a greater achievement than it sounds. With all the new and old governments fearful of espionage, codes were forbidden. This did not hamper resourceful Americans with native slang at their command. In their dispatches one dignified statesman always figured as Mutt, another as Jeff, a third as The Chump.

The most famous of these dispatches was seized as a war curiosity by Clemenceau, who had lived in America and appreciated its humor. Captain Tom Gregory, in Budapest, had instructions to inform the Archduke Joseph, who had assumed power in

Hungary, that the Allies wanted no Hapsburg for that job. On August 23, 1919, over his own wires, Hoover received the following message:

"Archie on the carpet 7 P.M. Went through the hoop at 8 P.M."

The shocking reports of the depredations of the typhus louse in the war zones of a shattered Russia could no longer be ignored when the epidemic, like a conquering army, began to move into Lithuania, Poland, the Ukraine, Rumania, and Serbia. Nearly a million cases of the dread disease were totaled in those areas and with each day the pestilence marched farther westward.

The most palpable and alarming information naturally came to Hoover, who alone among the men in Paris had representatives everywhere. He pressed the Supreme Council to take action. But finally he could wait no longer. With a sigh he also shouldered that battle. By the time the Council was ready to act, there was no need for it—Hoover had command of the situation.

With Colonel H. L. Gilchrist in charge, Americans formed a battle line that stretched from north to south across the whole continent. The American Army contributed vast amounts of medical and hospital supplies and equipment and a few other armies in time came through. The German Reichswehr turned over millions of dollars' worth of delousing machinery. No one was allowed to pass the battle line from east to west without a certificate of delousing. Having strayed to the wrong side of the cordon sanitaire, Hugh Gibson had to obtain a delousing document the hard way despite his diplomatic eminence. From June to December the war on typhus continued. The line was pushed steadily eastward and finally total victory could be announced.

In the scheme of this book there is, unfortunately, no space for the detailed accounts of how the crusade was fought and won in each of the twenty-odd countries. Any one of those battlefields provides enough drama to fill volumes.

Consider the Baltic wedge where three new-hatched republics —Lithuania, Latvia, and Esthonia—had their violent being. Their aggregate population was under five million, but their aggregate sufferings and bloodlettings were incalculable. Governments rose and fell in cyclones of terror, with Bolshevik termites always boring in the debris. Latvia writhed in agony nearly six months under a Soviet orgy of loot and murder of nauseating memory. The streets of Riga were still littered with corpses when American food arrived to the rescue.

Hoover tells one minor incident in the relief of Riga which I cannot resist retelling. A Yankee sergeant asked if there was an American consulate in town and was directed to an obscure address. Tacked on the door was a small American flag and under it a typewritten notice in Lettish and English warning the world in general not to molest the premises, and signed "Acting Consul of the United States of America."

The sergeant knocked. After a while a girl peeked out; at the sight of the American uniform she burst into tears of joy. It turned out that she was an American of Lettish origin, the stenographer in the consulate. When everyone else retreated before the Germans she chose to hold the fort, and promptly reopened her "consulate" when the war ended.

Much shrill nonsense has been written by Communist propagandists about Hoover and the short-lived regime of murder under Béla Kun in Hungary. It was the fixed policy of the relief not to deliver food to governments anywhere which could not be trusted to distribute it equitably, without political bias. That by definition ruled out Communists, to whom food and famine were "class weapons."

Yet Hoover insisted that twenty-five trainloads of supplies en route to Budapest at the moment Béla Kun took over be delivered to its destination, since the Hungarian Government had paid for them. The Supreme Council yielded to him on this but specifically forbade any more shipments. Though the decision was not his, Hoover agreed with it, knowing that supplies surrendered to Bolsheviks would never reach the people.

Just as soon as the reactionary Kun mob was ousted, at the initiative of the trade unions, provisioning was resumed. Then, when a Hapsburg briefly enthroned himself, it was a Hoover man, acting for the War Council, who unseated him; we have already cited Captain Gregory's cryptic message on that occasion. Hoover knew and Gregory knew—but the Archduke didn't—that the Allies were bluffing; they had no forces available to oust him if he had told the American to mind his own business.

Throughout the great relief effort Hoover was especially vigilant for the well-being of children. Subordinates, knowing his softest spot, could get anything they wanted by showing that it involved help for the little ones. In part his life-long concern for the young rests on cold logic—without a healthy, normal new generation there can be no hope for any future, he argues. But that is merely the façade for a solicitude that is of the heart, not the mind. Perhaps it harks back to his own harsh childhood, as some biographers surmise. The fact is that the very thought of children in pain or in hunger strikes to the deepest core of his being.

Beyond the general rationed relief Hoover therefore set up special services which in time embraced eight million boys and girls in Poland, Finland, Czechoslovakia, and other countries. Since no official American appropriations could be diverted to former enemy countries, the child relief work in Germany was conducted, by Hoover's arrangement, by the Quakers on a straight charity basis. The children's relief continued for years after the rest of the work was ended.

Nearly thirty years later, in 1946, Hoover found himself in Warsaw on his round-the-world trip for President Truman. He was conferring with a group of Communist officials there. Suddenly a woman physician present turned to him and said in effect: "I am one of the children you fed after the first war. If it were not for you, Mr. Hoover, I wouldn't be alive now—and I guess the same is true of others in this room." True it was: one after another the officials smilingly acknowledged that they had been sustained by Hoover charity as children. At a public meeting in Belgrade, in the course of the same mission, the Yugoslav Foreign Minister in his speech made the identical admission; he, too, had been among the millions at the tables spread by American benevolence in schoolhouses throughout eastern Europe.

All in all, in the twelve months following the armistice, the Hoover organization distributed twenty-seven million tons of food and other supplies, valued at about five and a half billion dollars. It saved millions of lives and headed off what would surely have been the most calamitous famine in mortal history. Again figures do not tell the whole story. Hoover and his associates put into effect an exchange of goods on a barter basis among the afflicted nations; they provided the initial push that started the machinery of reconstruction rolling; they became the mouthpiece of stricken populations and the conscience of mankind.

Amazingly, the man in charge of this colossal effort found time for tangential activities. The super-executive did not wholly blot out the scholar. He had read about the difficulties of posterity in understanding past events because contemporary documents so rarely survived. Since he had men all over the continent, he decided to have them gather such documents as the future might value; hundreds on his staff made a game of his treasure hunt for archives, posters, and other historical data.

The resultant material, tons and tons of it, formed the nucleus of the famous Hoover Library of War, Revolution and Peace at Stanford University. Grateful governments and individuals consigned carloads of records and archives to Hoover; even the Soviet Government later came through with immense and valuable Czarist archives. To this day full-time agents of the library scour the world for vital documents reflecting the tides of human history.

3

Sprawling Russia, riven by violence, presented a special problem. After the overthrow of Czardom, Hoover had urged that the fledgling democracy receive food and other supplies. Had the Allies possessed the wisdom to provide timely and generous support to the moderate forces under Alexander Kerensky, the handful of fanatics under Lenin might never have managed to seize power; the multiple world tragedies deriving directly or indirectly from that seizure—including Fascism and Nazism—might have been averted.

After the armistice Hoover continually wrestled with the puzzle of how to help the Russian people without helping their Bolshevik oppressors rivet the chains of terror on them more firmly. In the upper stratum of Paris advisers he was almost alone in urging relaxation of the Russian blockade to allow food and medicaments to enter.

In the confusions of our time it is almost forgotten that the

Lenin-Trotsky group did not overthrow the old regime or "make the revolution." On the contrary, they hijacked the revolution from its makers, the people of Russia, washing out in blood the first efforts of those people to establish a democratic pattern of life. It has been forgotten that the Russians, in the election of the Constituent Assembly after the Bolshevik coup, voted overwhelmingly against the interlopers. That, of course, was why Lenin suppressed the Constituent Assembly; why his regime thereafter relied exclusively on police terror and the mental terror of controlled propaganda to retain power.

But in 1919 these simple truths were too fresh to be overlooked. Hoover's sympathy for popular Russian aspirations to freedom was even deeper than his detestation of the Bolshevik concepts and methods. On March 28, 1919, he wrote a long letter to Wilson outlining his views on the Russian problem.

"It simply cannot be denied, that this swinging of the social pendulum from the tyranny of the extreme right to the tyranny of the extreme left is based on a foundation of real social grievance. The tyranny of the reactionaries in Eastern and Central Europe for generations before the war, the sufferings of their common people, is but a commonplace to every social student. . . . The poor were starved and driven mad in the presence of extravagance and waste."

Having indicted the Red terror in scorching language, Hoover declared that some way must be found, notwithstanding, to bring help to millions of starving Russians. If the Soviet Government should prove willing to remain within fixed frontiers, renouncing plans to carry its minority domination into neighboring countries, the outside world—and America in the first place—should agree to give unlimited and completely non-political relief.

Specifically, he proposed formation of a commission headed by a prominent neutral acceptable to Moscow and operating on about the same basis as the Belgian Relief. President Wilson agreed. Fridtjof Nansen, the celebrated polar explorer, was the man Hoover selected to head up the project.

The Big Four, in an exchange of letters with Nansen, accepted the Hoover plan. Clemenceau was frankly reluctant and contemptuous. Indeed, French sabotage delayed Nansen's formal message to Lenin, dated April 17, by more than two weeks, during which the French press assailed the idea and limited it in a way that made Moscow's rejection a certainty.

When Chicherin, Bolshevik Foreign Commissar, finally received and answered the Nansen proposal—an answer again delayed by accidents which were not accidental—it was in the negative, as expected. Hoover was profoundly disappointed and blamed the French more than the Russians for the failure of his intercession.

"I believed the reply left a crack open," Hoover subsequently wrote about the Chicherin statement, "and that the many words were for internal consumption. I wanted to pursue the question further, but the French in the meantime emitted vociferous denunciations of the whole business and so the effort died at no cost but words."

Knowing what we know today about the Bolshevik mentality, he was probably naïve in believing Lenin might agree to compromises of any sort. The Kremlin then had high hopes (as it was to have them a second time after World War II) that all Europe would go Communist. What were a few million Russian corpses more or less against the interests of world revolution? But the Russian people, if ever they throw off the yoke of their Red oligarchy, will learn for the first time that the same Hoover who did feed millions of them in subsequent years tried desperately to bring them relief as early as 1919.

To finish with the subject, I shall again ignore chronology. In 1921 weather and Soviet economic barbarism combined to bring a terrifying famine. That July, Maxim Gorki, the Russian novelist, appealed to the American people for aid. Hoover was then Secretary of Commerce. He had kept the American Relief Administration alive and it still had $7,000,000 in its coffers.

Hoover replied to Gorki, indicating that the A.R.A. was eager to help. He made some reasonable conditions, such as the release of Americans held in Soviet prisons, full liberty of travel for relief workers, equal treatment of all Russians regardless of "class origins" in distributing food. At the same time he pledged that the undertaking would be rigidly non-political at the American end.

Negotiations followed, and on August 20 an agreement was

reached in Riga. The first American meals were served in Russia just one month later, on September 21. Americans responded generously to the appeal, although it coincided with hard times at home. There was little hope that our government would contribute to the work. But the Grain Corporation had a balance of $20,000,000 in its account, and Hoover induced Congress to authorize the diversion of that sum to Russian relief. About $25,000,000 from Russian gold reserves was added with the Kremlin's consent.

In all, $78,000,000 worth of assistance was brought to the struggle with famine. It was administered by a veteran of the earlier relief work, Colonel William N. Haskell, and a corps of devoted "Hoover men," among them graduates of the hard Belgian and East European schools of experience. They stuck to the job until the crisis ended. The calamity was horrible beyond description. That it was not worse was owing entirely to American assistance; estimates of lives saved ranged as high as fifteen million.

The Soviet Government and individual officials were loud in praise of the work as long as it was under way. A few hysterical anti-Hoover bombs thrown by Americans fanatically attached to the Soviets proved to be duds. The full-blown Communist charges that the A.R.A. was "political" were of much later vintage.

I can contribute two minor bits of personal information. While the Hoover organization was raising funds for Russian relief, appeals were also made by an American Communist "front" group, the Friends of Soviet Russia. It published a propaganda monthly, *Soviet Russia Pictorial*—and I was its editor. As a non-Communist liberal sympathizer, I was not taken into secrets, of course; but it was scarcely a secret in our offices that little of the money raised by this organization—and other pro-Soviet outfits —ever reached the famine victims. It was diverted to Communist propaganda purposes here and in other countries.

These men and women who robbed the famished and defrauded the charitable were not evil people; some of them were even high-minded and idealistic people. It was their politicalized code of conduct that was evil. They had no sense of personal guilt, since "the cause" purified any and all actions. They were not interested in helping the Russian people but in promoting world revolution.

The second piece of personal testimony relates to the six-year period from 1928 to 1934 when I lived in the U.S.S.R. as a press correspondent. By that time Hoover had become a favorite target of Communist attack the world over. But I know as an inexpungable fact that his name was still venerated among Russians, including some of the Russians who were obliged to lambaste him publicly. Whether in Moscow or in remote villages, I found that mention of America instantly recalled the great humanitarian job of A.R.A. I met dozens of people who told me they owed their lives to the Hoover organization, hundreds who were anxious to have me know that Russians are not ungrateful or forgetful.

When the task in Russia was wound up, the Moscow press paid off in the coin that has made Communist sportsmanship so admired. Hoover, the Soviet papers said graciously, had provided relief hoping that "his mines in the Urals would be returned to him." The circumstance that he retained no mining interests in Russia did not deter American comrades and others from repeating that obscenity.

But officially the Soviet Government did present Hoover with a decorative scroll expressing extravagant appreciation. It was inscribed in the name of the Council of People's Commissars and signed by some of its top commissars. I have a photostat of it before me as I write. Dated July 10, 1923, and addressed to the American people, it specifically thanks Hoover and the whole A.R.A. through whose "entirely unselfish efforts . . . millions of people of all ages were saved from death."

Maxim Gorki was even more explicit. In a letter to Hoover he thanked the American people and expressed "complete satisfaction with the humanitarian work of the American Relief Administration of which you are chairman." Then he went on: "In the past year you have saved from death three and one half million children, five and one half million adults. . . . I know of no accomplishment which in terms of magnitude and generosity can be compared to the relief that you have actually accomplished. . . ."

In announcing the completion of the A.R.A. mission, Hoover pleaded with Americans to continue to provide help for Soviet children. In a public speech he paid his respects to people whose anti-Soviet sentiments blotted out their humane instincts. "I would rather have implanted the love of the American flag in the hearts of millions," he exclaimed, "than to have added to the American Navy all the battleships that the Atlantic Ocean can float."

James Rosenberg, lawyer and philanthropist, has described to me a scene which provides a sufficient answer to Communist slurs on Hoover's motives in relation to Russian relief. In August 1921, at the request of the Secretary of Commerce, representatives of many social-work agencies met in Washington to plan co-operation on the Russian appeal. Rosenberg attended for the Jewish Joint Distribution Committee. At one point in the discussion a lady raised doubts about the wisdom of the whole business.

"Mr. Secretary," she said in effect, "aren't we going to help Bolshevism by feeding these people?"

For once Hoover's celebrated calm broke down. He stood up and banged the table angrily. "Twenty million people are starving," he declared. "Whatever their politics, they shall be fed!" The problem for him was not whether the Russians should be aided but how to do it most swiftly and effectively.

4

As I have already indicated, Hoover played a considerable role in the Paris deliberations, quite aside from his specific economic functions. He saw clearly that a peace of vengeance was being hammered out which could not endure. Like other liberals on the scene, he was especially distressed by the economic absurdities, amounting to crimes, that were being perpetrated.

A confidential copy of the completed draft of the treaty was delivered to Hoover in the middle of the night. He read it in bed till dawn, in mounting sorrow. His own and other voices of moderation had been disregarded. He felt that the document did not so much mark the end of a war as the prelude to another war.

Agitated and depressed, he arose and went for a walk in the deserted streets of Paris to think about what he had just learned. Suddenly he found himself face to face with another agitated and sorrowful figure in the dawn: General Smuts of South Africa. Each of them recognized at once what had driven the other into the streets! They compared notes, agreed that the document was a tragic business, and pledged to do what they could to have the more senseless clauses modified. Neither of them, of course, succeeded.

In the great debate that was to follow in America, Hoover supported ratification as well as American membership in the League with reservations. He believed that even a bad treaty was better than none; that Europe needed above all to resume some sort of settled life.

But that is ahead of the story. On April 11, 1919, Hoover addressed a long memorandum to President Wilson. It was outspoken. The President, weary, despairing, in failing health, more and more intolerant of criticism, was not grateful for the candor. In the weeks that followed, when Hoover's conscience drove him to make yet other proposals for salvaging some remnants of our investment of high idealism, Wilson stopped seeing him. Along with Colonel House and other advisers, he thus ended in the presidential doghouse. Two paragraphs in the April 11 memorandum, however, are revealing of Hoover's mind and emotions as the Peace Treaty was reaching the climactic stage. They throw light on certain of his attitudes in the second war yet to come.

"It grows upon me daily," he told Wilson, "that the United States is the one great moral reserve in the world today and that we cannot maintain the independence of action through which this reserve is to be maintained if we allow ourselves to be dragged into detailed European entanglements over a period of years.

"In my view, if the Allies cannot be brought to adopt peace on the basis of the Fourteen Points, we should retire from Europe, lock, stock, and barrel, and we should lend to the whole world our economic and moral strength, or the world will swim in a sea of misery and disaster worse than the Dark Ages. If they cannot be brought to accept peace on this basis, our national honor is at stake and we should have to make peace independently and retire."

Hoover does not set himself up as a prophet. He was simply a clear-headed, scientifically trained American who had been more deeply immersed in European reality than any other American in Paris. He was not offering inspired prophecies but making deductions from available data. Certainly the disaster and misery and medieval darkness he foresaw came in vast and bitter measure.

With the signing of the Treaty, Hoover's principal tasks in Europe were ended. He began winding up the multifarious departments of his organization. Three months after the fifty-room offices on Avenue Montaigne were closed a plaintive note reached him from a humble sergeant who had been checking trains in Central Europe and sending in reports to the vacated headquarters; he wanted to know when he would be relieved. He was the original "forgotten man."

Europe did not forget. Respecting Hoover's strange aversion to decorations and citations, countries, cities, villages, millions of individuals found other ways to show their gratitude. The Belgians, as we have already seen, made him the sole recipient of a new order: "Citizen and Friend of Belgium." Dozens of cities struck special Hoover medals in his honor. Warsaw erected a statue to him. In all of the twenty-five countries ancient street names were discarded in favor of the name Hoover. Letters and collective scrolls poured in upon him from all over Europe, often signed by the entire citizenry of communities, and totaling nearly four million signatures.

It was essential that he make a final personal inspection of relief centers in various countries. Try as he did, he could not avoid public meetings, demonstrations, press eulogies. In Warsaw he reviewed the most touching parade of his career—the parade of more than fifty thousand children whom he had been feeding, and which I have already mentioned in another chapter.

The prestige which American idealism lost in Paris it regained through the length and breadth of Europe, wherever "Hoover relief" had penetrated.

CHAPTER XIV

Faith of an Old-fashioned Liberal

THE FORTY-FIVE-YEAR-OLD HERBERT Hoover who departed from Europe on September 5, 1919 was physically exhausted. "A weary Titan" Keynes once called him. For more than five years he had labored an average of eighteen hours a day, commanding campaigns on a score of fronts in a widening war on hunger, disease, chaos, blind vengeance, and official callousness. Not one of his stalwart lieutenants could quite keep pace with him, for few human beings are so blessed with reserves of energy and inner discipline.

It was, besides, a deeply saddened Hoover who left the scenes of his activity. The officer on the front is sustained by the passion and pageantry of war, by the goad of a tangible foe. Hoover dealt with the plodding, depressing, amorphous materials of famine, typhus lice, human wreckage, and economic rubble—in a war with only some amelioration rather than the glory of total victory at its finish. He saw at close range the emergence of new and frightening ideologies that canceled out centuries of liberal progress. He was one Republican who had no delusions of "normalcy" for his own land or the world.

With every aching muscle and nerve in his body he yearned for an interval of leisure and forgetfulness, for the joys of normal family life. He needed his sturdy sons, now twelve and fifteen, as much as they needed him. The family had been united for only a few fitful and harried months in all these years.

Besides, now that he paused to survey the landscape of his life he realized that his fortune had been sadly depleted. He had given no personal attention to the companies in which his savings of fifteen years were invested. He had paid every last cent of his expenses out of his own pocket; the drain grew more serious as his prominence and obligations expanded. After a good long vacation, he promised himself, he would begin to repair the family finances.

The idyll crumbled rapidly, since it was based on the false assumption of retreat into a sheltering obscurity. From the sheafs of invitations, requests, and demands that awaited him it was clear that his countrymen were massed to block his retreat. About a thousand letters a day reached him, each a trap baited with heart appeal to snare his time and energy. Cables, telegrams, phone calls pursued him even to the hills and streams when he went fishing.

Hoover had underestimated his own celebrity and his hold on his country's imagination. The struggle to avert the limelight had failed. Worse, his very reticence, the very edge of mystery, added dimensions of popular excitement to his personality. A New York *Times* opinion poll on the ten most important living Americans showed him that he was disturbingly high in the list.

He found, moreover, that America was in a confused, restless, and in some areas embittered state of mind and nerves. The letdown from the heights of wartime dedication had set in. A sobering cynicism was the reaction to patriotic intoxications. Counsels of violence, intolerance, and social extremism were gaining ground. Having seen the results of equivalent moods abroad, Hoover was alarmed for his native land. The zeal to make the world safe for democracy was petering out in impatience to withdraw from the world altogether.

He was conscious of his own tensed powers at that zenith of his maturity. His experience and intuitions—ripened into a philosophy of life—weighed on his spirits like a public trust. In declining the public services that were being urged upon him, he felt almost as if he were deserting in an hour of danger.

He actually went as far as opening an office in San Francisco with a view to resuming some old business associations. He threw himself spiritedly into the job of completing the home on a hill overlooking his beloved Stanford campus which had been begun before the war. But the pressures from without, and even more so the pressures from within, were too strong for him. "Reluctantly I gave way to conscience," he explained in viewing that personal crisis across the years.

To begin with, there was plenty of unfinished business to occupy him. He must give a detailed accounting to the Supreme Economic Council, the United States Congress, and the American people of billions of dollars and a multiplicity of organizations under his stewardship. When the accounting was completed, not even his boldest detractors ever raised any doubts about it.

His, also, was the main responsibility for setting up endowments with the $33,000,000 residue in the Belgian Relief. When that task was in order, he put his friend Perrin Galpin in executive control. Above all, there were the millions of children in Central and Eastern Europe dependent on continuing American funds. He undertook to raise the money, and kept his hand on the machinery of this undertaking for years.

As for the American scene, he set himself—in his characteristic organized fashion—a series of immediate objectives. He would do what he could to swerve the Republicans from their ultra-isolationist course in foreign affairs; and from the reactionary domestic course of men such as Penrose, Grundy, Knox, Watson, and Lodge. He would pull his full weight for moderation, liberalism, and social reform—against standpat futility at one extreme and socialist fallacy at the other.

To say that he had no political ambitions is to understate the matter. He was uncomfortable and embarrassed in the political orbit. As a realist in self-appraisal, he knew that he lacked the flexibility of opinion, the talents for compromise and flattery, so valuable in the political trades. The Hoover-for-President clubs mushrooming all over the country and the campaign for him by the liberal New York *World* depressed him far more than the vituperative attacks on him in the Hearst press.

Yet he could not disown his engineering mind, which told him that government offered the most effective medium for his influence. For a man like Hoover it was not enough to oppose exploitation of children, to favor better conditions for labor, to believe in more equitable division of the fruits of our free economy, to visualize improved living standards through lessened waste in industry. He must translate these preferences into concrete measures, and in a democracy he could not snub the democratic processes.

He had supported Wilson in 1918, because he feared the effects of a politically divided government on the prosecution of the war; the mistaken notion that he was a Democrat or a man without a party therefore spread. In fact, while he disliked the so-called right wing of Republicanism, he believed "the rank-and-file membership of the party in the North, comprising the majority of small businessmen, skilled workmen, farmers, and professional men, gave it a core of true Americanism." The Democratic party, rightly or wrongly, seemed to him a hodge-podge of "three elements: a reactionary Southern oligarchy with the social ideas of the sixteenth century, a set of plundering political machines in some large cities, and a group of men high in New York finance who exerted an invisible government." (The quotations are from a letter to a former secretary.)

When his direct protests against the presidential booms did no good, he issued a public statement on February 9, 1920: "I have not sought and am not seeking the presidency. I have no organization. No one is authorized to speak for me politically." In letters to overactive friends he insisted he was interested in issues, not office. But he did believe that a strategic cabinet post might give him the leverage for the public effectiveness he craved. It was this delicate balance of impulses—to avoid political embroilments without stultifying his potential for national service—that had him worried, and it was the problem he brought to an old Quaker friend who was also a shrewd and experienced political leader, William Ward of New York.

Ward convinced him that the way to win a cabinet post was to let the presidential boom gain some momentum, since he was in no danger of winning the nomination in any case. Except in his home state of California, Hoover withheld his legal consent to the election of delegates pledged to him. In a number of states where no such consent was prescribed, he appeared on the primary ballots. In Michigan he was entered in both Democratic and Republican primaries; it was the Democratic, not the Republican, delegation that went to its convention pledged for Hoover. He drew 210,000 Republican votes in California against 370,000 for Hiram Johnson, which was an impressive showing by a candidate without political background.

Though thirteen votes was his high point on the floor of the Republican convention, the acclaim from the galleries was without many precedents for fervor. The nomination of a mediocre compromise politician, Warren Gamaliel Harding of Ohio, was a great disappointment to Hoover. As for the Penrose-Grundy-Johnson forces, they never forgave Hoover's alignment with the liberal wing of the party.

Soon after the election Harding offered Hoover his choice between the Interior and Commerce Departments. Commerce was at that time rated among the least important cabinet offices, but Hoover saw its value in specific relation to the program that most concerned him. Before the appointment could be made definite, however, Harding had to overcome embittered party opposition to the inclusion of such a "radical." The President-elect forced agreement by refusing to designate Andrew Mellon as Secretary of the Treasury unless he could balance him with Hoover.

Meanwhile Hoover, while considering the cabinet offer, was confronted with another temptation, perhaps the strongest in his life, to return to the fleshpots of business and great wealth. In January 1921 Daniel Guggenheim went to see him. The Guggenheim brothers owned the greatest mining and metallurgical company in the world, one of the most fabulous empires of wealth in America's history. The brothers, Daniel explained to Hoover, were getting old, and their sons were not interested in taking over. They needed someone to carry on—and had decided that Hoover was the man. Their offer was probably without precedent in the annals of business: a full partnership and a guaranteed *minimum* income of $500,000 a year.

Hoover asked for a week to think it over. As on that critical occasion in London in 1914, he and Mrs. Hoover weighed the alternatives—the self-same alternatives, great fortune or public service. Not even their closest friends, let alone the public, realized the magnitude of the sacrifice he was making when he announced his readiness to serve as Secretary of Commerce. Hoover gave up a slice of the Guggenheim empire and half a million dollars a year for life for the uncertainties and headaches of a political office paying $15,000 a year—which salary would never go into his own pockets.

While these events were shaping up there was a strange interlude harking back to the Belgian adventure. The King and Queen of Belgium, in October 1919, paid a visit to the United States as guests of our government. Apprised of President Wilson's serious illness, the royal pair fell in with a State Department suggestion that they spend in California the week originally apportioned to the White House.

Accordingly Hoover was asked whether he could put them up on his "estate." Their party, he was informed, counted only sixty people. Since there was only one spare bedroom in the cottage which constituted the Hoover "estate," that presented problems. In the end an old engineering associate helped him find two homes in Santa Barbara which by dint of crowding could care for thirty each.

The generous hosts and other local folk collected plenty of Belgian "buttons" for their posterity, and the royal visitors had a wonderful time. Santa Barbara at the time still boasted an old-style sheriff complete with boots, a ten-gallon hat, and two revolvers. The sheriff and his deputies assumed the task of guarding King Albert's quarters. Monarch and sheriff became good friends at once. Being shy on protocol, the sheriff addressed his charge as "O King," until someone set him straight and he switched to "Your Majesty." His Majesty, however, would have none of this and requested him to switch back to "O King."

San Francisco staged a great parade for the royal pair. But Mr. Rolph, the mayor, was scared to death that the Order of the Crown, second class, awarded him by King Albert, might hurt him politically in the election scheduled for the very next day. Hoover stepped into that great emergency by suggesting that Rolph accept the award not for himself but for the city. The election was saved. Years later, when Rolph (by that time governor) died, Hoover was among the pallbearers. On the governor's breast lay the Belgian Order of the Crown, second class.

2

As early as 1908, when he lectured to engineering students, Hoover held views on labor considered advanced and even radical for his time, as we have already noted. The economic and political challenges of our modern world were never far from his mind, and certainly his opportunities for observing and judging were unsurpassed.

He had lived and worked in areas of this planet where every variation of new and old social dogma was in control. Each of these he had studied and judged not in a vacuum but in reference to all the others—and against his American background. During and immediately after the war he had been at the very center of what he called "a gigantic laboratory of fierce ideas and change." Always he related those experiments to his native heritage: "During my whole European experience I had been trying to formulate some orderly definition of our American system."

He felt he had come close to such a definition and was impelled by his social conscience to share his awareness with the rest of the country. In the year or two after his return from Europe Hoover declared himself. His ideas had "jelled." With the same gift that made him supreme in the domain of mining, he had separated the gold from the dross, the lofty verbal trimmings from the base realities.

Words have never been his most effective tools. As a literary stylist he will certainly not be bracketed with presidents such as Jefferson, Lincoln, or Wilson. Yet he proved himself extraordinarily effective when, in his middle forties, he was ready to present the ripened fruit of his long years of pondering. He was not elegant or scintillating; too often he relied on phrases worn thin by much handling in American oratory. But he achieved what he aimed at, which was not sensation but *lucidity*.

In a series of speeches and articles—and practical proposals— in this period he summed up his personal philosophy. In 1921 he distilled most of it in a little book which he called *American Individualism*. It might with equal justice have been called American Liberalism, for that is what it came down to; in his writings, as a matter of fact, he frequently used the terms interchangeably.

Already Bolshevik and other collectivist dogmas were eroding the concept of liberalism. In time they were to make "liberal" almost a synonym for its antipodes—state regimentation, totalitarianism, the melting of the person into some abstraction of mob, society, class, race, or nation. Men and women robed in self-righteousness would before long steal the vocabulary of liberalism and progress for their most illiberal and retrogressive beliefs—in the greatest semantic victory of all time. That monstrous social mongrel, the "totalitarian liberal," would take command at the left, and would dedicate himself especially to pushing genuine liberals into the extreme right where they did not belong.

In the 1940s a Dutch architect would seriously proclaim that "The individual is losing significance; his destiny is no longer what interests us," and self-styled American liberals would quote such views in warm approval. In orgiastic fervor they would boast, "There is no more I, but only We!" Which was like celebrating self-extinction.

But in the 1920s that semantic conquest was still in an early stage. The vulgarization of liberalism which was to be its death sentence had not gone so far that an instinctive liberal like Hoover needed to apologize or to dissociate himself from the totalitarian impostors. The kind of "progressive" who whooped it up for concentration camps, slave labor, one-party dictatorship, was yet to emerge in his full magnificence of lunacy.

The more reactionary Republicans and the manipulators of "invisible government" who feared Hoover and fought him were quite justified. He was not and by his nature could not be one of them. They sensed the implications of his assertion that "No civilization could be built or endure solely upon the groundwork of unrestrained and unintelligent self-interest." Reactionary thinking at the extreme left and right alike saw menace in his inclination to quote Alexander Hamilton's aphorism, "A power over a man's subsistence amounts to a power over his will."

A personal philosophy is significant largely in the measure that it is impersonal and universal. It is little more than an intellectual curiosity unless it sums up an important current of thought and experience; unless it gives voice to real and living forces in a man's time—forces rooted in the past and pointed to the future.

Hoover's "orderly definition," as first expressed at this juncture and fortified in later years, is deeply meaningful because it is close to the core of traditional American feelings. It did not once occur to him to claim originality. He sought merely to give conscious expression to quintessentially American historical memories and preferences and urges. "Our Individualism," he said, "is in our very nature. It is based on conviction born of experience."

The individualism he championed was not a party program or an academic concept, but the pragmatic principle of American life as a whole. It was not, that is to say, a dogmatic belief to be held inviolate as if it were of divine origin—in the way that orthodox socialists, for example, hold to "economic determinism" or "dialectic materialism."

American individualism, as Hoover described and defended it, was not an absolute law handed down from some sociological Mt. Sinai. It was simply a system that had worked—worked so well in its American version that the American people were incomparably better off, healthier, better educated, and above all freer than any other people in human history.

Because it was a living reality, not merely a memory of the past or a promise for the future, its economic, political, and ethical contents were intimately interlaced, and each inseparable from the other. To revolutionize one of these elements—the economic system, let us say—without revolutionizing the others in about the same measure was therefore impossible.

Hoover claimed for this individualism no miraculous powers which, applied anywhere, would evoke an American type of life. He saw it rather as a peculiarly American flowering. Nor did he claim for it the arrogance of perfection. On the contrary, recognition of serious faults, serious injustices, and the impulse to reduce them without destroying the whole system, were part of the genius of individualism.

Thus, having credited our economic system with stimulating "invention . . . enterprise . . . individual improvement of the highest order," he followed up with a catalogue of problems to be solved:

"The congestion of population is producing subnormal conditions of life. The vast repetitive operations are dulling the human mind. The intermittency of employment due to the bad co-ordination of industry, the great waves of unemployment in the ebb and flow of economic tides, the ever present industrial conflicts by strike and lockout, produce infinite wastes and great suffering. Our business enterprises have become so large and complex that the old pleasant relationship between employer and worker has, to a great extent, disappeared. The aggregation of great wealth with its power to economic domination presents social and economic ills which we are constantly struggling to remedy." (Washington, November 19, 1920.)

Our individualism, moreover, was a system that had its own "dialectic," as Marxists would put it. It contained seeming opposites in a balanced whole. It combined the supremacy of the individual with a passionate concern for the health and advancement of the community of which he is a part. It saw the successful society as the by-product of free, wholesome, adjusted individuals. It regarded as degenerate the community in which personal values are discounted or wholly proscribed.

"Progress of the nation is the sum of the progress of its individuals," Hoover declared. And at another time: "The primary duty of organized society is to enlarge the lives and increase the standards of all the people." Which is to say that organized society is not an end in itself. It has no prerogatives to which the individual must knuckle under—except, of course, purely functional rights needed to protect the individual.

In the spectrum of social ideas this view (which is American liberalism unalloyed) is at the remotest remove from totalitarianism in any of its guises. It accepts the human being—not state or race or class—as the unit of social value. Virtue, it assumes, resides in the person and not in any impersonal entity like society. Its final test for the good, the true, the beautiful is in the effects on individual men, women, and children. Hence there can be no general freedom based on specific enslavements.

Hoover, being a genuine liberal rather than a know-nothing defender of the status quo, did not allow himself to be trapped by any of the free-enterprise absolutes. For every attack on socialism there is in his writing and thinking a corresponding attack on laissez-faire assumptions. His experience as a "self-made" leader is tempered by his Quaker certainty that man is his brother's keeper.

"Private property is not a fetish in America," he declared. He cited the crushing of the liquor trade without a cent of compensation as one proof that human rights take precedence with us over property rights, and added: "Our development of individualism shows an increasing tendency to regard right of property not as an object in itself, but in the light of a useful instrument in stimulation of initiative in the individual." Where control of property and control of government fall into the same hands, our individualism reacts to smash the amalgam.

A revealing note running through Hoover's definition relates to leadership. He sees it as "a quality of the individual," but not one that should be perpetuated by inheritance. Under a liberal dispensation leaders "can arise solely through the free-running mills of competition. They must be free to rise from the mass; they must be given the attraction of premiums to effort. . . . Human leadership cannot be replenished by selection like queen bees, by divine right or bureaucracies, but by the free rise of ability, character, and intelligence."

He abhors the equality that averages human endowments; it is for him at the opposite pole from the equality which provides unlimited room for each individual to develop to the utmost the best that is in him. He argues for variety as against uniformity, for individual creativeness as against adherence to a prescribed pattern.

"Amid the scene of growing complexity of our economic life," he wrote, "we must preserve the independence of the individual from the deadening restraints of government, yet by the strong arm of government equally protect his individual freedom, assure his fair chance, his equality of opportunity from the encroachments of special privileges and greed for domination by any group or class."

His support of free economy by definition implied opposition to monopoly, whether in the mild forms of business oligarchies or in its virulent extreme of government regimentation and dictatorship. For him, capitalism carried to its utmost logic in one direction would be anarchy; carried to the extreme in the other direction it would be fascism. (That, incidentally, was why he was destined to reject the N.R.A. scheme when it was broached to him by the representatives of Big Business when he was in the White House; why he would be quick to denounce it, as we shall see, as a camouflaged fascism.)

That kind of individualism has nothing in common with dog-eat-dog, survival-of-the-fittest behavior and justifications. It is not an ideological cover for exploitation of the weak by the strong, but implies at every point a moral obligation toward the weak. Its heart is charity. Its true ideology is not in Adam Smith or Darwin but in the Hebrew prophets from Moses to Jesus who prescribed love of one's neighbor as the first law for man. "Our individualism insists upon the divine in each human being," Hoover wrote.

In the very first pages of *American Individualism* he declared:

Individualism cannot be maintained as the foundation of a society if it looks to only legalistic justice based upon contracts, property, and political equality. Such legalistic safeguards are themselves not enough. In our individualism we have long since abandoned the *laissez faire* of the 18th Century—the notion that it is "every man for himself and the devil take the hindmost." We abandoned that when we adopted the ideal of equality of opportunity—the fair chance of Abraham Lincoln. We have confirmed its abandonment in terms of legislation, of social and economic justice—in part because we have learned that it is the hindmost that throws the bricks at our social edifice, in part because we have learned that the foremost are not always the best nor the hindmost the worst—and in part because we have learned that social injustice is the destruction of justice itself.

We have learned that the impulse to production can only be maintained if there is a fair division of the product. We have also learned that fair division can only be obtained by certain restrictions on the strong and the dominant. We have indeed gone even further in the 20th Century with the embracement of the necessity of a greater and broader sense of service and responsibility to others as a part of individualism.

He insisted that "the most potent force in society is its ideals." America, he said, "has become not merely a physical union of

States, but rather is a spiritual union in common ideals of our people. Within it is room for every variety of opinion, every possibility of experiment in social progress. Out of such variety comes growth, but only as we preserve and maintain our spiritual solidarity."

He was at all times aware of the risks:

"No doubt individualism run riot, with no tempering principle, would provide a long category of inequalities, of tyrannies, dominations, and injustices. America, however, has tempered the whole conception of individualism by the injection of a definite principle, and from this principle it follows that attempts at domination, whether in government or in the processes of industry and commerce, are under an insistent curb."

The principle he has in mind is "an equality of opportunity," backed by "that sense of service that lies in our people." Progress, he said a few years later, "will not come from crushing the individual into a shapeless mass but in giving him enlarged opportunities."

Nations which have learned from America, he believes, have gained in temporal and spiritual vigor. But the philosophy he cherishes is too identical with a particular national experience to be exported or imposed on other communities. It is "our sort of individualism," the kind that "has been the primary force of American civilization for three centuries." Its symbol has been the pioneer—sensitive to "the challenge of opportunity, to the challenge of nature, to the challenge of life, to the call of the frontier." And there can never be an exhaustion of these challenges: "There are continents of human welfare of which we have penetrated only the coastal plain. The great continent of science is as yet explored only on its borders."

The individualism of the Old World, as Hoover saw it with his own eyes, was far removed from the American variant; because it was superimposed upon the remnants of feudalism, upon class stratifications. America, for Hoover, was not an extension of European culture but a break with that culture.

"For myself," he attested, "let me say at the very outset that my faith in the essential truth, strength, and vitality of the developing creed by which we have hitherto lived in this country of ours has been confirmed and deepened by the searching experiences of seven years of service in the backwash and misery of war. . . . And from it all I emerge an individualist—an unashamed individualist. But let me say also that I am an American individualist."

He warned against "the equal dangers both of reaction and radicalism," and even then refuted "the perpetual howl of radicalism . . . that it is the sole voice of liberalism." These men, he said, "would assume that all reform and human advance must come through government. They have forgotten that progress must come from the steady life of the individual and that the measure of national idealism and progress is the quality of idealism in the individual. . . . Most theorists who denounce our individualism as a social basis seem to have a passion for ignorance of its constructive ideals." But he showed just as little tenderness for "those who insist that the future must be a repetition of the past; that ideas are dangerous, that ideals are freaks."

3

"In every society, however perfected," Hoover wrote at this time, "there will always be at the bottom a noxious sediment and at the top an obnoxious froth."

He did not agree with those who in anger or impatience demanded that the entire perfected society be jettisoned because of those unpleasant excrescences. For this he was denounced as a radical at one extreme and as a reactionary at the other. In truth he was an earnest reformer—though not the kind who is willing to kill the patient for the sake of a beautiful operation.

I was once asked to give my definition of a conservative in about a hundred words. This was my try:

"A conservative is one who seeks to conserve the true-and-tried values of his particular society. He has a wholesome respect for tradition as the repository of a people's experience. He regards change as in the nature of life itself and for that reason wants it slow, systematic, and natural. The life of mankind, he recognizes, is an ordered growth, not a series of wild, explosive jumps. The fact that conservatism is so often confused with 'reaction' is merely a triumph of dogmatic propaganda. Because the whole tradition of America is liberal, an American conservative is in the final analysis the guardian of genuine liberalism."

In the sense that Hoover sought to safeguard the central values of our American society, he was ever the conservative; sometimes especially so when he seemed most radical to his reactionary critics and most reactionary to his radical critics.

His lifelong emphasis on child welfare—his automatic acceptance of the child as the test of a society's health—has in it the primordial logic of the farmer's concern with the new crop. It is in the pattern of his life that one of his first speeches after returning from Europe was on this theme. Addressing the Associated Charities of San Francisco, he said:

"If we could systematically grapple with the whole child problem in the United States, if we could insist on the proper conditions of birth, upon proper safeguarding of their general health, on proper education, we could then say with confidence that . . . in twenty years . . . public health, efficiency, sanity, morals, and stability of the whole population would be advanced beyond anything that any nation has yet aspired to."

He proposed a program to give all children "an equal opportunity at their start in life." Out of this proposal and others on the same order there ultimately came the American Child Health Association; and later, in his own administration, the "Children's Charter" familiar to all social workers in this field. But the feature that made headlines on this occasion, and to which he returned persistently in the following years, was his demand for a constitutional amendment to outlaw child labor.

Clearly such a proposal does not fit easily into the distorted representation of Hoover as the fanatic foe of any sort of government action on social problems.

From the first he supported a sensible, socially responsible labor unionism. He insisted that freedom was indivisible: spiritual and political freedom could not flourish without a free economic base. But this freedom carried with it obligations; it required regulation to prevent abuse. Writing in the *Saturday Evening Post* (December 27, 1919), he said:

The organization of workers to better the conditions of labor is undoubtedly a safeguard of equality of opportunity and in accord with basic principles. The essence of combination of workers is collective bargaining, and the recognition of the right to combine cannot be separated from the right to bargain collectively.

Every such combination, he added by way of caution, "can be used for domination of the community," whether it be labor or farmers or capitalists. Other groups and individuals therefore must have adequate means of heading off this domination.

In July 1920 he wrote:

"No one doubts that the modern consolidation of the employers over large units of employees gives every justification and right for the organization of the employees similarly into units for the exertion of equality in bargaining powers. Such organization has a right to present its own representatives in bargaining, but those representatives must truly represent the employees for whom they speak."

He was, of course, too optimistic in supposing "no one doubts" this view. There were plenty of doubters and they bore no great love for Hoover in this connection. It is worth recalling at this point that Hoover in 1922, as a cabinet member, protested vigorously against federal injunctions against railway men on strike; and that as President he signed the bill which outlawed "yellow-dog" contracts in the face of loud conservative protests.

In the *Post* article cited above Hoover sought to put his philosophy of individualism into a few sentences:

This view—that every individual should within his lifetime not be handicapped in securing that particular niche in the community to which his abilities and character entitle him—is itself the negation of class. Human beings are not equal in these qualities, but a society that is based upon a constant readjustment of the relative influence and rewards of individuals in the community, upon the basis of ability and character, is a moving virile mass—it is not a stratification of classes. Its stimulus is competition.

The American plan, as he called it, has given the United States immense advantages, for all its admitted flaws. "Our plan," he wrote, "does not enable us to take our neighbor's home overnight, but it does enable us to build a home of our own."

There was another facet of Hoover's individualism which hardly enhanced his standing among the excessively rich. This was his repeated proposals for higher inheritance taxes. He believed that "congestion of wealth and control of tools of production were limitations on equal opportunity and laid a dead hand on industrial progress." The vice, as he saw it, was not in accumulation but in inheritance. Hereditary economic power, he contended, made as little sense as hereditary political power.

His thoughts on taxation as a useful instrument in supporting individualism he embodied in 1921 in a memorandum to President Harding which said in part:

"If we are to lessen the stifling of initiative we should make lower schedules applicable to individual incomes from wages, salaries, professions, and business transactions, than to those from dividends and interest and rents. That the Government takes up to 50 per cent of the profits from professional earnings or business transactions, while the individual takes all the risks, is intensely discouraging to initiative. It is fundamentally wrong to charge at the same rate these two types of income, 'earnings,' and 'property income,' because a person who possesses 'property income' has already the capital protection of his dependents while a part of 'earned' income must be put aside for such a purpose."

It is no part of my intention to make a complete inventory of his views; I hope only to suggest their general temper and direction. Hoover demanded government regulation to curb vicious speculation, and in particular rigid supervision of "blue-sky" promotion. He asked for better planning and organization of public works. He suggested creation of machinery for mediation and arbitration in labor disputes, but opposed the compulsory arbitration being widely advocated at the time. Much of his emphasis was on co-operatives for farmers, producers, and consumers. Private co-operation in the economic domain, without government coercion, seemed to him fully in the free-enterprise tradition.

Small wonder that the standpat schools of business and political leaders began to look at him askance, as a possible mischief-maker.

At the end of 1919 Wilson placed Hoover on a national commission of industrialists, labor leaders, economists, and public figures to study the growing economic tensions and submit proposals for dealing with them. Hoover played a leading part in the commission's work; and, in any case, its findings reflected his personal beliefs.

The resulting report marked a milestone in the history of American trade unionism: it was the first time an independent body recommended collective bargaining by agents of labor's own choosing. The report also asked for an end to child labor, for reduced hours of work, better housing, and health insurance. It recommended the development of plans for old-age insurance, or what came to be known as social security. Naturally these findings were hailed with enthusiasm by true American liberals.

Several weeks after their publication Hoover addressed the Boston Chamber of Commerce. He defended his social program and asked his listeners to face the facts and implications of "a desire on the part of workers to exert more organic influence in the processes of industrial life." This concept of labor as a partner in the productive scheme, not just another commodity, is the core of liberalism as related to labor-employer relations.

His reception on that occasion, he was to remark in retrospect, was "frosty," and when he concluded, "the applause would not have waked a nervous baby."

I have quoted passages and facts almost at random to make the point that Hoover, far from being the "mossback" of the hostile propaganda version, was in the front ranks of our American liberal tradition. Where his path diverged more and more from that of the "official" liberals who gradually obtained a monopoly of the designation was in his fear of excessive government, distrust of bureaucratic agencies, insistence on decentralizing political power.

In *American Individualism* he identified two schools of thought: those who believed "that all human ills can be cured by government regulation" and those who believed "that all regulation is a sin." He denied both schools. To him government was "the umpire in our social system." In that capacity, he pointed out, it had been remarkably successful, having provided equality before the law and authorities in restraint of evil instincts. His explanation of the increasing intrusion of government in the economic field was tantamount to a justification:

The entrance of the Government began strongly three decades ago, when our industrial organization began to move powerfully in the direction of consolidation of enterprise. We found in the course of this development that equality of opportunity and its corollary, individual initiative, were being throttled by the concentration of control of industry and service, and thus an economic domination of groups builded over the nation. At this time, particularly, we were threatened with a form autocracy of economic power.

Our mass of regulation of public utilities and our legislation against restraint of trade is the monument to our intent to preserve an equality of opportunity. This regulation is itself proof that we have gone a long way toward the abandonment of the "capitalism" of Adam Smith . . .

To curb monopolistic and autocratic forces in business "and yet to maintain the initiative and creative faculties of our people" —this was the problem as he saw it. Neither of the purposes, he declared, was served by an approach to socialism, however it might be camouflaged. Nationalization of business or commerce is itself the ultimate in monopoly, destructive of initiative and opportunity, and especially dangerous because it puts economic and political authority in the same sets of hands. The difference between trusts running the government and government running the trusts is more seeming than real.

Because the views Hoover expressed at this time remained valid for him all his life, I do not hesitate to reach into the future for two more quotations on this subject.

During his first campaign for the presidency, in 1928, he said:

"You cannot extend the mastery of the government over the daily working life of a people without at the same time making it the master of the people's souls and thoughts. Every expansion of government in business means that government, in order to protect itself from the political consequences of its errors and wrongs, is driven irresistibly without peace to greater and greater control of the nation's press and platform. Free speech does not live many hours after free industry and free commerce die."

During his second campaign, in 1932, he was contending with "big government" sentiment.

"Every step in that direction," he insisted, "poisons political equality, free speech, free press, and equality of opportunity. It is the road not to more liberty but to less liberty. True liberalism is found not in striving to spread bureaucracy but in striving to set bounds to it. True liberalism seeks all legitimate freedom first in the confident belief that without such freedom the pursuit of other blessings is in vain."

Perhaps he put his keen consciousness of the risks of state regimentation into one pregnant sentence when he asserted in 1929 that "every time the government is forced to act, we lose something in self-reliance, character, and initiative."

The Hoover philosophy of life and public affairs as he sketched it by word and act in the early 1920s he adhered to in the following decades. A second and more detailed definition appeared in his book *The Challenge of Liberty*, written after his experience in the White House, and after a few years' observation of the New Deal in action. It did not in essence diverge from the thesis of *American Individualism*.

For Hoover, truly, has been "no politician." He has never trimmed his fundamental convictions to the prevailing trade winds of politics. He has been unable by his nature to invent "principles" in order to forestall attacks or placate powerful attackers. Election promises—and for that matter the promises implicit in his whole life—could not be to Hoover just vote-getting devices.

His life, his work, his policies, his convictions are not separate departments but different names for the same man. He could not, especially as President of the United States, adopt measures merely because they might have greater political sex appeal and provide a more diverting "show." In an era of rampant opportunism and declining standards of moral leadership, he has remained integral, true to his country because he has been consistently true to himself, whatever the price in political terms.

Hoover despised the "strong men," the ruthless ones so fashionable between the two world wars—whether economic oligarchs or political oligarchs. Strength without compassion has ever seemed to him a species of savagery. To the new-style "liberals" who take no account of the individual and his freedoms, men like Hoover no doubt seem leftovers from a bygone epoch. To the monstrous Darwinists of the "social engineering" which treats people as the raw stuff for experiments men like Hoover are not even comprehensible. They dismiss such men sneeringly as "old-fashioned" Americans, Rotarians, reactionaries.

Neither the piecemeal presentation of Hoover's philosophy in speeches and articles nor its organized presentation in a book created much stir. It seemed to Americans in the early 1920s simply a summation of widely accepted and respectable liberal ideas—sufficiently "left of center" in their day to annoy extremes, but not enough so to shock anyone. They had been so much a part of the mental climate in America for so many generations that few had felt it necessary to articulate them in succinct fashion.

Only in the perspective of time has his formulation acquired a quality of the sensational. In the intervening decades social tendencies in the world, and in America itself—especially the deepening of totalitarian moods—helped bring into clear and even startling relief the values that he defended.

Whether those values will survive only the future can tell. At this writing they seem again in the ascendency, at least in the United States, after a period of decline; one senses a renewed concern for individual rights and dignities and a new respect for the moral springheads of American history. But that is no guarantee that the Hoover type of philosophy will not be submerged in the floodtide of collectivism; unfortunately World War II, in defeating one segment of the encroaching slave state, has strengthened and inflamed another segment. Perhaps we are irrevocably on what Professor Hayek called "the road to serfdom."

Be that as it may, it seems to me likely that Herbert Hoover will emerge more sharply and in increasingly heroic stature, as the prophet of the "old-fashioned liberalism" he calls American Individualism.

His virtue may well seem to reside in the fact that he represented, not only in words but in deeds, a set of disappearing values. He is likely to loom in the historical perspective as almost a personification of those values, since his life story has been a uniquely American blend of practicality and idealism, earthly social purposes informed by a spiritual intensity. I don't like to sound dramatic, but his personal experience holds some of the elements of the classic prophet, for it contains a time of crucifixion and a day of resurrection.

CHAPTER XV

Consulting Engineer to the Nation

ONE OF HIS PREDECESSORS AS SECRE-
tary of Commerce, the elder Oscar Strauss, assured Hoover that
a couple of hours a day would be all the post required. Few men
had ever given it more. The accepted idea about its scope was
packed into the jest that a Secretary of Commerce was expected
only "to put the fish to bed at night and turn on the lights around
the coast."

That was not Hoover's idea of any job. The Enabling Act
establishing the department had not skimped on territory in defining its province: "To foster, promote and develop the foreign
and domestic commerce, the mining, manufacturing, shipping
and fishing industries, the labor interests, and the transportation
facilities of the United States."

Hoover meant to explore the whole of that province and got
President Harding's support for his intentions before entering
the Cabinet. He made it a full-time office—and full time in the
Hoover vocabulary was a literal phrase. Within a year or two
after he took over Commerce ranked with State among the most
influential executive departments.

These eight years, though they held their quota of griefs and
disappointments, were among the happiest and most creative in
Hoover's career. The long separations from his wife had been
great trials; Mrs. Hoover was his helpmate in far more than the
conventional sense. Now she could be with him continually.
Their boys were in college; Herbert, Jr., entered Stanford Uni-

versity in 1921 and Allan in 1925. The comfortable brick house and garden at 2300 S Street which became their Washington home was replete with affection and friendship. It was constantly filled with associates so dear to them that they seemed part of the family. And the solace of a Quaker meetinghouse which they missed in the long travels was again open to them regularly.

But now, as always, vital work was Hoover's main and often sole "recreation." The department was rapidly reorganized. Somnolent bureaus were wakened into dynamic activity; routine functions suddenly turned into service stations and repair shops for a nation's entire economy. Even "putting the fish to bed" ceased to be a joke, now that their nursemaid began replenishing rivers, fighting pollution, protecting Alaska salmon, and serving as patron of all amateur fishing folk as president of the Isaak Walton League.

The spirit in which he tackled his new opportunity was well described by his friend Mark Sullivan: "One may say that Hoover has regarded our entire business structure as a single factory, conceiving himself, as it were, consulting engineer for the whole enterprise. Having this conception, Hoover set about applying to the whole business structure of the United States principles similar to those which Henry Ford applied to the manufacture of automobiles."

Shallow comment on this effort judged it merely in relation to Hoover's genius for efficiency. Hostile comment related it merely to profits. Both failed to comprehend that for Hoover efficiency was a tool, not a goal. The goal was set by his social conscience, his concept of the good life for America. His eight-year offensive against waste rested on a revolutionary idea: *the enrichment of existence for the whole population through maximum use of modern productive potentials.*

In the voluminous record of that offensive there is scarcely a trace of the profit motif. Its whole purport is to provide more of the necessaries and luxuries of life for more people. The riches siphoned off by material and human waste, it insisted, spelled the difference between comfort and penury for tens of millions. In 1919, that is to say before he was in the government, he outlined the basic idea in a magazine article thus:

The standard of living is the quotient of the amount of commodities and services that are available among the total population. Therefore the standard cannot be maintained or improved unless there is a maintenance and increase in the production of commodities and services up to the maximum need of the entire number.

There is no equality of opportunity to the consumer with deficient production. The maximum production cannot be maintained unless there is combined and co-ordinated action in effort, intelligence, and skill of all elements of production, whether workers, tools, or managers; unless there is an elimination of waste, whether it be due to the support of non-producers, oversized armies and navies, to extravagance, strikes, lockouts, or lack of skill in either labor or administrators; unless every member of the community works up to his maximum ability and ceases to agitate for reduction in effort below his real capacity, for there is no equality of opportunity if some are to work six hours and others twelve hours; unless the physical, moral, and intellectual welfare of the producer is properly safeguarded as to hours, conditions of labor, opportunities of education, and so forth.

In short, conservation of wealth and creation of ever more new wealth and its spread among all the people, now that intelligent use of knowledge and skill made this possible. Here was the ancient dream of an economy of abundance, asserted not as a rhetorical wish but as a practical plan.

This vision was his theme in a speech accepting the presidency of the American Engineering Council in November 1920. He followed it up by mobilizing seventeen top engineers, their combined experience covering the whole of the nation's economic life and setting them to find the "leaks" of wastage. These men served without remuneration, and Hoover raised $50,000 from private sources to finance their work. In a foreword to their report four months later he wrote:

"We have probably the highest ingenuity and efficiency in the operation of our industries of any nation. Yet our industrial machine is far from perfect. The wastes of unemployment during depressions; from speculation and overproduction in booms; from labor turnover; from labor conflicts; from intermittent failure of transportation of supplies of fuel and power; from lack of standardization; from loss in our processes and materials—all combine to represent a huge deduction from the goods and services that we might all enjoy if we could make a better job of it."

To correct this situation was the program he sought to work out beginning with March 4, 1921. His warning at this early stage against "speculation and overproduction in booms" is the more remarkable because it was made in a time of depression. He would reiterate it continually in the boom years that followed. His was a program aiming at the abolition of poverty through the fertility of modern machine methods. And he applied it not by compulsion of law but on the principle of voluntary co-operation which had served him well in the past.

Hoover insisted and demonstrated that America could save as much as thirty billion dollars a year by cutting out waste motion; that this wealth equitably spread through the whole population could cancel out destitution. Obviously this could not be achieved at once, but we could make an immediate beginning. At the end of his two terms as secretary, in accepting the presidential nomination, he would say:

"One of the oldest and perhaps the noblest of human aspirations has been abolition of poverty. By poverty I mean the grinding by undernourishment, cold and ignorance, and fear of old age of those who have the will to work. We in America are nearer to the final triumph over poverty than ever before in the history of any land. . . .

"My conception of America is a land where men and women may walk in ordered freedom in the independent conduct of their occupations; where they may enjoy the advantages of wealth, not concentrated in the hands of the few but spread through the lives of all; where they build and safeguard their homes, and give to their children the fullest advantages and opportunities of American life; where every man shall be respected in the faith that his conscience and his heart direct him to follow; where a contented and happy people, secure in their liberties, free from poverty and fear, shall have the leisure and impulse to seek a fuller life."

There (except for those who persist in wilfully misunderstanding him) was the idea which he symbolized picturesquely as "two chickens in every pot and a car in every garage." Despite the clowning ridicule to which it was later subjected, it still stands up as an inspiring ideal. In being mocked for his daring vision, Hoover is in the good company of idealists through the centuries.

Unfortunately the most important facts do not always make the most entertaining reading. At the risk of wearying the reader, I want to list some of the myriad objectives set, and in some measure achieved, by Hoover's crusade for conservation of wealth as Secretary of Commerce:

Elimination of waste through improved equipment and methods in railway transportation; better and fuller use of water resources for cheap transportation, flood control, reclamation, and power; enlarged electrification to save fuel and labor; reduction of seasonal fluctuations in employment in construction and other industries; reduction of waste in manufacture and distribution through more sensible standardization of sizes, qualities, and methods; more uniform business documents and bookkeeping procedures; government aid in developing pure and applied science looking to labor-saving devices and practices; co-operative marketing and better terminal facilities to avoid waste in agricultural distribution; greater commercial arbitration to eliminate the wastes of litigation; reduction of losses through preventable labor-management conflicts; a scientific approach to reducing industrial, traffic, and other accidents; preservation of competitive freedom and protection of the public interest in new fields like aviation and radio (both the Civil Aeronautics Bureau and the Federal Communications Commission were Hoover creations).

This by no means exhausts the program. Each of the items was sufficient to occupy one man for a lifetime. Hoover undertook them all simultaneously, and made some progress in all. He did not think of them as isolated problems, but as aspects of the same goal of abundance.

And despite the intervening tragedies of depression and war he is still convinced that it is a proper goal for the human race. I talked with him about this recently. In the physical sense, poverty is no longer necessary, he believes. It is a hangover from a primitive past, perpetuated by inertia and human stupidity. With the advent of atomic energy, with the marvels of the new chemistry, with modern facilities for exchanging the world's total products, the civilization based on abundance which was possible a quarter of a century ago in America is possible now for the whole human race.

To trace his labors in each of the categories he tackled would require many volumes. I must content myself with mere listings. The Department of Commerce, without benefit of new laws or powers, stimulated self-regulation for efficiency in literally dozens of industries. Through thirty or forty "commodity divisions" it provided the data and the guidance on which exports and imports flourished as never before. It linked all the elements in the process—actual and would-be homeowners, unions, builders, architects, planners—in a co-operative drive called "Better Homes in America."

The department explored water resources and started processes that ultimately gave the country great hydroelectric stations, deepened waterways, better flood control. Hoover himself administered a $20,000,000 fund for research in pure and applied science. He simplified and systematized standards and sizes in hundreds of fields, as various as paving blocks and the care of child health. There were few corners of national economic life where he did not penetrate, and at all times by stimulating voluntary action in a spirit of mutual understanding.

The planning and stimulation of a whole country's economy had been tried before—in our own time in fascist and bolshevik countries—but only on the principle of force. Always they failed because without freedom there can be no initiative, no stimulus of reward, no wide gateways to opportunity. Always their substance was eaten away by the blights of bureaucratic wastefulness and police invasions.

Hoover tried it (in so far as one man with limited authority in a limited time could do so) on the principle of consent. He did not fail—because the hundreds of gains he made have not all been dissipated; the techniques he developed are available to carry the experiment forward; principles of self-regulation and co-operation he was the first to promote have been widely accepted; the goals he set remain to inspire new generations of Americans.

He met many and serious setbacks, of course. For instance, he failed to obtain the better control of banks and financing which he pleaded for. President Coolidge, content with the prosperity of the moment, yielded to financial interests in blocking his Secretary of Commerce. The President "rejected or sidestepped all our anxious urgings and warnings to take action" on "the rising boom and orgy of speculation," Hoover would recall in after years. As for the professional speculators and economists drugged with optimism, they called Hoover a "spoil sport" and "crepehanger." They resented the attitude in such a typical Hoover statement as this:

"No sensible businessman wants either a boom or a slump. Our working folk should dread a trade boom above all things, because it means an afterclap of unemployment and misery. Our farmers should resent a boom, because they inevitably get the worst of the deflation which is bound to follow."

Hoover's spirited objections were successful in 1925 in blocking an expansion of credit by the Federal Reserve Board, under pressure from foreign and domestic sources: Benjamin Strong of the Federal Reserve Bank of New York, Montagu Norman of the Bank of England, Charles Rist of the Bank of France, Hjalmar Schacht of the Reichsbank, Bertil Ohlin of Sweden. In a letter to one of the Reserve governors, referring to policies then under consideration, Hoover declared:

"As to the effects of these Reserve policies upon the United States, it means inflation with inevitable collapse which will bring the greatest calamities upon our farmers, our workers, and legitimate business."

Two years later the "easy-money" policies were put over notwithstanding. Probably Montagu Norman, Hjalmar Schacht, and the others would have succeeded in 1927 in any case, but Hoover's total dedication to a gigantic lifesaving task at the time—the removal of 1,500,000 people from the path of the Mississippi floods—made their victory easier. As he had foreseen, the vast new credit inflation fed the speculative madness. And in due time he would be castigated and stoned for the very calamities he had sought to divert and then labored to keep within bounds.

Neither did Hoover get very far in his campaign against foreign and domestic cartels for price-fixing and apportioning markets. To him these devices were fascist in spirit and a menace to the individualist economy he was defending. He did in some degree liberate his country from complete dependence on British sources for rubber by encouraging rubber plantations in other areas, especially in Latin America. And he did lay down policies which preserved the radio airwaves for the people—"this is just as important as to keep the channels of navigation open for ships," he said—and ruled out their monopolization.

One of the defeats he felt most keenly was in the realm of bureaucracy. He made various studies of the operation of our government, showing the kind of duplication of effort and confusion of methods which would not be tolerated in any rationally run private enterprise. Again and again he demanded action to eliminate waste in federal administration. But there were too many vested political interests in the status quo; he could get no action. Only in 1947, when he was appointed to head a committee for this very purpose, was he able to undertake in earnest this cherished project.

The frustrations of depression and war have tended to obscure Hoover's achievement as Secretary of Commerce from 1921 through 1928. A pervasive national cynicism has operated to distort the very objectives which he had set himself. History, one dares hope, will make amends.

2

Hoover had lived and worked for many years in tough mining towns, among hard-drinking, hard-playing men, without being one of them. In that lusty gambling and toping crowd the young Quaker must have seemed incongruous; if he was not resented, it was because he was the best miner of them all.

The same edge of incongruity attached to him when he found himself among the "Ohio gang" whom President Harding gave the run of the White House. After a sad experiment or two Harding had sense enough no longer to invite Hoover (and for that matter Charles Evans Hughes, Andrew Mellon, Will Hays, and certain others) to his poker parties.

But the President and his Secretary of Commerce became friends. The man from Ohio, being without illusions about his own limitations, liked to consult Hoover on all sorts of problems. He took pride in the versatile and well-stocked Hoover mind. It was known to insiders that Harding repeatedly went to bat for his Secretary against Penrose and other party bosses who feared his innovations. Hoover came to know that he could depend on the President's common sense in any appeal for liberal ideas.

Harding, according to Hoover, was a dual personality: a man of noble instincts with a weakness for ignoble company. He "sincerely wanted to be a good President" but could not cut himself off from his highbinding cronies. There was a juncture when Hoover was so disgusted by Harding's associates and the whole poker aura that he discussed seriously with Mrs. Hoover the temptation to resign. The importance of the work he had under way—and Harding's helpfulness in that work—swung the balance in favor of remaining.

Shortly before President Harding went on his trip to Alaska in the summer of 1923—the trip which was to end in his sudden death on the return stage—one of his friends, Jesse Smith, committed suicide. Though Harding enjoyed an amazing popular affection, ugly rumors were already in circulation.

On his summons, the Hoovers joined the President at Tacoma on July 3. They found him morose and distracted, his genuine gaiety of the past now a transparent mask for inner distress. He played bridge from breakfast to past midnight as if it were a drug. Hoover and others organized a schedule of relays to keep the President supplied with partners yet escape the treadmill for a while. "I grew a distaste for bridge and never played it again," Hoover says.

A few days out, on the way to Alaska, after a gloomy luncheon, the President asked the Secretary of Commerce to come to his cabin. He had obviously mulled over what he intended to say, for he at once asked a startling but carefully formulated question:

"Hoover, if you knew of a great scandal in our administration, would you for the good of the country and the party expose it publicly or would you bury it?"

Hoover replied without hesitancy. "Blow it out at once," he said. "The blowing will prove the integrity of the administration."

Then he asked for more particulars, and Harding seemed willing to give them. He had heard some rumors of irregularities, he said, centering around cases in the Department of Justice and involving Jesse Smith. He had sent for Smith one evening and informed him, as a matter of friendship, that he would be arrested the following morning. That night Smith burned a lot of papers at home and killed himself. Harding gave Hoover no intimation about the nature of the irregularities. When asked whether Attorney General Daugherty was mixed up in the affair, the President "abruptly dried up" and the interview terminated.

Did Harding give anyone else on board that much of a glimpse of what was preying on his mind? Hoover could not know. Not until the Teapot Dome and the other scandals broke did he realize the nature of the weight on Harding's mind.

When the President first took ill in Seattle on July 27, his personal physician diagnosed poisoning from bad sea food. A younger doctor attached to the party suspected a heart ailment, and Hoover wired ahead to his friend Ray Lyman Wilbur to have reputable specialists meet the presidential train in San Francisco. They confirmed that it was heart trouble. Harding died on August 1. Whether he was planning to "blow it out" on his return to Washington, whether the knowledge of the piracies committed by his "gang" hastened his death—these are anyone's guess.

In the housecleaning under President Coolidge after the scandals a man of sterling integrity, Harlan Stone, became Attorney General. Stone asked Hoover to recommend an able and reliable man to head up the Federal Bureau of Investigation. He recommended a namesake who is not a relative, J. Edgar Hoover.

A stage director could scarcely have figured out a sharper contrast to Harding than his New England successor. Lusty, openhanded hospitality, a bit on the rowdy side, gave way in the White House to quiet and parsimonious hominess. Coolidge's favorite recreation—the myth of taciturnity notwithstanding—was conversation. He often invited Hoover alone of an evening for a few hours of "gab," and drew on a rich fund of Yankee stories as they discussed public affairs and people.

He also had a store of wisdom, which he passed on in copybook style. "If you see ten troubles coming down the road," according to one of his home-brewed proverbs, "you can be sure nine will run into the ditch before they reach you and you have to battle with only one of them." He was a lucky President—the man who followed him discovered that when ten troubles came down the road they somehow multiplied to a hundred by the time they arrived.

After Hoover was elected in 1928, Coolidge offered him some fatherly advice of the kind that explains his fame for silence: "You have to stand every day three or four hours of visitors. Nine tenths of them want something. If you keep dead still they will run down in three or four minutes. If you even cough or smile they will start up all over again."

Coolidge proved less interested and less co-operative than Harding in the ambitious reforms of his Secretary of Commerce. The charge that would one day be made falsely and stupidly against Hoover—the charge of "doing nothing"—did apply to Coolidge. Letting things ride amounted to a passion with him; the less we meddle with it, the more chance nature has to work its ancient healments. Hoover's zeal for changing the world therefore disturbed the President. He sought to restrain it. He opposed the child-labor amendment; he dissolved the controls over foreign loans worked out by Hoover; he yielded on the Hoover Dam and other federal construction projects most reluctantly. And in particular he closed his mind to Hoover's pleas for timely curbs on credit inflation and the thundering catastrophe called Coolidge Prosperity.

3

Depressions after periods of boom are no new phenomena. Another depression arrived in the first year of the Harding administration, in 1921. Never in the past had the Federal Government assumed any responsibility in such emergencies. A depression was something that "ran its course," like measles.

But Hoover, in opposition to the dominant opinion in his party and in the Cabinet, decided to "do something." By September 1921 unemployment had assumed serious dimensions and the winter ahead promised to be hard and bitter. With Harding's approval, he summoned a conference of business leaders, labor men, farm-organization people, economists, social workers.

The time for quiescence had passed, he told them in an opening speech. In modern society the pain and suffering are too immense to let nature take its cruel course.

"There is no economic failure so terrible in its import," he said, "as that of a country possessing a surplus of every necessity of life in which numbers, willing and anxious to work, are deprived of these necessities. It simply cannot be if our moral and economic system is to survive. . . ."

In line with discussions at this gathering Hoover set up volunteer groups to deal with immediate relief and others to study the business cycle with a view to moderating future slumps. In retrospect he wrote:

"To alleviate the immediate situation in co-operation with state, municipal, and charity organization officials during the next winter we created an organization of committees in every state and county where relief was needed and mobilized behind them such funds as were necessary. We further created an organization in the Department to stimulate public works by the co-operation of governors and mayors with the Federal Government. We arranged that employers should 'divide time' so as to give some work to all of their normal complement of employees and that industries should expand their own construction work."

Nor was that all. Special agencies to stimulate home construction were formed; banks were induced to finance larger exports. The nation lived through the winter without real suffering. A precedent for federal intervention in economic depressions was set, rather to the horror of conservatives. "The obvious way to lessen the losses and miseries of depression," Hoover declared publicly at this time, "is first to check the destructive extremes of booms." His words were too soon forgotten.

Long before he entered the government Hoover had spoken out firmly against the ten- and twelve-hour day and the seven-day week which prevailed in the steel and other industries. The subject was one of his main specific concerns when he became Secretary. Immediately he undertook an investigation which gave him ammunition in the form of clear and incontrovertible information. Then, on May 18, 1922, he got Harding to call Charles Schwab, Judge Elbert Gary, and other top steel men to a White House conference.

The President let Hoover run the show—and the industrialists squirmed as he spread the record of their industry. It was clear to him from their attitude that they would not move unless dynamited by public opinion. He had small faith in the committee under Judge Gary which they agreed to set up to "look into the problem."

Hoover therefore deliberately "broke the story" to the press. The President, he told the American people, was attempting to persuade industry to adopt a reasonable working day. He had the engineering societies issue a report in support of the President—with an introduction written by Hoover and signed by Harding.

The Gary committee delayed its report until June 1923; it was obviously stalling for time. Hoover expressed publicly his own and the administration's disappointment and fed fuel to the fires of popular resentment. The result was that the steel industry soon capitulated. When Hoover reached Tacoma to join Harding on July 3, he was just in time to write a few powerful paragraphs into the presidential July Fourth address, announcing the voluntary abolition by industry of the twelve-hour day and the eighty-four-hour week. The language was so different from the rest of the speech that Harding stumbled over it in the reading. While the great assemblage applauded the announcement wildly, the President whispered to his neighbor on the platform, "Damn it, Hoover, why don't you write the same English as I do?"

I can only mention a few of the myriad episodes of Hoover's fight for justice to labor. Horrified by a federal injunction against striking railway workers, he sought Hughes's support in the matter. Knowing that Daugherty was the key culprit, they decided to tackle the issue at the very next cabinet meeting, in the Attorney General's presence. Hoover raised the subject, Hughes backed him up with a learned legal opinion—and Daugherty, on Harding's order, undertook to have the injunction vacated.

Among the strikes in which Hoover acted as negotiator as the President's representative was that of the railway shopmen. His chief difficulty was not with labor but with the railroad interests. Their committee of two hundred tried to repudiate terms agreed to in principle by its spokesman, Daniel Willard, of the B. & O., but Hoover was in no mood to permit this.

"I certainly had a freezing reception," he said later. "Paradoxically, my temperature rose somewhat and I delivered a modest preachment upon social relations which, to most of them, only branded me as a wild radical. Among other things I stated that such attitudes would sooner or later bring great disaster upon industry itself."

In these years, as always, child welfare occupied a lot of Hoover's attention. He co-ordinated existing health and educational agencies for children and took the lead in most of the fund-raising efforts in those connections. The designation of May Day as "Child Health Day" grew out of his suggestion.

While promoting home-owning, through reduction of costs and standardization of processes, Hoover decided to help solve a housing problem close to home, in Washington itself. He lined up the banking and building support for the construction of comfortable small apartments for federal employees; they were to be self-liquidating at rentals considerably lower than those prevailing in the capital. The scheme was wrecked, however, by the real-estate interests of Washington.

An amusing by-product of his department's action in the radio field involved the famous woman evangelist, Aimee Semple McPherson. The eloquent lady built a radio station in connection with her church, but could see no reason why she should not use any wavelength and power volume she pleased. When the Department of Commerce intervened, she denounced it—and Hoover specifically—for thwarting God's freedom of speech.

In the end Hoover decided to assign a young radioman to manage the McPherson station and keep it from wandering out of its appointed channel. The radio troubles were cured, but the young man, alas, embroiled himself subsequently in an alleged love tangle with the evangelist that made headlines through the nation for many months.

Hoover's double term as Secretary, as we have seen, began in its initial year with a great relief job for the victims of a depression. Its final years were highlighted by a greater and more dramatic work of rescue, in the Mississippi floods in the spring and summer in 1927. Neither of these undertakings was strictly within his official province. But Harding in the first instance and Coolidge in the second as a matter of course turned to him to take over. One can understand why Will Rogers, when an earthquake hit the Near East, thought it strange the Levantines were not calling in Hoover. "Bert was only resting between calamities," he said.

And the calamity of the floods was Hooveresque in dimension: the largest peacetime disaster in American history at the time. A congestion of Mississippi waters without precedent for volume ultimately flooded the Lower Mississippi for a thousand miles, from Cairo to the Gulf, for a width as much as one hundred and fifty miles.

Two hundred people were drowned before the Federal Government took over in the person of Hoover—after which only three lives were lost. He mobilized local and state authorities, the militias of the six endangered states, the coast guard, the Red Cross, a naval air contingent and Army engineers. As the waters moved southward—a process that took about two months—rescue workers were a few safe steps ahead of them; populations had been evacuated.

Commanding the grandiose war on disaster, first from Memphis and then from other cities, Hoover organized the removal of about 1,500,000 men, women, and children with such goods and animals as they could manage; then saw to their feeding, health, and rehabilitation. Some two million acres of crops were washed out and millions in property and livestock destroyed. Forty river steamers, each with a flotilla of small boats, worked continually at lifesaving. In ten days, at Hoover's urging, a thousand new boats, rough but serviceable, were built and thrown into the breach. About 200,000 people were sheltered in eighty tent colonies, under Red Cross and government supervision. Health workers plied their needles so efficiently that there was no sign of the epidemics normally associated with such catastrophes; indeed, the refugees under Hoover's control were healthier than in normal times.

The same Will Irwin who reported the Belgian Relief for the American press and the pre-armistice relief in Europe was now reporting the Mississippi miracle. In one of his dispatches he expressed wonder at Hoover's calm effectiveness: "It was like seeing a master play billiards. You may not know much of the game, but you recognize supreme skill when you see it . . ."

Bringing to a close a brilliant biography of Hoover that he published soon after this event, Irwin wrote:

I . . . would like to leave him as I saw him one May morning of 1927—standing on the tottering Melville levee, his aeroplanes scouting overhead, his mosquito fleet scurrying below, a group of prominent citizens about him listening to the wise, quick, terse directions which were bringing order out of chaos. It symbolizes the man, that scene—"The one tranquil among the raging floods," the transmuter of altruistic emotion into benevolent action. On that side of him his friends and intimates base their fanatical affection.

He could not know, as he wrote those words in 1928, what history had in store for Hoover. But having talked to Will Irwin shortly before his recent death and to many others among those "fanatical" friends, I know that they have not altered their opinion by one iota. Quite the contrary, Hoover's almost single-handed struggle with multiple disasters as President confirmed their fanaticism. Watching his desperate duel with economic, political, and psychological forces more devastating than the Mississippi ever mustered—watching it close up and in sympathetic understanding, not at a distance in bitter hostility—they continued convinced that he was "the one tranquil among the raging floods."

Hoover's nomination by the Republican party at its convention in Kansas City was expected, inevitable, despite the opposition of the more conservative leadership. The late Charles Michelson was right when he wrote at the time that the Old Guard "don't like Hoover, don't understand him, and are doubtful of their ability to deal with him. . . ." It was an open secret that the finance-speculator elements symbolized by Wall Street felt deeply affronted by his strictures on the boom.

But small business and more enlightened leaders of big business were for him; the American Federation of Labor, the miners, the railway workers, and the mass of unaffiliated workers were for him. Groups which had never before taken a political stand, such as organized engineers, women's societies, and social workers, were for him; in the actual vote, it was estimated, about three quarters of all women were for him, as the man who thought unceasingly about the welfare of their children.

He had no personal political machine. He didn't need one. The Chicago *Daily News* did not believe its own doggerel, of course, when it rhymed in irony before the convention:

> *Who'll never win presidential position,*
> *For he isn't a practical politician?*
> *Hoover—that's all!*

The telegram notifying Hoover of his unanimous nomination was so worded as to imply that he had "earned" the right to be President. To this implication he reacted at once.

"My country owes me no debt," he declared. "It gave me, as it gives every boy and girl, a chance. It gave me schooling, independence of action, opportunity for service, and honor. In no other land could a boy from a country village, without inheritance or influential friends, look forward with such unbounded hope. My whole life has taught me what America means. I am indebted to my country beyond any human power to repay. . . ."

In November 1928 he was elected President of the United States by an overwhelming majority.

There were aspects of the campaign against Alfred E. Smith, the Democratic candidate, which hurt Hoover to the quick; whisperings that made him ashamed of some of his supporters. Religious bigotry is alien to his character, to his Quaker upbringing and cosmopolitan experience.

In his acceptance speech on August 11, 1928, Hoover said:

"In this land, dedicated to tolerance, we still find outbreaks of intolerance. I come of Quaker stock. My ancestors were persecuted for their beliefs. Here they sought and found religious freedom. By blood and conviction I stand for religious tolerance both in act and in spirit. The glory of our American ideals is the right of every man to worship God according to his own conscience."

And six weeks later, on September 28, taking cognizance of ugly outcroppings of intolerance, he declared:

"Religious questions have no part in this campaign. I have repeatedly said that neither I nor the Republican Party want support on that basis. There are important and vital reasons for the return of the Republican Administration but this is not one of them."

Hoover and Al Smith were good friends before the campaign. They became even better friends after the campaign. That should suffice to shame those who accused Hoover of religious bias into apologizing but it won't. Al Smith was known to stand up and defend Hoover's reputation on this score, and on most other scores, when people in his presence attacked his successful opponent on the mistaken supposition he would relish it.

On a blustering Monday in March 1929 Herbert Clark Hoover took the oath of office as our thirty-first President. When the Quaker blacksmith in West Branch, Iowa, nearly fifty-five years earlier, announced that "another General Grant"—meaning another American President—had just been born in his tiny cottage, he spoke more truly than he could possibly suspect.

CHAPTER XVI

Boom into Bust

IN A PRESS CONFERENCE A FEW DAYS before he turned over his office to his successor, President Coolidge assured the nation once more that its prosperity was "absolutely sound." John J. Raskob, chief financial backer of the defeated Democratic candidate, announced that common stocks were still a fine buy. Franklin Delano Roosevelt, governor of the state where three quarters of all the gambling madness was centered, saw everything "in a healthy and prosperous condition."

No reproof attaches to such citations, which were simply typical of 1929. To censure individuals for not foreseeing calamity around the corner is as futile as blaming fishermen on a sunny day for the hurricane that is sweeping down upon them. Why should politicians, in particular, be better weather prophets than the meteorologists of the big financial institutions?

The country was on an economic binge. All the laws of gravity seemed suspended as America rode the towering crests of its optimism, recklessly, drunkenly, mistaking its giddiness for high spirits and the flush of fever for the color of health.

The incoming President's first chore was a thankless one— how thankless should be apparent to anyone who has ever tried to sober an obstreperous drunk—and a hopeless one. The frenzy had gone too far to be arrested without a smashup and a terrifying hangover. The significant fact, for our understanding of Hoover, is that he was among those who saw the danger and did try to head it off.

He failed. Of course he failed. No mortal man could have succeeded. He was one man against an avalanche that had been piling up for fifteen years. Mordecai Ezekiel, New Deal economist, wrote in 1947, "The catastrophe of 1929–32 had its roots in policies we adopted, actions we took, from 1920 on." They went even deeper, those roots, into the devastations and dislocations of a world war; into the economic blunders of the peace, the social upheavals in Russia and Italy.

Millions of Americans had been plunged into a great debauch of greed. When the day of reckoning arrived they needed a sacrificial goat. The man in the White House was "it." He would have been "it" had his name been Smith or Roosevelt instead of Hoover.

Hoover's had been one of the killjoy voices crying caution drowned out by the uproar of the carousers. Now that he could make himself heard it was too late. On assuming the presidency he stated that he considered market values inflated and the speculation a madness. But he did not shout these truths—to shout them from the White House might have precipitated the very calamity he sought to prevent, or at worst to cushion. He had to talk discreetly and work behind the scenes.

It would be too much to say that he knew the smashup was coming. Like the rest of the small and despised company of the sober in that time of intoxication, he knew only that the boom was unwholesome; that capital was being poured into unproductive speculation rather than productive investment; that the stock-market indices were galloping far ahead of prices and employment.

Frightened by the cyclone of speculation let loose by their own "easy-money" policies of 1927, Federal Reserve officials wanted to reverse themselves but dared not so long as the complacent Coolidge was President. Only after the election of Hoover, whose support they could count upon, did they begin to restrict speculative credit. Within forty-eight hours after his inauguration the new President assembled them at the White House to authorize additional and drastic measures.

On March 15 Secretary of the Treasury Mellon, at Hoover's behest, announced that "bonds are low in price compared to stocks." This was an indirect warning, the first to come from such a source, that stocks were inflated. Governor Young of the Federal Reserve followed it up next day with an appeal to all banks, a public appeal, to curb speculative loans. At the same time Hoover invited leading newspaper and magazine editors to the White House, individually and off the record, and implored them to speak out against the mounting mania of easy profits. A few complied; the majority thought him an alarmist.

The President then sent his friend Henry M. Robinson around the country, from Los Angeles to New York, to warn the bankers and promoters behind the frenzied markets. They scoffed at his pleas for self-restraint; had they not found the secret of Midas? Thomas W. Lamont of the House of Morgan, as spokesman for the banking fraternity, dispatched to Hoover a long and solemn report "proving" that official doubts of the health of the New Era were unfounded.

As a result of the President's efforts the rates on market loans rose as high as 20 per cent, but the tide of madness could no longer be stemmed by interest barriers. Housewives and millionaires alike were intent on 100 and 200 per cent "killings" in a few weeks or months. The country resented Hoover's evident intention to douse its daydreams. Speakers at the newspaper publishers' meeting in April voiced that resentment. Blistering attacks on the new restrictive policies echoed through the halls of Congress.

Wall Street treated the President's actions as a declaration of war.

Hoover believed then, and still does, that the inherent weakness of our banking system, further enfeebled by unscrupulous men and methods, was mainly to blame for forcing the country into the valley of shadows and keeping it there for ten years. His conviction is supported by the startling fact that though industrial bankruptcies in the first three years of depression were only $1\frac{1}{2}$ per cent of the total, bank failures reached almost 25 per cent. Most of the 24,000 banks were state institutions, operating under forty-eight conflicting, inadequate, and often vicious codes of laws; thousands had insufficient capital, more thousands inefficient management.

The evils of this setup, however, were too deeply rooted in time and American psychology to be reformed overnight. The President set in motion studies of the complex situation looking to corrective legislation even before the market collapse came to complicate the problem; he fought for a bank-reform program to his last day on Pennsylvania Avenue.

The focal point of the great speculative infection was Wall Street. Unfortunately the legal authority to deal with the Stock Exchange rested in Albany, not Washington, and there Governor Roosevelt resisted all counsel of moderation. Until the day he resigned from his Wall Street law firm to run for governor, Roosevelt had himself been involved in the speculative orgy as a stock promoter. His closest associates were people who geneflected before the Stock Exchange. In all honesty—I intend no reflections on his public spirit—he saw no excuse for interfering with the ticker-tape Santa Claus. Even the failure of the Bank of the United States late in 1930, affecting 400,000 depositors, did not shake Albany out of its profound torpor.

The President had only one small-bore weapon at his disposal, and it could reach only the lower strata in the pyramid of greed: the tipsters and bucket-shop operators. He instructed the Department of Justice to go after them hard for using the mails to defraud. This it did so energetically that hundreds of the parasites were driven into hiding. The Better Business Bureaus called it the greatest clean-up of Wall Street up to that time.

Hoover then summoned Richard Whitney, the president of the New York Stock Exchange, to the White House, and apprised him that the federal authorities were aware of grave abuses in the Exchange, even if the state officials seemed indifferent. Unless there was a genuine house cleaning, he warned, Congress would be asked to step in, much as he disliked intruding on the state precincts. It was in pursuance of that threat, indeed, that Hoover in time forced the Senate (over the bitter resistance of Democratic leaders) to investigate the Stock Exchange, disclosing manipulation, price-fixing, and plain thievery on an awe-inspiring scale.

Seven months after the President entered the White House

his struggle against the boom was converted into a struggle against the bust. In October the stock market crashed.

Those old enough to remember that debacle know that one big spill was not enough to sober the joy-riders. Press and radio were flooded with reassurances. "Even in the present high market the prices of stocks have not caught up with their real value," said Professor Irving Fisher of Yale. "Yesterday's break was a shaking out of the lunatic fringe that attempts to speculate on margin." The New York *Times* reported: "Confidence in the soundness of the stock-market structure notwithstanding the upheaval of the last few days was voiced last night by bankers and other financial leaders." At a conference of governors in Salt Lake City, Mr. Roosevelt defended the soundness of the financial situation, arguing that only "gamblers" were being hurt by the collapse.

Statements in the same general vein were made by Charles E. Mitchell, John D. Rockefeller, Thomas W. Lamont, John J. Raskob, Democratic Senator Carter Glass, a thousand others. Stuart Chase declared that "the stock markets will not affect general prosperity." William Green, president of the American Federation of Labor, announced that "all the factors which make for quick and speedy industrial and economic recovery are present." "Business is sound," said Alfred P. Sloan, Jr., president of General Motors.

Quotations of this character could be multiplied for pages. They came from every direction. It was an attempt to shoo away bad times by choral incantation. President Hoover, though in more guarded language than most, contributed to the chorus. "The fundamental business of the country, that is, production and distribution," he said, "is on a sound and prosperous basis." The industrial and labor leaders who conferred with him in those weeks know that he spoke more gloomily in private than in public. Editorial demands that the White House urge people to invest in stocks "notwithstanding" were steadfastly ignored.

Hoover devoted himself to action with a minimum of talk and public posturing. He was determined to head off panic. He began that grinding, brutal, self-lacerating labor, often eighteen and twenty hours a day, or clear around the clock, which would continue unbroken until the blessed hour of release more than three years later. No galley slave of old was ever more firmly riveted to his drudgery, for he was chained by his surpassing sense of duty.

He began that long ordeal of unsparing exertion—physical, mental, and spiritual—for which he would be rewarded with the infamous legend that he "did nothing." For already, as we shall see, an efficient, well-oiled smear machine geared to just one job, the defamation of a President, was in operation.

2

Hoover came to the White House keyed for a supreme job of building. Instead he was obliged to patch. That is the nub of his private tragedy. He was like a mariner, starting off on a journey of discovery to bring home rare treasures, who is forced by sudden storms to pour all his energies into just keeping the ship afloat.

It was not a nebulous do-good urge that he brought with him but a detailed and ambitious blueprint of basic social reforms and ameliorations. That much can be deduced from the things he initiated in the few months of clear weather allowed him by history; from what he accomplished and attempted in a hundred directions even in the midst of violent storms. The record has been blurred by trouble and blotched by misrepresentation, but those who bother to examine it are impressed and astonished.

As Secretary of Commerce he had laid the groundwork in some fields—child welfare, home ownership, flood control, labor relations, more equitable distribution of the fruits of industry. He had reached out for the presidency as a God-given chance to extend his philosophy of liberalism to the whole of American life. But he had barely unrolled his constructive plans and assembled some of their raw materials when he was overwhelmed by destructive forces.

Because he has generously enabled me to read his unpublished notes, I happen to have a sense of the magnitude of his intentions and of the care with which he had prepared to translate them into action. For fifteen years America had been absorbed in war, in sheer growth, in digesting such new developments and inventions as mass-produced automobiles, radios, aviation; it had not paused to take stock of its social structure. Vital changes were long overdue.

"The prolific soil of individual liberty produces not only magnificent blossoms but noxious weeds," Hoover says, "and we had grown a lot of thistles. . . . I had come to the White House not only convinced of the necessity of easing the strains of growth and giving impulse to progress but in high hopes that I might lead in performing the task."

In foreign affairs he aimed to break through America's deepening isolationist fixations. His inaugural address stressed "the profound truth that our own progress, prosperity, and peace are interlocked with the progress, prosperity, and peace of all humanity." His blueprint called for a sensible adjustment of relations with Latin-American nations; adherence to the World Court; full co-operation with the League of Nations in its non-political activities; an end to debilitating naval competition; agreement to give full immunity to food ships in time of war. It called, above all, for co-operation with other nations to prevent economic and political disasters.

Between his election and inauguration he journeyed to Latin America on the battleship *Maryland* with a contingent of American newspapermen. He promulgated what he called a "good-neighbor" approach to Western Hemisphere relations. That this phrase, which he used innumerable times in one American republic after another, should be arbitrarily credited to his successor proves for all time the superiority of fable over fact. As President, Hoover followed up by withdrawing American troops from Haiti and Nicaragua; by pledging hands off in the internal affairs of neighbor nations; by enunciating the principle that Americans investing capital in foreign countries did so at their own risk.

Except on the issue of limiting naval armaments, he was blocked in his major efforts to overcome the isolationist mood. Congress rejected his every formula for adherence to the World Court or collaboration with the League. His cherished plan for outlawing the use of civilian food as a war weapon—by guar-

anteeing the immunity of food ships—was hailed by the press
of the world, except the official mouthpieces of Japan and England, but it never got beyond the stage of abstract enthusiasm.

In the economic dimension he was more successful only because the interdependence of all nations was made so tragically
clear by events. His moratorium on intergovernmental debts and
his "standstill" agreement on private international debts marked
the first great reversals of the nationalist patterns set at Versailles.
The retreat to total economic isolationism by his successor
(dramatized when Mr. Roosevelt torpedoed the London Economic Conference) had much to do with prolonging the depression at home and intensifying those forces abroad which
led to World War II.

The highly intricate subject of tariffs may be mentioned in
this context. Hoover was not among the Republican extremists
on the issue. The platform on which he was elected committed
him to tariff revision in the interest of hard-pressed farmers, but
the moderation of his proposals displeased protectionists. He
was opposed by a virtually united front of lobbyists for his insistence on flexibility in tariffs; his plan, in which he was only
partly successful, called for a bipartisan tariff commission with
authority to make adjustments as conditions changed, after public
hearings by judicial procedure. Thus he hoped to remove tariff-
making from politics.

The Smoot-Hawley tariff, passed in July 1930, was unsatisfac-
tory to the President but the best he could obtain. It suited some
political critics in the next presidential campaign to blame the
whole depression upon the moderate increases in this bill. They
simply ignored the fact that the crash came nine months before
the law was enacted; and the further fact that some forty countries had raised their tariff walls before America did. In addition, numerous nations had set up rigid import quotas and exchange controls which made customs barriers quite secondary
controls by contrast. The whole world had moved grimly toward
autarchy long before Hoover reached Pennsylvania Avenue; the
tariff measures of his administration were minimal defensive
tactics.

Democratic talk of sharp reductions in the tariff during the campaign of 1932 was what evoked Hoover's much-chewed warning that "grass will grow in the streets of a hundred cities" if that were done. The test was never made, since the New Deal did not dare to keep its campaign promises. On the contrary, through a devalued dollar it actually raised American tariff walls to unexampled heights; the whole Roosevelt program aimed at American self-sufficiency. But the fanciful grass-will-grow phrase, which referred specifically and only to tariffs, was cynically misquoted in later years to apply to the Democratic reign generally in order to mock an ex-President.

Hoover's domestic program amounted to a room-by-room overhauling of the American social structure. It ranged from simplification of government to social security for the aged; it embraced revision of bank and bankruptcy laws, prison reform, improved judiciary and law-enforcement practices, collective bargaining rights for labor; extensive government intervention to aid children, widen the boundaries of education, promote lowcost housing, and, above all, care for the victims of social calamities.

Soon after Hoover became President, he began the organization of a national conference on the health and protection of children. The $500,000 expended on this undertaking did not come from the Treasury; he raised every dollar of it from private sources. A suggestion for the use of public funds for such a purpose would have horrified every Democrat and Republican alike at that stage. Besides, Hoover regarded voluntary, co-operative action for great social objectives as more wholesome, more safely in the tradition of freedom.

To bring the voluminous findings and tangible proposals of the several thousand men and women involved in the enterprise within the mental compass of the average American, the President himself, in longhand, reduced them to what he called "The Children's Charter." As a succinct, practical assertion of society's responsibility to its young—the fundamental social security offered by a physically and morally robust new generation—this document has never been surpassed.

Its nineteen clauses, not merely in what they say but in the goals of a perfected humanity which they envision, amount to a Magna Charta of social idealism within a framework of freedom. "For every child spiritual and moral training to help him stand firm under the pressure of life. . . . For every child understanding and the guarding of his personality as his most precious right. . . . For every child a community which recognizes and plans for his needs, protects him against physical dangers, moral hazards, and disease. . . . For every child an education which, through the discovery and development of his individual abilities, prepares him for life. . . . For every child these rights, regardless of race, or color, or situation, wherever he may live under the protection of the American flag." Merely high lights, these, in a plan rounded and complete as an engineering graph. As an index to Hoover's view of the good life that charter is worth tomes of research and interpretation.

Having gotten the survey on child welfare started, the President initiated an even more comprehensive examination of larger problems—one of the most ambitious studies of the American scene ever undertaken. This was his Committee on Social Trends, appointed on September 9, 1929, and financed again by private contributions. The committee mobilized several hundred specialists in diverse fields—public-welfare activities, taxation, social security, rural life, utilization of national resources, education, trends in economic institutions, national planning (not in the coercive but the co-operative sense), crime and punishment, labor-management tensions, a score of other basic areas. They analyzed the problems, lined up the pertinent data, and offered alternative solutions. In issuing the report of the committee in the final months of his administration, the President declared:

"The significance of this report lies primarily in the fact that it is a co-operative effort on a very broad scale to project into the field of social thought the scientific mood and the scientific method as correctives to indiscriminating emotional approach; to secure factual basis in seeking for constructive remedies of great social problems."

I have chosen these two projects for the light they throw on Hoover's conception of presidential leadership. Together they cover every aspect of American life and therefore represent a sharp break with the theory—unchallenged until Hoover's day—

expressed by President Cleveland in 1887: "Though the people
support the Government, the Government should not support
the people." Hoover, of course, did not accept the principle that
government *should* support the people—carried to extremes that
means a paternalistic and ultimately a totalitarian state—but assuredly he renounced the Cleveland precept which rejected all
responsibility.

* Those surveys have had a profound effect on social thinking
in the years that followed; but acknowledgment of Hoover's pioneering contribution became an obsessive taboo in those years.
Implementation of that thinking was made impossible by the
growing load of immediate problems of depression and destitution. Both as a matter of necessity and of principle Hoover addressed himself to first things first: to buttressing a caved-in economy, warding off recurrent threats of panic unlimited, and
caring for millions of needy.

He happened to believe deeply that disasters and distress must
not be made the pretexts for risky social experiments. He could
not accept the cynical assumption—the point where Marx and
Nietzsche intersect—that human beings were the expendible raw
stuff for "social engineering" by men in power. He turned away
in revulsion from those who greeted mass suffering with great
glee as a wonderful chance to put over this or that "revolution"
while the masses, paralyzed by fear, were helpless to resist.

If this sounds theoretical, the fault is mine. To the man in the
White House the problem posed by events was concrete enough.
The question was not about *ends*—all decent-minded men wanted
to restore normal life and relieve misery. His problem was a
wise choice of *means*—not the means best for Hoover or the
Republican party, but those best for the country.

Only fools still believe that Hoover was a fool. He knew as
well as the most demagogic soap-boxer or pork-barrel impresario
that he could reap applause and votes by providing sensational
temporary solutions at the price of permanent impairment of
the American concepts of life and government. Those solutions
were no recondite secret. He needed only to look across the
Atlantic, where totalitarian regimes were "solving" fiscal problems and "abolishing" unemployment with the greatest ease.

Every one of the solutions subsequently tried, discarded, re-tried until war came to wash them all out, from devaluation and the N.R.A. to made work and pump priming with inflated billions, was urged upon him by friend or foe. He was familiar with every ancient and modern trick in history's bag. Being human, he was under temptation to use them. But he rejected them deliberately, firmly, in full knowledge of the political risks. His obligations to his office took precedence as a matter of course over obligation to himself and his party. Let me cite an instance:

The scheme which in due time proliferated as the N.R.A. and was hailed as a noble common-man invention was brought to Hoover by spokesmen for business interests in 1932. The idea had its genesis, actually, in a plan published by Gerard Swope of the General Electric in September 1931. It proposed to "stabilize prices" through industry associations under government super-vision, in effect suspending the anti-trust laws.

The President's office memorandum that day recorded his im-mediate reaction. He saw it as a fascist-type proposal and a deathblow to American free economy. The parallel with Musso-lini's "corporate state" was, as a matter of fact, all too apparent. Hoover asked his Attorney General for a legal opinion on the Swope suggestion and was informed that it was wholly uncon-stitutional.

The idea was taken up by the United States Chamber of Com-merce and developed into substantially the future N.R.A. It is amusing to reflect on the fact that this program for regimenting and monopolizing all economic life (eventually ruled uncon-stitutional by the Supreme Court) originated in the citadels of free enterprise.

In September 1932, with the presidential campaigns about to start, the president of the Chamber of Commerce, Henry I. Har-riman, called on Hoover. He wanted a pledge that if re-elected the President would support the N.R.A. scheme. Hoover would have none of it. He wanted it inscribed on his tombstone, he said in effect, that he had stood firm against an unconstitutional attempt to smuggle fascism into America through a back door.

Mr. Harriman—this according to Hoover's private notes—then revealed that the Democratic candidate had already agreed to go along on the idea; and that if Hoover remained obdurate the cash and influence of leading industrialists would be thrown to Roosevelt. The President did remain obdurate, and Roosevelt did, in consequence, get immense big-business backing.

"We have not feared to adopt unprecedented measures," Hoover explained in 1932, though few understood him. "(But) we have resolutely rejected the temptation, under pressure of immediate events, to resort to those panaceas and short cuts which, even if temporarily successful, would ultimately undermine and weaken what has slowly been built and molded by experience and effort through these one hundred and fifty years."

Hoover's concepts of social justice were so advanced that he has himself on occasion described them as "revolutionary." But in achieving them he was strictly the evolutionist. His study of history, his close-up observation of postwar Europe, had convinced him that unless a people conserves its essential heritage even while refining and adding to it, social justice may expire in a welter of slogans.

3

A unique factory was opened up in Washington about three months after the inauguration of President Hoover. An understanding of the administration and of Hoover's personal ordeal is impossible without awareness of this strange enterprise. And the date of its organization is significant. It was not, as some people later pretended, a reaction to the slump or an answer to the President's "fumbling" of depression problems, for these things were still in the future.

The factory might be called Michelson's Mills, although technically it figured as the press division of the Democratic National Committee. Its products were smear stuff, rumors, verbal tar-and-feathers, and high-grade literary ectoplasm manufactured by Charlie Michelson and his associated ghosts. The plant occupied nearly a whole floor of the National Press Building and it specialized in "processing" every word and act of the President —including words he never uttered and acts he never committed —into proofs of his ineptitude, callousness, and confusion.

It mattered little what went into the Michelson Mills at one end. The genius of its presiding chemists transmuted it to evil-smelling stuffs at the other end. Hoover's pessimism in seeking to restrain speculative forces served as well as his optimism in envisioning recovery after the October smash-up. His refusal to roll out the pork barrel was parsimony; his budget for public works and economic rescue agencies was extravagance. Many of the very agencies and procedures which this factory later dressed up as proofs of New Deal genius were mocked and mauled here when Hoover first proposed them.

No President, not even Washington and certainly not Lincoln, escaped vilification while in office and after. But in Hoover's case the process was put on an organized, systematic, and scientific basis. The techniques of smearing, after all, had been amazingly improved since Lincoln's time. Every accusation against Hoover was endlessly multiplied, as in repeating mirrors, through press syndication, canned speeches, quickie books, bushels of cartoons, miles of radio broadcasts—all of it on a mass-production basis.

There is, of course, nothing new about disloyal oppositions in American politics. The novelty of the Michelson Mills was that it functioned from the very beginning of the Hoover incumbency and on a truly daring scale. Normally, as Herbert Corey wrote when the project was still fresh, "it had been the Democratic party's habit to sink into an irritated stupor during Republican administrations and only waken for the four months of its appeal to the people."

This time the opposition organized for continuous attack before they had the faintest knowledge what they would be called upon to attack. A shrewd politico, Jouett Shouse, was hired as general manager and Charles Michelson, an astute Washington correspondent, as production chief; each of them was paid $25,000 a year and expenses. The lush financing came from John J. Raskob ($462,000), the du Ponts, and other men of immense wealth.

The Democratic National Committee raised nearly $3,000,000 for the undertaking. Part of this went to cover campaign deficits. The rest, estimated at no less than $2,000,000, went to oil the wheels of the smear mills. It was the largest partisan expenditure *between campaigns* in the whole history of American political life.

Two other novel features need to be mentioned. The first is that this great effort was not directed especially against the Republican party but specifically against one man, Herbert Hoover. The theory, and a mighty smart one for all its indecency, was that some Republicans, too, could be incensed against their standard bearer who was certain to run for re-election. The second is that the systematic process of character assassination was not soft-pedaled after its victim had been ousted from the White House; on the contrary, it was even stepped up and infinitely refined, until Hoover was turned into a synonym for all the sins and fears and angers of a troubled time.

It should be recalled that the crisis in national economy and morale during the Hoover administration was as serious as war itself. It demanded some measure of national unity, some relaxation of the partisan spirit, at least a moratorium on the more egregious varieties of mud-throwing. No President in peacetime had ever made more earnest and self-effacing proffers of bi-partisan action to find solutions for problems threatening the very survival of American civilization. No President had ever been so completely and insultingly rebuffed.

In effect Hoover found himself with the responsibilities of a wartime President but without wartime powers, wartime prestige, and, most important, any wartime command of non-partisan support. The Shouse-Michelson offensive, far from easing off when catastrophes such as market crashes, economic collapse, floods, drought struck the country, went into high gear. The factory thrived on disaster and therefore hailed the approach of every new one with whoops of joy.

Besides being hired propagandists, the Michelson staff were also Americans and human beings. But one would never guess this from their output. In all the millions of ghost-written words there was not one paragraph of constructive criticism; not one expression of genuine sympathy, understanding, and encouragement. The smear mills were conducted wholly in the spirit of high-powered shyster salesmen tearing down a competing product.

In September 1930 the extraordinary enterprise had barely

found its full stride. It had not as yet had enough human misery to feed upon. But already in that month an intelligent press observer, Frank R. Kent, of the Baltimore *Sun,* could write in *Scribner's* about "The political agency in Washington that more than any other has helped mold the public mind in regard to Mr. Hoover, magnifying his misfortunes, minimizing his achievements . . . an illuminating illustration of the amazing power of *unopposed propaganda* in skillful hands."

He described the Michelson Mills as "the most elaborate, expensive, efficient, and effective political propaganda machine ever operated in the country by any party, organization, association, or league." The goal set for Mr. Michelson, he wrote, "was to 'smear' Mr. Hoover and his administration. That is what he is there for and all he is there for."

I have italicized Mr. Kent's phrase "unopposed propaganda." It packs a great truth. Neither the President nor the Administration nor the Republican party fought back.

The succeeding administration also came under violent attack—by many of the same men who were now providing millions for the Michelson Mills. But it disposed of veritable armies of defenders and counterattackers: not only the Michelson machine which it inherited but hundreds of special "public-relations" officers on the federal pay rolls attached to every one of the teeming New Deal agencies.

There was no such propaganda force, defensive or offensive, under Hoover. The shooting was all in one direction, with the President as the sole target. The Republican party—softened by the fat years of prosperity, sabotaged by self-styled progressives at one end and standpatters at the other—did not react to the smear campaign, and the President did not possess a personal political machine to take up his cudgels.

To complicate matters there was Hoover's almost pathological aversion to squabbling on the plane of personalities. When associates urged him to respond to ugly insults, he merely shrugged his shoulders in disgust. He had more important things to do, he insisted, than deny that he had robbed Chinese, promoted fake mines, made money on food relief, or remained indifferent to the misery of the unemployed. "If the American people choose to believe such nonsense," he once remarked to a secretary, "there is nothing I can do about it."

The unopposed propaganda hit the mark. Millions of well-meaning Americans still carry in their minds "facts" and "opinions" about Hoover which had been artfully invented and planted there by the Michelson outfit.

The job was so expertly done, indeed, that the self-same Raskob, du Ponts, and the rest in due time had to put up yet more millions *to undo their own handiwork*. For these are the gentry who organized and operated the Liberty League, with Jouett Shouse as director! In undertaking the campaign against Hoover, of course, they had not bargained for a New Deal. Only Michelson himself, who did not much care whether his $25,000 and expenses came through a Shouse or a Farley, remained after the original organizers disowned the New Deal epoch.

The partisan Democratic drive, of course, was supplemented by a prodigious private campaign that was, likewise, to continue long after Hoover left the White House. In 1932 Arthur Train, lawyer and author, could describe the published anti-Hoover stuff as "a veritable library of scurrilous books . . . written in terms of foulest abuse . . . conceived in partisan animosity, in the mere lust for profit, or in a surreptitious hope of blackmail."

The principal product of the Michelson Mills was so skillfully fashioned, so continually reinforced by repetition, that it persists to this day. It was the myth of a President who "did nothing." Not, mind you, that he did the wrong things but that he rejected responsibility and dawdled quiescently while his country went to hell. It was a cruel and indecent invention. It infuriated those around Hoover who begged that he relax from his exhausting labors and actually feared he might be crushed by the staggering weight of the responsibilities he assumed.

Of all the personal attacks hurled at him from all sides in the second election campaign, this was the only one the President deigned to answer. Speaking at Fort Wayne, Indiana, on October 12, 1932, he said:

"During my public life I have believed that sportsmanship and statesmanship called for the elimination of harsh personalities between opponents. . . . I shall say now the one harsh word that

I have uttered in public office. I hope it will be the last that I shall have to say.

"When you are told that the President of the United States, who by the most sacred trust of our nation is the President of all the people, a man of your own blood and upbringing, has sat in the White House for the last three years of your misfortune without troubling to know your burdens, without heartaches over your miseries and casualties, without summoning every avenue of skillful assistance irrespective of party or view, without using every ounce of his strength and straining his every nerve to protect and help, without using every possible agency of democracy that would bring aid, without putting aside personal ambition and humbling his pride of opinion, if that would serve—then I say to you that such statements are deliberate, intolerable falsehoods."

The "nothing" that he did, presented in bare outline, fills a closely printed book of 550 pages by Professor William Starr Myers and Walter H. Newton, *The Hoover Administration*. It fills the 640 pages of *The Hoover Policies* by Ray Lyman Wilbur and Arthur Mastic Hyde. I can touch only a few of its episodes, and that sketchily, in the chapters that follow.

CHAPTER XVII

In the Valley of Shadows

WHEN PRESIDENT HOOVER AN-
nounced from the White House that in any major economic
breakdown the Federal Government must assume responsibility—
that no American willing to work should go hungry—he was
establishing a new and audacious principle in federal theory and
practice.

Popular memory is lamentably short. Because that principle has
been widely accepted since then, few bother to recall that it was
first launched by Hoover, or that he was denounced on its account
by the guardians of economic and political orthodoxy.

The country suffered economic slumps and depressions in the
administrations of Van Buren, Buchanan, Grant, Cleveland, Theodore Roosevelt, and Wilson. In not one of them did the government take serious official action to relieve individual or business
distress. It would have been considered a shocking federal intrusion. The established theory was that an economic calamity must
run its ordained course, squeezing out the weak for a new start.

The latter-day myth-makers imply that the country from 1929
forward clamored for Washington intervention but that President
Hoover stubbornly resisted. The truth is the exact reverse. In pro-
jecting the government into the situation he was cutting boldly
across prejudice, tradition, and honest opposition within his own
official family.

Two schools of thought, reflecting national and historical
opinion, clashed in the Cabinet. Neither of them was wicked or

selfish or unpatriotic per se. Neither of them could claim a monopoly of human sympathy and good will. All those men had the commonweal at heart, but differed on how it could best be served.

One school, typified by Andrew Mellon, might be called "liquidationist"; it would permit depression to purge our economy the hard way, without government meddling. The other, typified by Hoover, was "interventionist," believing that the government must act to cushion the blows and care for the victims. Hoover being President, his school prevailed, and the rest loyally upheld his policies.

Those who thought like Mellon felt that after a runaway boom a sobering bust was not entirely evil. They held that it performed painful but needed service in liquidating swollen prices and wages, inflated real estate, and a gambling psychology. If not artificially restrained, it would squeeze out incompetents, misfits, parasites, driving people to work harder and live more austerely. It could be a forced retreat to sanity, an escape from unwholesome something-for-nothing delusions.

Mellon despised the Wall Street boom makers and wished to see them chastised. His was at bottom the attitude of the self-made small-town banker, distrustful of the New York manipulators, disdainful of their phony financial values. He was no more "heartless" than the surgeon who recommends a major operation. The great panic of the 1870s was fresh in his memories; the distress had been cruel; innocents had suffered with the guilty; but recovery came within a year. Now, he argued, the sum total of suffering would be less if economic nature had its way unhampered; official tinkering would prolong the agony without curing it. The fact that the depression did last eleven years, yielding finally only to the major surgery of war, makes one hesitate to dismiss his viewpoint out of hand.

The President countered, of course, that this was 1929, not 1870. In our industrialized society starving city dwellers cannot go back to the farm, as in the past. The farmers themselves were no longer self-sufficient. Unless the government intervened to keep depression within tolerable bounds, our complex social system would break down entirely, and a desperate people would reach out for false ideologies.

This was the liberal view. It stemmed naturally from Hoover's attitude to life. Given his deep-seated solicitude for suffering humanity, it was indeed inevitable. His own actions as Secretary of Commerce in the 1921 slump offered a point of departure. Thus it was that Professor Myers and Newton were able to write in their monumental study of the Administration:

"President Hoover was the first President in our history to offer federal leadership in mobilizing the economic resources of the people, and in calling upon individual initiative to accept definite responsibility for meeting the problem of the depression. This leadership, pioneering as it was, he confined to an arena of action clearly within the constitutional powers of the Federal Government. In some cases, where the threat to our economic or financial system came from abroad, he extended this leadership to world-wide action."

One can understand, therefore, why more conservative critics of the New Deal link Hoover with Roosevelt in their indictments. They charge that Roosevelt merely built on foundations laid by his predecessor; that he carried to devastating extremes the principle of federal intervention introduced by Hoover.

To a laissez-faire economist such as B. M. Anderson, for instance, the tragedy figures as the Hoover-Roosevelt depression. He is not "just another professor." From 1920 to 1937 he was editor of the influential *Chase Economic Bulletin*. In an essay included in a book on *Financing American Prosperity,* published in 1945, he writes:

We were probably still strong enough at the end of 1929 to have gone through an orderly reaction and depression, and to have come through with an orderly revival, if the government had refrained from interference. . . .

But the New Deal was in the saddle. The President of the United States, Mr. Hoover, the back-seat driver, called in the leaders of business, railroads, and public utilities to urge upon them the policy of not cutting prices, not cutting wages, and increasing capital outlay, and called upon the States and municipalities to increase public borrowing for public works. Purchasing power must be kept up! There must be no letdown! . . .

The Republican New Deal demoralized the markets and brought about the unprecedented depression and unemployment of 1932.

. . . The Democratic New Deal intensified the demoralization of the markets and perpetuated the depression and the unemployment.

The intrusion of government, cited by Dr. Anderson in blame, was cited recently from the other extreme in praise, by a left-wing economist. *Depression Decade* by Dr. Broadus Mitchell, published in 1947, is frankly pro-New Deal and weighted against Hoover. But Dr. Mitchell has respect for facts, and so we find him saying:

President Hoover . . . did much through domestic measures to allay the effects and even to reverse the course of the depression; as indisputable need dictated, he more and more laid aside his inhibitions for direct, forthright government action. His policies, explicit and implied, came closer to the program of the New Deal than has been generally recognized. And he was more mindful of the need of international treatment of the depression than the New Deal was. . . . Roosevelt, after a brief interval in which it seemed he would throw his force into the World Economic Conference, abandoned international responsibility, even disparaged it by fostering nationalist devices. . . .

Strictures by business spokesmen on Hoover's use of federal prestige did not have to wait for historical perspective. The Guaranty Trust Company of New York, for instance, declared soon after the market crash:

"The vigorous measures undertaken by the Government to combat the downward tendency in business have also injected an element of uncertainty. . . . Never before have public agencies interceded in such a direct and intensive way to alter the course of business, and the results (are) necessarily unpredictable."

Whether it rates praise or blame, the facts are crystal clear. Hoover did face up to the challenge of depression. Without precedents to guide him, against severe opposition, he did act quickly and sharply. Those who would strip him of credit for courage have said, "But this was not an ordinary depression; any President would have been forced to intervene." They blithely overlook the fact that the magnitude of the depression was not yet apparent in 1929–30 when Hoover made his pioneering decisions. Neither he nor anyone else could know what America was in for. Theirs is the wisdom of hindsight. "Yes, we could have done better—in retrospect," Hoover once remarked.

His intervention was twofold: through economic measures to cushion the impact and stave off panic; through direct relief to the needy. Though they are really inseparable, I must, for clarity sake, deal with them separately, and with small regard for chronology.

The great depression continued from October 1929 to November 1940, when World War II came bloodily to the rescue. It was not until the latter date that the pre-collapse peak of business was regained; and it is too generally forgotten that even on Pearl Harbor day we still had about 4,000,000 unemployed.

In deference to elementary facts, the reader should keep in mind that the artfully misnamed "Hoover depression" lasted eleven years, eight of them under President Roosevelt. In the spring of 1936 the score was about even, so to speak—Roosevelt had presided over as long a stretch of the tragedy as Hoover before him. At that point an eloquent liberal publicist, John Spargo, wrote an angry pamphlet demolishing *The Legend of Hoover Who Did Nothing.*

"It is a simple fact," he stated, "that on the day Franklin Roosevelt was elected President there were less workers unemployed, less people needing relief, than there have been on any day since then."

This is a literal truth, and a sobering one for over-zealous New Dealers. Roosevelt scored magnificently as a showman. He rallied mass sympathy and provided a three-ring circus. Jovially, almost as if it were an ingenious solution of all problems, he reconciled the country to a "permanent emergency." He compelled almost as much applause for his failures—as proof of noble intentions and high daring—as for his successes.

President Hoover, by contrast, was stoned for failures without the tiniest bouquet for achievements. He got none of the benefit of the doubt, for he dealt with a public opinion not yet acclimated to foul economic weather.

Besides, Roosevelt would dispose of endless billions of dollars and virtually "blanket" powers without parallel in time of peace and not many parallels in time of war. In effect he would be accountable only to himself, his Congress being servile and self-abasing.

Hoover had neither the billions nor the powers. He actually rejected them when they were urged upon him, because neither accorded with his concepts of government and free economy. Recently, in a speech by Secretary of Defense James Forrestal, who has learned a lot about government in time of national emergency, I found this striking statement:

". . . It's an easy thing for a man at the head of a state to acquire power if he wants it. And it sometimes takes the sharpest discipline not to accept that power."

President Hoover exercised that discipline at the price of political suicide. He not only abided strictly by the rules of the democratic game but blocked attempts to alter them in his favor. In the first year of the depression he faced a headstrong Congress, in the rest of his term a brutally hostile Congress. But out of devotion to the principle of separation of legislative and executive power, which is the heart of our democratic theory, he used none of the available tricks for circumventing Capitol Hill.

The point is not merely that Hoover did not seek to centralize control in the Federal Executive but that he continually pleaded with our people not to force it on him. In a radio address on Lincoln's Birthday in 1931, for example, he said:

"The moment responsibilities of any community, particularly in economic and social questions, are shifted from any part of the nation to Washington, then that community has subjected itself to a remote bureaucracy. . . . It has lost part of its voice in the control of its own destiny. . . ."

This dread of inflating government powers runs through all his acts and words. To safeguard constitutional government seemed to him as important as any of the colossal economic problems with which he wrestled. Writing on March 11, 1931, to a reporter who suggested enlargement of the federal functions, he said:

"I have the feeling that if you could sit in the middle of the government and see the tools with which we have to work and the disasters which confront us at all times in the use of these human tools, you would not want us to extend the area of government, but rather to keep the government as nearly as we can in its greatest function—the safeguarding of human rights."

The juggling of billions and the juggling of powers seemed to him equally dangerous in terms of the gigantic trust in his hands: the conservation of liberty. "Never was the lure of the rosy path to every panacea and of the easy ways to imagined security more tempting," he told the American people at a difficult juncture, when miracle cures were being peddled on a thousand political corners. At every turn he warned against "the equally specious claim that hired representatives of a hundred million people can do better than the people themselves in thinking and planning their daily life." It was precisely because he understood the fatal allure of the siren song of "the easy way for the moment of difficulty" that he begged his fellow countrymen to close their ears to it. Instead, and in full awareness that the advice was not good politics, he urged "the part of self-reliance, independence, and steadfastness in time of trial and stress."

2

The depression had its ups and downs, its seasons of illusive revival. The forty Hoover months—October 1929 to March 1933—divided into three distinct stages. The first and mildest began with the market crash and was almost entirely domestic. Signs of recovery were noted early in 1931. But within a few months, by April 1931, economic disasters in Europe blighted American hopes and touched off the second stage.

With several bright but disappointing reprieves, the movement was then dizzily downward until July 1, 1932, when the most clean-cut improvement began not only in America but in most of Europe. On the other side of the Atlantic it continued to the point of genuine recovery. In the United States, alas, it was violently arrested, as we shall see, and then turned into a tragic rout, largely by a presidential election.

The third stage covered the brief and disastrous interval between the election and inauguration of Roosevelt. The ship of state was in effect without a pilot in those bitter months: the defeated President was stripped of authority and the incoming one—who, not in law but in fact, had all the power—for reasons of his own "did nothing."

"During the administration of Hoover," Myers and Newton were to record, "the country was five times turned back from a like number of crises, any one of which threatened to produce the destruction which can come from an acute public and banking panic. . . . On each of these occasions the tide was turned almost wholly through the battles fought by President Hoover and his associates. The country gradually gained strength after each crisis was passed—only again to be swept by a new hurricane of economic trouble."

The sixth of these hurricanes, because it swept down on the nation after his defeat and in largest measure as the direct reaction to that defeat, the President could not turn back. That was when the banking panic of February and March 1933 overwhelmed us. It was in the Hoover portion of the depression only by the calendar; in simple justice it belongs in his successor's portion.

In the weeks after the stock-market bubble burst, the White House was turned into a first-aid station for emergency treatment of a nation even more shocked than burned. But few people— then or since—could see the picture whole or savor its stirring drama. There were no official press agents to blazon it in black type. And the unofficial ones, the correspondents, had to deal with a President seemingly allergic to headlines.

Hoover did what the head of a big business organization in sudden danger of bankruptcy would do, and with the same accent on privacy. He immediately called in the ablest and most responsible people in every department—agriculture, industry, labor, construction, railways, public utilities, social work—to consult on what could be done. In the final analysis he told them what he thought should be done.

Remember that he had no power from Congress or under the Constitution to compel any of them to co-operate. The heartening fact is that on the whole they did co-operate. The entire effort was voluntary—without directives, threats, or penalties. The President quieted those who were paralyzed by fear and alerted those who seemed too complacent.

A Federal Farm Board backed by $500,000,000 of federal capital had been established at Hoover's instance in the initial months of his administration. The very day after the market debacle he set this agency into motion to brace agricultural marketing co-operatives. Again and again it helped millions of farmers to weather the first storms.

One morning Hoover conferred with leading industrialists and key men in business organizations, among them such people as Henry Ford, Julius Rosenwald, Owen D. Young, Walter Teagle, Pierre duPont. That afternoon be conferred also with the spokesmen for organized labor, among them William Green, John L. Lewis, Frank Morrison, William L. Hutcheson, A. F. Whitney.

The result was a balanced agreement—the first of its kind on a national scale in American history—to maintain prices, wages, and industrial peace. The President warned industry that for its own good it could no longer treat workers as a "commodity," without regard to their human rights and needs. There would be no wage slashes, it was agreed, and as far as possible available work would be spread to hold layoffs down to a minimum. Industry also pledged itself to undertake capital repairs and construction. Labor at its end promised to avoid strikes and actually withdrew certain wage demands already announced.

Leading railroad officials, summoned to the White House, undertook not only to keep up but to expand construction. Similar understandings were reached with leaders of utilities (only Samuel Insull refusing), merchant marine, building, and construction.

Simultaneously the President instructed all federal departments to rush public works already authorized, amounting to $240,000,-000; and he lined up congressional leaders to support his request for an additional $423,000,000. This total of $663,000,000 in public works seemed gigantic at that time and brought outcries of extravagance.

Hoover also sent personal messages to all governors and leading mayors pleading for generous appropriations without delay for useful construction work. Governor Roosevelt's response had to be filed among the most lukewarm. He agreed to recommend a "much-needed construction program . . . limited only by estimated receipts from revenues without increasing taxes." As a tip-off on what he might have done had he presided over a nationwide, rather than merely statewide, depression the response makes interesting speculation.

Without ballyhoo or appeals to class antagonisms, 1930 thus witnessed an increase of $1,130,000,000 in construction activity over the boom year 1929. Some three billions in *stimulated* building, most of it the direct result of White House measures, made up for unavoidable construction declines, with one and a quarter billions to spare.

In his first post-depression message to Congress on December 3, 1929, the President necessarily avoided scare talk. Yet he left no margin for doubt as to the seriousness of the coming challenge. He asked for drastic banking laws (which Congress failed to enact), appropriations for job-making construction, economies in government to keep the budget in balance.

In its New Year issue at the end of that month the A. F. of L. official journal commended the President for his pressure on industrialists who "in earlier recessions . . . acted individually to protect their own interests." Corresponding praise for the new mood in labor appeared in business publications. It is a little-known fact that only 4,000,000 man-hours were lost annually through labor conflicts in the three depression years of the Hoover administration as against 19,000,000 annually in the three years after Hoover. There was actually no major strike or lockout in the entire Hoover period.

His various measures (I have mentioned only a small fraction of them) did not bring cure, but they assuredly brought improvement. "Indications are that the patient at the end of January has begun to recover," the New York *Times* declared on February 12, 1930. Six days later the President could announce that the Department of Labor index of employment, which dropped from 93.3 in October to 86.0 at the end of December, had now bounced back to 92.8. By May the financial pages reported tangible upturn in nearly all fields. We had reached a "point of improvement" and a "decidedly encouraging" one, William Green announced in June.

To keep the slump from degenerating into a panic, the President fought a hundred battles at the same time. He was a commander in chief of a war without trumpets and banners; a war fought mostly in the shadows, under continuous sniping by the very groups he was trying to help. Anyone interested in the detailed picture, at once heroic and heart-rending, of a President who ate and slept and lived with his work, driving those around him and especially himself to superhuman exertions, should read Theodore Joslin's *Hoover Off the Record*.

It was all, unfortunately, too much off the record. Activities which rated the number-one spot on the nation's front pages Hoover deliberately muffled in secrecy. Often important visitors were smuggled into and out of the White House through back doors to bypass publicity. Repeatedly the President betook himself to a rendezvous outside the White House to keep news hounds off the trail of some urgent scheme of salvage under discussion. He was the first President to install a telephone on his desk, so that he could consult people without the press notoriety attending a personal visit.

It is unhappily true that his relations with the press corps became ever more strained. That helped shape the unfavorable portrait of the Chief Executive projected to the public. Too many of the vital things he did during these years, Hoover felt, would be spoiled if exposed too soon to the limelight. His primary purpose was to prevent panic—but the spectacle of a President continually patching, conferring, pleading, pressing for action would have created justified alarm. He was much like the head of a family who keeps disturbing news from his loved ones. Because he had no stomach for white lies and no deftness in smiling evasions, Hoover repeatedly called off scheduled press conferences, though he knew the pressmen would be bitter.

Speaking in Des Moines in his second campaign, and referring to his entire depression struggle, Hoover said:

"Many of these battles had to be fought in silence, without the cheers of the limelight or the encouragement of public support, because the very disclosure of the forces opposed to us would have undermined the courage of the weak and induced panic in the timid, which would have destroyed the very basis of success.

"Hideous misrepresentation and unjustified complaint had to be accepted in silence. It was as if a great battle in war should be fought without public knowledge of any incident except the stream of dead and wounded from the front."

His position was scarcely a pleasant one. From where he sat the appalling facts of life were too clear for optimism. Yet it was his plain duty to sustain public morale and block the descent into defeatism. He knew that a depression feeds on bad news. Often the only road open to him was a retreat into silence, which would be misunderstood by friends and exploited by enemies.

A time came in 1932, for instance, when only passage of the Glass-Steagall Bill could save American currency from forced devaluation. Yet Hoover could not tell the country why he fought so desperately for the law; to do so would have brought on the catastrophe he was determined to intercept. Even in the election campaign that autumn, when he did finally tell the story, he withheld some parts of it because there was still danger in revealing them.

Neither at the start of the troubled time nor ever thereafter did President Hoover utter the phrase "prosperity around the corner." It has been exploited *ad nauseam* by the very tricksters who invented it and deliberately pinned it on him.

But even if he had said it, what, in all conscience, is the crime imputed to him? Simply that he seized upon symptoms of improvement to inject some confidence into a despairing people. Did his detractors expect a President of the United States to pronounce funeral orations over the living body of America? With so many others eager to assure the American people that faith in recuperation was an imbecilic delusion, should the Chief Executive have joined the dismal chorus? Has there ever been a President, before or after Hoover, who did not in time of stress invoke the nation's tradition of faith in survival?

Franklin Roosevelt, year after year, decried defeatism. His very smile was a banner of all-out optimism. He played variations on the theme "We have nothing to fear but fear itself," this in the face of stagnating industry and ten million unemployed and growing relief rolls. How did that theme differ in essence from Hoover's assurances that "We are suffering today more from frozen confidence than we are from frozen securities," and that renewed normality was not an impossible goal?

It was the goal to which he dedicated every thought, every waking minute, every fiber of his robust spirit. The most important fact is that he did believe in America; that in the larger, historical sense he remained optimistic always. "No one can occupy the high office of President and be other than completely confident of the future of the United States," he said in October 1930. "Perhaps as to no other place does the cheerful courage and power of a confident people reflect as to his office." And he added:

"There are a few folks in business and several folks in the political world who resent the notion that things will ever get better and who wish to enjoy our temporary misery. To recount to these persons the progress of co-operation between the people and the government in amelioration of this situation . . . only inspires the unkind retort that we should fix our gaze solely upon the unhappy features of the decline. . . . This is no time to talk of any surrender . . . the spirit of this people will never brook defeat."

3

As if nature itself were conspiring to undo his work, one of the worst droughts in national history hit huge areas of the Midwest and the South in the late summer of 1930. Its effects destroyed the marginal gains made in the preceding months. The President's friends smiled sadly: "Hoover will probably be blamed for this too." The jest nearly came true. If he was not blamed for the drought, he was blamed for its consequences.

About a third of all the states, about a million families and twenty million animals, were affected. The President induced the railroads to haul feed to drought sufferers at half the normal rates. He instructed the Department of Justice to report publicly any attempts to profiteer on food. He summoned the governors to Washington and with them worked out plans for swift relief. His orders went out to all federal departments to speed up highway, waterways, and flood-control projects in the afflicted regions to make new jobs.

In agreement with the President and the governors, the Red Cross assumed responsibility for a comprehensive job of direct succor. It earmarked funds for the purpose and undertook a public appeal, with the President's help, for more. Hoover asked Congress for a special thirty-million-dollar appropriation for drought relief, but this was over and above the Red Cross part of the job.

Never before had a problem of drought been met so promptly and fully by Washington. Yet even this new and extra emergency was grist for the Michelson Mills. To demonstrate that they were more charitable than the President, Democratic senators sought to raise his requested appropriation to sixty millions and compromised for forty-five. Then one of them, Harrison of Arkansas, introduced a bill granting twenty millions to the Red Cross—though Judge Payne, its chairman, and then its entire central committee, assured Congress that they did not need or want government gifts. The very proposal had the effect of freezing up private contributions, which are the lifeblood of the Red Cross.

Under its humane habiliments, the senatorial measure was of course strictly political; after two months of acrimonious debate it was defeated. For opposing it firmly, however, the President was pilloried from coast to coast as "heartless" and impervious to cries for help. Only a few months before this writing an acquaintance said to me in all earnestness, "But didn't Hoover refuse to help the Red Cross in the drought business?" The episode helped fortify the fable of a callous Chief Executive.

The Red Cross, in the final checkup, used only twelve of the fifteen million dollars it raised privately. Had Congress drawn on the taxpayers' money, few of those millions would have been obtained on the age-old basis of human sympathy. While the Senate debate was under way, a hue and cry was raised about "hunger riots" in Arkansas; army investigators rushed to the scene could find no trace of them.

The "easy" solution of every problem obviously was to take a billion or two out of the Treasury. In December 1930 depression appropriations before Congress, above those requested by the President, totaled nearly four and a half billions; in later sessions the ante was raised. Hoover set his face stubbornly against these assaults on the taxpayer. "We can't spend ourselves into prosperity," he insisted.

The very fact that the bills were nearly all on a purely geographical basis, rather than on the basis of need, supported the general suspicion that they were of the pork-barrel, vote-getting variety. The President did not hesitate to charge that some men were "playing politics at the expense of human misery." In a statement to the public at the end of 1930 he declared:

"Prosperity cannot be restored by raids on the Treasury. . . . Some of these schemes are ill-considered; some represent the desire of individuals to show that they are more generous . . . than even the leaders of their own parties."

By firm resistance and when necessary the use of his veto, Hoover defeated nearly all these proposals. He sought to provide jobs through public works; *more was spent for this purpose in his administration than in the preceding thirty-six years, including the building of the Panama Canal.* Immediately after its formation, the Reconstruction Finance Corporation was authorized to loan up to $1,800,000,000 for public works in addition to specific appropriations. Hoover, in fact, held himself ready to recommend as much federal aid as necessary for direct relief—to be administered through the states—as soon as the need arose. But he would not yield to pressures for mere political spending.

Which provided a Roman holiday for those who charged him with excessive caution, unfeeling stinginess. But amazingly this did not discourage charges—often by the same people—of reckless spending and failure to balance the budget. "Throw the spenders out!" was to be one of the prime anti-Hoover slogans in the 1932 campaign, along with sub-slogans implying that he did not spend enough.

Early in 1931 a movement for immediate payment of a bonus of $1,300,000,000 gained force. The President favored steps to care for unemployed and otherwise needy ex-soldiers, but not indiscriminate largesse. The bill was passed over his veto, to the accompaniment of catcalls in the direction of the White House. Charles G. Dawes, then Ambassador to London, watching the drama from afar, wrote a letter to the President which is worth quoting. To veto a bonus is politically risky and calls for high courage at any time, he said, but

"To veto one during the worst of an unprecedented business depression, at a time when the bill prompted by demagogism could be represented as one to relieve suffering, is an heroic thing. . . . You stood for a principle when you knew you would go down with it. . . ."

He stood for that principle again six months later, when a bill for an even larger bonus was filed. Hoover took the issue personally to the American Legion convention on September 21, 1931. To the amazement of politicians, the convention adopted a resolution supporting his view. This did not deter Congress from passing the measure.

Hoover himself initiated a series of reforms which had the effect of extending direct help to hundreds of thousands of veterans who really needed it. The arithmetical proof of this is in the fact that by the end of his term 853,000 disabled and destitute ex-soldiers or their dependents were on federal pay rolls compared with 376,000 at its start; the figure fell fast after he left the White House. But he considered the time unpropitious for payments to veterans who were working and well.

In the nature of the case I cannot here even allude to the hundreds of skirmishes and all-out battles marking the first stage of depression. The public saw only a tiny segment of its President's incessant contest with forces of destruction.

But by February of 1931 the press, business, labor, nearly everyone hailed clear signs of improvement. March marked a rise in the index for factory pay rolls from 68 to 75 in two months. In the first quarter, industrial output was up 5 per cent, pay rolls 10 per cent, stock prices 11 per cent.

Few had the grace or the insight to offer a word of appreciation to the man who had steered the ship of state safely through more shoals than were visible to the naked eye. The American Federation of Labor, which had co-operated with the White House right along, was among these few.

In his congressional message in December 1930 the President warned that "in the larger view the forces of depression now lie outside the United States." Five or six months later his prognosis came true. Disturbing, then terrifying news began to arrive from Europe. The *Kreditanstalt* of Vienna was in trouble. German banks tottered. The rest of the continent shook with these tremors. And American banks, loaded up with European obligations, began to feel the pinch. The green shoots of recovery which Hoover had coaxed into life were instantly withered.

He has been light-mindedly reproved for too much optimism. Yet when he argued that this country must soon feel the full impact of the European earthquakes, the chairman of the Federal Reserve, Eugene Meyer, denied that the danger was as grave as he claimed; other financial leaders insisted the President was seeing ghosts.

They soon turned out to be such lusty and mischievous ghosts that they all but pushed America over the precipice of full panic. The deepest slough of the world depression was reached between July 1931 and July 1932. Unemployment touched the ten million point. This was the year in which Hoover conducted not one but a series of desperate, soul-searing campaigns to save the nation from total economic chaos. He conducted them almost single-handedly—under the terrific handicap of a confused and partisan Congress; and under unceasing and ever uglier personal attacks and appeals to know-nothing mob angers.

"These events," Hoover later said about the world depression, "were not as children playing with blocks. They brought revolutions, mutinies, riots, downfall of governments, and a seething of despair which threatened civilization."

4

The President's initial plan for containing the world catastrophe was his proposal for a year's moratorium on all inter-government debts. Even his most cynical opponents conceded after a while that it was a daring and imaginative piece of financial statesmanship; for a moment the assembly line in the Michelson plant faltered.

The moratorium was conceived and hand-tooled by Hoover. He took congressional leaders of both parties into his confidence —one of them promptly violated the pledge to keep the idea secret, and thus nearly killed it aborning. Later, the President's mere announcement of the plan had a quieting effect on world finance. A full month the President labored day and night to put it over. He remained in hourly touch with American and foreign diplomats by transatlantic telephone—the first use of that instrument in international negotiations. At this end he bludgeoned political-minded congressmen into agreement.

Rarely had any action evoked such nearly unanimous acclaim. A British editor was quoted as exclaiming, "We look upon it as the greatest thing since the signing of the armistice." Prime Minister Ramsay MacDonald called it "an action of great wisdom, courage, and deep insight." The New York *Times* declared: "We cannot but wonder with the rest of the world at the happy revulsion of feeling which everywhere followed."

It was no more Hoover's fault than yours or mine that the effects of the moratorium were short-lived. Europe was much too sick for American medicine. It was beginning to pay the price of seventeen years of troubles postponed and compounded. And the American financial structure, after long years of unregulated foreign loans and credits, was organically linked to that shattered continent. The second and vastly more severe stretch of the depression was under way.

Consider the plight of the President, and the country, when he received the appalling news that staggering German banks, if they fell, would cancel out $1,700,000,000 in paper held by American institutions. This in addition to billions more in uncollectable foreign debts about which he was aware. European banks outside Germany, too, carried mountains of bad paper. A German default would have tumbled most of Europe and a large part of America into a common pauper's grave. Matters were not made easier for the President by the absolute need to conceal the extent of the looming disaster—the news would have toppled the whole shaky financial world into a helpless heap.

It was then that Hoover again saved the situation with what came to be known as his "standstill" agreement, under which a year's leeway on large quantities of short international credits was conceded by all the nations affected. To safeguard his own country the President had to assume firm world leadership, and that he did. As usual, great pressure was exerted to make the American taxpayer foot the bill. But Hoover insisted that it was entirely a banker-made crisis which the banks themselves must finance, and exacted world-wide acquiescence by main force.

Together, the moratorium and the standstill saved the United States from the second of the potential panics to which Myers and Newton referred. Other such threats came in rapid succession, each of them loaded with dynamite to blow our enfeebled economy to smithereens.

The third major crisis arose on September 21, 1931, when England went off the gold standard, and fifteen to twenty other countries quickly followed suit. The President had authorized two loans, totaling $625,000,000, to Britain in a desperate effort to prevent default on gold. But it could no longer be prevented. For the first time in a century the expression "safe as the Bank of England" became a joke.

The impact on America was stunning. Convinced that this country was next, foreigners began to withdraw gold as fast as bottoms could be found to ship it. In five months our pay rolls fell off 20 per cent, meaning millions more on relief; stocks declined 40 per cent. Dozens of banks failed. It was into this maelstrom of disaster, incidentally, that calculated demagogy tossed a three-billion-dollar bonus time bomb.

What little hope remained for the world resided here in America which became, in Hoover's apt phrase, "the Verdun of world stability." In off-record meetings with the press and other groups of opinion leaders he begged for co-operation in bolstering morale and keeping the boat steady. By a hundred devices, always under the dampers of a stepped-up personal smear campaign, the President avoided a third panic.

In this period Hoover called a secret conference with bankers. He knew what some of them only guessed. A calamitous breakdown of the national bank structure—the kind that did come ultimately, when Hoover no longer had the power or machinery to prop the structure—was imminent. He convinced them that they must act together by pooling resources to reinforce the weakest links in their chain. Out of this came the National Credit Association, with a half billion dollars and Federal Reserve support. Chaos was again headed off.

He also met with insurance, mortgage, building and loan groups. Together they worked out a program that soon took form in the Home Loan Discount Banks, which saved hundreds of thousands of homes and farms.

The Seventy-second Congress, elected in November 1930, was under firm Democratic control and seemingly dedicated to embarrassing, hamstringing, and ultimately defeating Hoover. Promises to co-operate with the Administration, made to reassure an alarmed country, were utterly forgotten in practice.

This Congress gathered again in December 1931, at a time when the crisis was global, the threat at its peak. Singly and in groups, Hoover conferred with one hundred and sixty senators and representatives of both parties. He pleaded for an end to obstruction, for constructive action. He humbled his pride of office and swallowed personal humiliations to obtain grudging promises of nonpartisan action on a patriotic basis. The promises were broken almost from the first day. A presidential election was just over the horizon; politics had the right of way.

In his message to Congress that month the President presented an extensive program of more than twenty sections which (even if there were nothing else) stands on the record to refute the do-nothing legend. "We must put some steel beams in the foundations of our credit structure," he warned. The sturdiest of these beams was his proposed Reconstruction Finance Corporation, with federal funds of half a billion dollars, authority to borrow up to three billions, and room for further expansion as needed.

In addition he asked for far-reaching revision of bankruptcy laws; cuts in appropriations and new taxation in the upper brackets; public works that would bring the total for the following year to $780,000,000; reform of the Stock Exchange and financial promotion methods; home loan banks to protect farms and residences; prompt improvement of banking laws to bring more of these institutions under reliable regulation; measures to unfreeze deposits in closed-down banks; expansion of federal reserve credit to meet the pressure of foreign withdrawals; continuation of Farm Board funds to prevent panic selling of farm products; specific types of co-operation with other governments to promote world recovery. He also asked for $300,000,000 for direct relief— to be used and administered through the states now that some areas were exhausting their own resources.

The President agreed to take Democratic leaders and recalcitrant Republicans into fullest confidence on his every move. If they preferred to legislate on a program of their own, or on a program combining features of his plan with their proposals, the White House stood ready and anxious to co-operate. The need was prompt remedial action in a dozen urgent directions.

But the opposition chose delay and obstruction. Now, as in the previous session, they would neither go along with Hoover's ideas nor offer a balanced counter-plan. Their job, they sent word to the President, was only to "scrutinize" his proposals. When pressed by the Republican House leader, Bertram Snell, his Democratic colleague, Rainey of Illinois, admitted with beguiling candor: "We intend to beat him—Hoover."

As one studies the story of that session, the feeling is inescapable that the hope of delaying recovery until after election had inflamed partisan sentiment to a disastrous degree. While blocking action on Hoover's requests, the Senate and the House merely pushed piecemeal "solutions" that came down to indiscriminate raids on the Treasury.

To ward off public wrath, the obstructionist group indulged in oratorical flights about the sufferings of the people. Practically, however, they held up the R.F.C. bill for six weeks, during which a new mass of suffering that could have been obviated by the R.F.C. came into being. Even at that they curtailed some of the powers asked for—powers which would be promptly accorded to the R.F.C. when Roosevelt asked for them. Congress took seven weeks to authorize additional funds for the Federal Loan Bank.

Not until February did they pass the Glass-Steagall Bill, proposed by Hoover, when the country was being swiftly forced off gold. That was another of the crises of which the nation at large knew nothing. By its very nature it had to be kept secret. But most of those who dawdled did know what it was all about. In finally pushing the bill through against massed opposition, Hoover made sure that American currency continued to "ring true on every counter of the world."

For six months that amazing Congress backed and stalled and played politics, doing little itself and tying the President's hands.

Its procrastination became a national scandal, so that the press, Democratic as well as Republican, spoke out more and more sharply in criticism. The President made scores of direct and indirect pleas, offers, demands for action on the budget and other financial legislation, as congressional obduracy became for a time the most serious barrier to recovery.

In connection with one of Hoover's messages, the Baltimore *Sun* (May 6, 1932) declared editorially: "Congress deserves what it has been given. It asked for all it has been given. Mr. Hoover's message is an unanswerable indictment. Bitter and savage as it is, in substance it is no more than a summary of the proceedings of Congress in the last two months. . . . Congress has flagrantly and disgracefully deserted its own standards. . . . Congress has missed no opportunity to disembowel the policy of orthodox finance. . . ."

The New York *Times* pointed out: "On the importance of federal retrenchment and the necessity of balancing the budget he (Hoover) has spoken in no less than twenty-one messages, statements, and addresses. . . . Responsibility for the chaos which now exists in Washington rests upon those members of Congress who have blocked the President at every turn and bolted their own party leadership."

This legislative paralysis, indeed, was the primary cause of the fifth of the crises to which we have made reference. On May 30, 1932, the President addressed the Senate in person to demand an end to the impasse. Luckily the almost unanimous press support and growing public disgust with the whole spectacle enabled Hoover to crash through. After his speech a sobered Senate remained in session until midnight and passed the revenue bill that had gathered dust for six months.

The prestige of Congress, as a result of its performance, was at its lowest ebb in this century. It was this, more than any other single factor, which made it possible for Hoover's successor to turn the legislative branch of our government into an ignominious rubber stamp for the executive.

The President could neither jolt Congress into tackling the problem of Stock Exchange abuses nor force action by the New York State authorities, with whom the primary responsibility rested. The press recalled that in a similar situation, when abuses by insurance companies were involved, another New York governor had not hesitated to act vigorously. But Governor Roosevelt, his eyes fixed on the next election, would not budge. In the end Hoover obtained a Senate investigation of the Stock Exchange despite powerful opposition inside and outside Congress. Subsequent federal regulatory laws, for which Hoover of course got none of the credit, grew out of this investigation.

A premonitory betterment in economic conditions could be discerned in the middle of March 1932. It was drowned in a flood of inflationary bills and buried by obstructionist tactics. Soon after Congress adjourned, however, the situation looked up again. In July a remarkable turn for the better became manifest and continued encouragingly until the election.

Shortly before he departed from the White House, the President summed up his dilemma, the dilemma of every President unlucky enough to serve during major depression, in talking to Joslin, who has recorded his words.

"What I have tried to do during these years," he said, "has been to save the American people from disaster. They do not know what they have missed. Because they don't know what they have missed, they are dissatisfied with what has been done. In such circumstances, they turn to other leaders.

"A former European official recently observed that statesmen, in trying to prevent disaster, kill themselves off. He might say that my tactics have been wrong, that I should have waited until the American people were half-drowned and then have waded in and tried to save them. In such an event, they would, of course, have known what it was all about. But it would have meant catastrophe!"

President Hoover's was the heartbreaking task of plugging leaks to keep the ship from sinking. The mean of spirit castigated the captain for failing to make port, instead of cheering him for keeping their battered vessel afloat.

CHAPTER XVIII

Relief Policies

THE PRESIDENTIAL CAMPAIGN OF 1932 which defeated Herbert Hoover was one of the most fiercely fought in our political history. The total output of the Michelson Mills—low-grade smear stuff manufactured at a cost of more than two million dollars to the millionaire backers—was at the disposal of the mud-gunners. Vicious anti-Hoover books compounded of falsehood and forgery (as the chief of the authors himself contritely confessed) were in circulation. Every real and fancied popular grievance was exploited to the limit.

But one hot issue was strangely, inexplicably neglected. This is the more curious when we recall that in later years, long after the election, it was promoted to the head of the list in the indictments of President Hoover. Looking back on the campaign from a decade's distance, Hoover himself would allude to the amazing oversight.

"Upon coming into office the New Deal Administration," he said, "claimed that millions of people were starving and that nothing had been done in the way of real relief. *Had that been true, they would not have failed to say so during the presidential campaign.* It would have been the best possible vote getter. But since it was manifestly not true, this charge would have antagonized that great body of devoted people who were carrying on the work efficiently in the spirit of neighborliness and kindness and patriotism."

There were as many Democrats as Republicans in that great

humanitarian army. They were not there under party labels but simply as Americans and as human beings. In the literature of that campaign of 1932, which I have examined with some care, there is scarcely a trace of the fairy tale of mass starvation. It made a timid debut here and there in the invective of extreme left-wing propaganda, but it did not figure in the basic Democratic thesis.

Clearly the idea was a fabrication of somewhat later vintage. At the moment such an accusation could not be made to stick. Every community knew that its own needy were being cared for by groups of local citizens; that private and public agencies in unexampled co-operation on a non-partisan basis were proving themselves effective.

The economic debacle of 1929 found at the helm in Washington the man who was unquestionably the world's greatest expert on large-scale relief of human suffering. In that fact one is tempted to trace a divine intention. Hoover had raised benevolence to a science. He had organized, administered, and financed the succor of hundreds of millions under the most unfavorable conditions. Because of his unique ability to mobilize good will, he had fed nations and a continent with unprecedented economy.

The premise that this man refused to use his rare talents to the fullest when his own flesh and blood faced destitution simply makes no sense. It is an indecent lie, to which only a generation drugged and dizzied by propaganda could have given a moment's credence.

There is ample room for debate as to the relative efficacy of the theory and methods of relief applied by President Hoover and his successor. The two systems were universes apart in spirit and substance. Hoover rallied primarily (though not exclusively) local, volunteer, non-political forces; the New Deal relied on a vast and costly federal bureaucracy. The first rested on the alerted neighborhood, the second on the welfare state. The first was frankly an emergency setup; it did not accept the notion that relief would be a permanent function of the Federal Government with its own civil service. The second was geared more and more to the assumption of eternal, systematized destitution.

Under both dispensations there were hardships, failures, in-

justices, and for the victims anguish of spirit. No effort of these
dimensions is without its faults and fumblings. But there is no
room for debate on the scope, the earnestness, the sincerity, and
the essential success of the relief enterprise under Hoover.

Throughout his experience Hoover had learned that the most
reliable measure of a relief effort was the health of the population involved. There is, indeed, no other way to gauge the progress of undernourishment. The reports of social workers "on the
spot" may be subjective, colored by irritation or the hope of
larger subsidies. Death and health statistics are matters of record.

Periodically, therefore, he had Surgeon-General Hugh S. Cummings provide him with surveys. They showed a declining death
rate, especially—the most sensitive and revealing area—among
infants under one year. On January 2, 1932, Dr. Cummings reported that "infant mortality during the past year was definitely
lower than in any preceding year on record." The president of
the American Public Health Association in October 1932 declared
in a formal statement that "By and large the health of the people
as measured in sickness and death has never been better despite
the depression."

Advocates of the relief theory subsequently adopted under
Roosevelt were sufficiently vocal from the start, in particular
the ambitious political leaders. They wanted centralized distribution of billions of dollars in federal grants. There were Republicans among them as well as Democrats. No doubt their system
would have "simplified" matters. There would have been no
recourse to private charitable instincts, no appeals to local communities to pitch in—and a vote dividend for the politicians commanding the largest slice of those billions.

President Hoover was profoundly convinced that such dependence on the Federal Treasury "would bring an inevitable train of
corruption and waste" and partisan exploitation of a people's
calamities. The alternative, his own conception, was not improvised. It was a strategy carefully developed through long
years of experience. Its essence can be summed up in four paragraphs:

1. Local resources—the neighbor, the existing social agency,
the municipality, the state—represent the first lines of defense

against distress. Being in lifelong contact with the victims of the depression, local volunteers would bring their hearts, not merely red tape and badges, to their undertaking. They would not easily be imposed upon by chiselers and malingerers, thus leaving more for the families in real distress.

2. The Federal Government is the last line of defense, in constant readiness to provide effective help if and when the first lines weaken. Meanwhile, however, it is not inert. It seeks to reduce the size of the problem by means of public works, the stimulation of capital investment, the spread of work, and other methods. Most important, it bolsters the whole economic structure, its financial institutions, its currency, its system of credit.

3. When it becomes necessary for the United States Treasury to make grants, the funds are not divided indiscriminately on a population basis but strictly in relation to actual needs, and their administration is left with the states through their local committees. This has at least three vital purposes: It makes unnecessary an immense federal personnel; it keeps down the incidence of patronage and pork-barrel diversions; and it continues to utilize human good will and voluntary services to the maximum.

4. The effort as a whole is treated as an "emergency program" for meeting specific needs. It is not an excuse "to implant a new social philosophy in American life in conflict with the primary concepts of American liberty."

"It is not the function of the Government," Hoover argued, "to relieve individuals of their responsibilities to their neighbors, or to relieve private institutions of their responsibilities to the public, or of local governments to the states, or of the state governments to the Federal Government."

While giving its guidance and when necessary its financial support, he added, "the Federal Government must insist that all of them exert their responsibilities in full. It is vital that the programs of the Government shall not compete with or replace any of them but shall add to their initiative and their strength. It is vital that by the use of public revenues and public credit in emergency the nation shall be strengthened and not weakened."

The self-respect and self-reliance of the community seemed to him values to be cherished, quite aside from the greater effi-

ciency and economy of his strategy. He saw only grief and moral
debility from "a cold and distant charity which puts out its sympathy only through the tax collector (and) yields a very meager
dole of unloving and perfunctory relief."

2

In pursuance of that strategy Hoover in October 1930 set up
the President's Emergency Relief Organization. This, in turn,
formed State Unemployment Relief Committees, whose work
was decentralized through thousands of county and city committees run by respected local leaders. The Washington staff,
except for purely secretarial work, was largely voluntary. Several
dozen inspectors crisscrossed the country to check complaints
and make sure there were no failures.

Periodically, until the end of his term, the President resurveyed
the situation, enlarging the organization to meet new demands,
and raising funds from many sources as needed. At his request
the Friends' Service, the Quaker organization, assumed the task
of feeding children in coal regions. Other such private agencies
were given special assignments to solve problems within their
special capacities.

Early in 1932 he determined to apply surplus commodities in
the hands of the Farm Board for direct relief. The grain earmarked for this purpose provided enough flour to supply six
million families for nine months. The cotton sufficed to clothe
four million families. This relief was administered by the Red
Cross.

No purely bookkeeping total of this kind of relief is possible,
since it did not flow from one source and was not managed by a
single agency. There is no arithmetic to compass the thousand
varieties of aid evoked by the continous appeals to self-help and
community spirit. It came abundantly from neighbors, employers,
social organizations, regional and state treasuries.

In later years these sources were for the most part choked off.
The national government undertook to do it all by taxing and
borrowing to the limit. Where the overhead for relief administration under Hoover rarely exceeded 3 per cent, it came to

consume from 25 to 50 per cent after his departure. Despite the launching of many new agencies, there were 10,000 fewer federal employees at the end of Hoover's term than at its start. At the end of the first New Deal term their number grew by 335,000. There was more than the proverbial man from Mars could have guessed in Hoover's remark at that later date:

"In his Jackson Day speech the President urged committees of one to support the New Deal. He has a good start with 335,000 committees—and their wives."

Relief on a regimented federal basis, he believed, would be especially tempting to politicians. Surveying the New Deal landscape after a few years, he felt justified in speaking of politicians as miners digging votes:

"They extracted this precious ore not only from the families dependent on the WPA, the CCC, and similar alphabetical organizations but from their relatives to the third and fourth degrees, from employees of the local bureaucracy formed to bestow these benefits. And they mined it in great nuggets from communities— preferably those on the doubtful list of political managers—on which they bestowed special favors at the expense of the government. Votes are the professional politicians' idea of the food of the gods, which is kept in pork barrels."

His obstinacy in barring the way to those barrels was deeply resented and the resentment now and then took startlingly petty forms. Thus on July 15, 1932, the President applied to Congress for an emergency appropriation of $120,000—thousands, not millions—to help pay purely clerical expenses of the nationwide relief effort. He pointed out that the organization was rigidly nonpartisan and that its members received no pay. Congress—the same Congress which a year later was shelling out billions and no questions asked—refused the appropriation. The President had to raise the money from private sources, one of them being his own pocket.

Hoover took no satisfaction in later years when the worst of his forebodings about waste and political corruption under a federalized relief system came true. By 1936 relief scandals, charges of vote-getting manipulation of relief projects, a swollen bureaucracy dedicated to its own perpetuation, were matters of common knowledge. Discussing relief procedures before a woman's organization in New York, Hoover asked his audience to go back and read the press of 1930–32 for contrast.

"It discloses that, aside from the sporadic accidents of any system, there were no criticisms for relief failure," he said. "No one starved. There were no daily headlines of fraud. There was much appeal for funds and painting of the need, but no painting of failure to provide. In the presidential campaign of 1932 . . . not a single charge against relief was made of politics, of waste, of corruption, or failure to prevent hunger or cold."

Each time he warded off another assault on the Treasury Hoover touched off new cries of "heartlessness." On one such occasion he felt it necessary to address the American people.

"This is not an issue as to whether people shall go hungry and cold in the United States," he declared. "It is solely a question of the best method by which hunger and cold shall be prevented. . . . The help being daily extended by neighbors, by local and national agencies, by municipalities, by industry, and a great multitude of organizations throughout the country today is many times any appropriations yet proposed. The opening of the doors of the Federal Treasury is likely to stifle this giving and thus destroy far more resources than the proposed charity from the Federal Government. . . .

"I am willing to pledge myself that if the time should ever come that the voluntary agencies of the country together with the local and state governments are unable to find resources with which to prevent hunger and suffering in my country, I will ask the aid of every resource of the Federal Government, because I would no more see starvation amongst my countrymen than any senator or congressman."

In the last year of his incumbency he made good on that pledge. Until then forty-seven of the forty-eight states (and the exception was *not* New York) had indicated officially that Washington grants-in-aid were not yet required. Then growing stringency of local resources made federal help necessary. Hoover obtained congressional consent for $300,000,000 in loans to states, to be administered through the existing committees, and made it clear that more would be available as the need arose. Meanwhile some 750,000 new jobs were created in public works and additional hundreds of thousands of veterans were placed on various pension roles.

Having outlined his philosophy of decentralized relief, Hoover was able to report in retrospect:

"This was the basis of organization for three years—1930, 1931, and 1932. At that time, when it was my duty to see that relief to unemployment was assured, we spread over the country a network of local volunteer committees free from political domination. As the need of relief increased, the number and authority of these committees were extended until there were more than three thousand of them. They were co-ordinated under state-wide committees by the national director of relief. They used existing organizations and the local authorities.

"This committee structure hired such paid staff as they required. The committees received no pay. Citizens of the type needed for such administration require no pay. They did the work with a minimum of administrative machinery and a maximum of volunteer services. They found jobs for the unemployed. They created a spirit in the community that held people from being discharged. They co-ordinated municipal, county, state, federal, and private funds.

"They knew their own people and the needs of their localities. They were able to act without red tape. They determined whether relief was to be applied in cash, or in kind, or by work relief, as the immediate local needs required. They gave particular solicitude to children. They gave encouragement and hope. They were doing neither politics nor social reform. They were taking care of distress. From 1933 that organization was replaced or reduced to a façade by federal centralization."

3

Let me quote a few interesting sentences. They date back to the time when Hoover was still President.

"I am opposed to any dole. I do not believe that the state has any right merely to hand out money. . . . People suggest that a huge expenditure of public funds by the Federal Government and

by state and local governments will completely solve unemployment . . . . let us admit frankly that it would be only a stopgap.
. . . Under no circumstances shall any money be paid in the form
of a dole or any other form by the local welfare officer to any
unemployed or his family. . . . Revenues must cover expenditures by one means or another. Any government, like any family,
can for a year spend a little more than it earns, but you and I
know that a continuation of that habit means the poorhouse. . . .
High-sounding, newly invented phrases cannot sugar-coat the
pill. Let us have the courage to stop borrowing to meet continuing deficits. Stop the deficits."

The man who spoke in this vein was not Hoover, but Franklin
D. Roosevelt in the course of his successful campaign to replace
Hoover. Even before that, at a conference of governors in Salt
Lake City, he denounced the "dole" as a "character-destroying"
device. Nor did he complain about his state and municipalities
being burdened with responsibilities that should have been shouldered by the Washington government.

What I want to indicate is that the stick with which Hoover's
character was so mercilessly belabored in subsequent years—the
charge of failure to give relief and refusal to open wide the Treasury for this purpose—was fashioned long *after* he moved out of
the White House. In so far as that charge was used at all by the
Democratic candidate, it was used carefully and sparingly.

Of the two conflicting sins imputed to Hoover, parsimony and
extravagance, it was the latter that was selected as the more deadly
by the anti-Hoover forces in the crucial hour. "Throw the
spenders out!" was the theme song, as I have already indicated.

The Democratic candidate pledged himself to "a saving of not
less than 25 per cent of the cost of Federal Government," and accused the Hoover administration "of being the greatest spending
administration in peacetime in all our history." Yet it was apparent to every open-eyed American that the excess spending was
for job-making purposes like new public works and business encouragement agencies like the R.F.C.

None of which jibes with the do-nothing legend in the domain
of relief any more than in other domains of the emergency activities of the Hoover years.

Another of the sticks for beating an ex-President shaped and embellished through the years has a tough knob in the form of an apple. The matter, for all the noise it has made, is so trivial that one blushes in writing about it. Suddenly unemployed veterans and others appeared on city streets selling apples. In all of those cities facilities for direct relief were available. The whole dismal project was worked up by Oregon and Washington apple-growers. Shrewdly exploiting the public sympathy for the unemployed, they mobilized salesmen for their excess wares, with lush profits for themselves and lush propaganda materials for others.

A more serious episode was the self-styled bonus march. This has been so outrageously distorted that the most significant fact about it should be stated at once. It is that the violence developed *before* the President intervened and ceased after his intervention. As General Patrick J. Hurley, then Secretary of War, put it to me in a recent personal letter: *"Not one single shot was fired nor was any person seriously injured after the arrival of the United States troops. Law and order was established in Washington."*

As a result of an agitation which was largely communist-inspired (as communist leaders subsequently boasted under oath) some 12,000 real and alleged veterans encamped in Washington to demand a huge bonus in June and July 1932. They were treated with the utmost patience by local authorities, though extremist leaders openly sought to provoke trouble. At the President's request, Congress voted return fare for those willing to leave and about 6,000 availed themselves of the offer.

Later the government obtained the names of more than 2,000 who had remained; it was established that less than one third of them had ever served in our armies and that more than 900 were ex-convicts. About fifty of the "marchers" occupied some old buildings scheduled for razing to make way for public constructions to give hundreds of men jobs. On July 28 the extremists had their way and the long-delayed "incident" was manufactured.

That day the Washington police requested the squatters to move. Suddenly about a thousand of the men camped outside the city limits concentrated on the scene, armed with clubs, and a riot was under way. Two policemen, surrounded and endangered, began to shoot, killing two men and wounding others.

At that point the civil officials—the Commissioners of the District of Columbia—appealed to the President in writing to send federal force to prevent further bloodshed. Hoover had little if any choice in the matter. As General Douglas MacArthur phrased it in a statement that night: "The President played it pretty fine in waiting to the last minute; but he didn't have much margin." His point, and there is no room for disputing it, was that had the President refused to act the situation, already out of hand, would have had far more tragic consequences.

With the arrival of Uncle Sam's soldiers, all violence ceased. Far from "shooting down bonus marchers," as communist propaganda has repeated for sixteen years and will repeat for sixteen more, Hoover's action put an end to shooting. The 600 troops carried no deadly weapons. Probably the military men went beyond the President's orders in dispersing all the encamped "marchers" instead of merely restoring order in the city as his instructions specifically stated. Be that as it may, no blood was spilled after the Army took over from the civil authorities. The accusations against Hoover, it thus appears, are not merely untrue but the exact opposite of the truth.

Few minor incidents in American history have been so viciously misrepresented. The decision the President made was under the circumstances unavoidable; he would have been criminally neglectful of his clear duty if he had done less. That did not save him from being reviled as a "killer" nor did it stop the political opposition from using garbled versions of the facts to rally veteran votes. A revealing light on the "build-up" that began in the camp of his political enemies almost immediately is provided by the behavior of the Hearst newspaper in Washington. In an editorial on the night of the riots it eulogized the President for his prompt action; but next morning it blossomed out with headlines accusing him of bloodshed.

The American Legion, it should be noted to its credit, did not then or ever after join in the unfair abuse. When Secretary Hurley came to its next convention and recounted the facts, he was accorded a warm and approving reception.

But to return to the subject of relief. That Hoover's fear of waste in a politicalized federal monopoly, as against the voluntary grass-roots system he put into effect, was amply justified became evident quickly. Speaking in 1936, he referred to a sample of such wastes:

"Recently I had the opportunity to observe comparative morals in the spoils systems by a contrast between Tammany Hall and the New Deal. In a Tammany-dominated borough in New York in early 1933 before the New Deal, there were about 11,000 persons on relief. Tammany had appointed about 270 additional officials under their particular spoils system to manage relief at a cost of under $30,000 a month for the officials. This job was taken away from wicked Tammany influence and directly administered by the New Deal.

"At a recent date there were in the same borough 2,000 federal officials appointed under the New Deal spoils system at a cost of $300,000 per month for salaries to manage 16,000 persons on relief. Tammany may learn something new in this spoils system. It was only 10 per cent efficient. And the same thing is going on all over the country."

The New York *Times* provided figures which should have shamed Tammany further. The Resettlement Administration, the newspaper claimed, employed 12,089 federal officials and was giving relief to 5,012 persons or families. The monthly cost for officials was $1,750,000 and the relief cost $300,000. Each family, in other words, had $350 worth of official supervision with its $60 of relief.

No doubt these are exceptional samples. In kind if not in degree, however, they are typical. They help explain why President Hoover was so anxious to keep relief out of the political arena.

The fable spread with unflagging industry by his foes that he was indifferent to the sufferings of the unemployed is ugly and threadbare. It should be lifted gingerly and dropped into the garbage can of history where such offal belongs.

CHAPTER XIX

Defeat—and Panic

THERE MAY BE DOUBTS AS TO WHETHER
President Hoover's system of relief through local self-help, from
the bottom up instead of the top down, was good public policy.
There is no doubt at all that it was wretched politics. It utilized
none of the vote-getting magic of open-handedness with public
funds. Worse, it guaranteed that his administration would garner
the most blame and the least appreciation.

The vote potential in food and funds to the needy would be
demonstrated on a gigantic scale in due time. But Hoover fixed
it so that all largesse, the federal contribution included, came
through the city, county, and state. These consequently reaped all
the credit, while a seemingly inert Federal Government reaped
only the odium of relief failure and confusion where these occurred. A billion dollars handed out by officials of the welfare
state, with appropriate demagogic noises, is one thing; the same
billion raised from many sources and administered by local volunteer committees is quite another thing.

Perhaps the most harmful fact about the Hoover system, judged
as politics, was that it provided maximum visibility for the grim-
mer side of depression and unemployment. It failed to sugar-coat
or conceal unpleasant realities. Hoover's repeated appeals to the
nation's charitable feelings kept the consciousness of destitution
always to the fore. You don't get contributions by minimizing the
needs. Every new fund-raising drive naturally played up the grave

sufferings. Hoover did not set millions to raking leaves, flailing water, daubing walls, writing guidebooks and gibberish.

Average annual unemployment during the Hoover administration was 6.2 millions. In the first two Roosevelt administrations, that is to say until war came, it was 9.9 millions. But the general impression is the exact reverse. The illusion that the country was "better off" in the New Deal era has little reference to economic fact. In largest part it was the product of superb showmanship. It is exhilarating to watch rabbits being pulled out of hats even if they are papier-mâché rabbits and inedible.

The mere passage of time, too, had a lot to do with the growing sense of well-being after Hoover. The man who loses a fortune or a limb is at first tragic and embittered, but in time he adjusts himself to the loss. Awareness of the economic disaster, of the contrast with recent prosperity, was painfully sharp in the early years. Then it gradually lost its sting; idleness and want became almost a new way of life, and dependence on government hand-outs became for thousands a preferred way of life.

The angers and frustrations of the slump were at peak points as the 1932 presidential campaign shaped up. The American people, distressed, confused, and afraid, needed a scapegoat. Hoover had been widely heralded—by others, never by himself—as a "miracle man," but no miracles were forthcoming. In the emotional shorthand of political folklore, which has nothing in common with fact and logic, his name came to mean hardship and despair. A President became the whipping-boy of his country.

It was a picture made to order for specialists in partisan malice. The Shouse-Michelson outfit, the self-styled Republican "progressives," the communists whose influence was then growing fast, the assorted prophets of "national planning," funny money, and other shortcuts to Utopia—all of them found a common focus in abuse of the President. Not content with assailing his policies, they impugned his motives and tried to besmirch his character.

He was blamed for all the aches and pains of a desperately sick world. In his book Michelson lightly flipped off the charge that his factory smeared the President; but a few pages further he alluded casually to "the gloomy occupant of the White House

whom we referred to as *the author of the depression.*" Perhaps he
was right—"smear" is too mild a word for such injustice.

During the recent war the English novelist Rebecca West wrote
as stinging an attack on Hoover as ever came his way. But she
had the decency to preface it with some sense.

"Mr. Hoover's term as President," she wrote, "was in the eyes
of others a tragical passage of American history, for reasons that
cannot be accounted to his discredit. It was not his fault that in
the autumn of his first year in office there broke on the United
States a dire economic catastrophe, a slump comparable to the
droughts and famines which afflict tropical lands."

No such common sense had a chance in that time of affliction.
The shameless phrase "the Hoover depression" is about as imbecilic as "the Teddy Roosevelt earthquake" in California or "the
Truman blizzard" of 1947 would be. But once it was insinuated
into everyday speech by the political profiteers of calamity there
was no need for other issues. What normal American could bring
himself to vote for the monstrous "author" of a depression?

Hoover had neither the temperament nor the machinery for
coping with personal calumny. It had been building up since the
first campaign; it saturated every minute of the second campaign
like an evil-smelling miasma. In December of 1930, talking to the
Gridiron Club, he referred sadly to "the sordidness and gossip
which oozes through the intellectual swamps of a great political
capital." But this was a rare departure from his conviction that
it was beneath the dignity of his office to take notice of vituperation. He could defend Hoover only by subjecting the presidency
of the United States to vulgarities, and this he would not do.

A few attempts to manufacture sensational scandals about his
administration were made and always fizzled out in absurdity.
The most ambitious of these had its start in the Michelson Mills
and was picked up, to its ultimate shame, by the New York
World. With a great beating of drums and cymbals that paper
announced a syndicated series of articles exposing "a second Teapot Dome," involving the President and his cabinet.

The charges were based on the say-so of a discharged government employee named Kelley, who received $12,000 for his stint.

It was alleged that vast oil shale lands of fabulous value were being lost to the people through contracts made by the Department of Interior; that documents relating to the deals had been "destroyed"; that someone somewhere was being paid off.

The advance ballyhoo was the first that Hoover or his Secretary of Interior, Ray Lyman Wilbur, ever heard of the affair. An immediate inquiry showed that Kelley had spun his fantasy out of his own confusions. The shale lands involved were without the slightest commercial value; the "destroyed" papers were all in their proper files; not a trace of misconduct or even irregularity could be found.

Walter Lippmann was then editor of the *World*. These sensational falsehoods made headlines from coast to coast. Later the *World* published an abject apology—in fine print.

Another "scandal" that failed was initiated in 1930 by John Nance Garner, later the New Deal Vice-President. He charged that Hoover had some shady association with sugar lobbyists. Democratic Senator Walsh seized upon the morsel with hungry glee and set up a senate inquiry. After having provided the press with a headline circus of insinuations, Walsh shamefacedly announced that there was not an atom of truth in the whole story.

Neither the new Teapot nor the sugar provided any real beverage of scandal. Both affairs were self-consciously buried by their instigators, buried so deep that they never showed up again even in the dirtiest of the anti-Hoover propaganda after Hoover left the White House.

Wilbur and Hyde, in *The Hoover Policies,* have attested that "all the search of bitter partisanship" failed to find "one particle of dishonesty . . . in the handling of over twenty-five billion of income and expenditure. . . . That was because of the Hoover policy in choosing men for probity and ability and not primarily for politics. Never has the public service been raised to as high a level as during the four Hoover years."

There was a joyous moment when New Deal probers did think they had found the illusive object of their search. Charles F. Adams had been Secretary of the Navy under Hoover. One day the Democratic chairman of a house committee announced in happy excitement that Charles F. Adams held stock in ten firms doing business with the Navy. The congressman might have spared himself and his party a load of humiliation had he done what Hoover did when the story reached the press. He phoned the ex-Secretary and learned, of course, that he had never owned a share in any of those firms; it was another Adams, neither known nor related to him.

The ex-President and the ex-Secretary decided to have their little joke. They let the New Deal proceed with the attack for another day before exposing the silly blunder.

2

Major libels like the shale lands and sugar charges could be met and exposed, but not a thousand corrupt whispers, distortions, and innuendoes. They came faster and traveled farther than a President burdened with a thousand urgent problems of state could refute.

Even in 1928 someone launched the tale that Hoover, a quarter of a century earlier, had robbed Chinese in a mine deal. It was, of course, an inside-out perversion of the London litigation I have recounted in an earlier chapter. The venerable Tong Shao-yi, twice Prime Minister of China, who had been a principal in the litigation, wrote a statement for America in which he set forth the true facts, made it clear that Hoover had acted honorably and in China's interests, and expressed his sorrow at the twisting of the story into its opposite.

Suddenly there appeared in circulation a photograph showing the gate of a Western ranch, with the scrawled sign "No white men wanted!" on it. It was a ranch Hoover had helped a friend acquire. No one was quite clear about the implication of the sign, unless it be that cheap non-white labor was employed. The fact, however, is that only white men worked on that ranch; local labor union leaders formally attested this. The whole thing was a stupid or malevolent practical joke, but it has plagued Hoover ever since.

The sky was the limit for malignity where Hoover was the target. The nation was shocked by the kidnaping of the Lindbergh baby. Ghoulish whispers had it that Hoover had helped Lindbergh "frame" the kidnap story for "publicity." Ivar Kreuger, the Swedish match king and speculator, committed suicide on the other side of the ocean as his financial empire collapsed around his ears. Instantly hostile stories identified him as "a friend of Hoover." The basis of this invention: a five-minute visit to the White House by Kreuger at the suggestion of the State Department, as a courtesy to the Swedish Legation which had asked for it.

John Spargo, in the pamphlet I have already mentioned, referred to "the most unscrupulous and shamefully dishonorable machine for systematic discrediting of a public man that this or any other nation has known in my time." Having sampled some of the products of that machine, I am prepared to agree that his language is less extreme than it sounds. The vilest of those products were in that "library of scurrilous books" which Arthur Train, a first-rate lawyer as well as writer, took apart in a *Collier's* article on February 20, 1932.

He was referring to five books so vicious that even the Michelson Mills steered shy of them—though they did not have the honesty to repudiate them in so many words. The most reckless of the poisonous confections, by an Englishman residing in the United States, John Hamill, was called the *Strange Career of Mr. Hoover—Under Two Flags.* Appropriately, it was published by a convicted dealer in pornographic books, who peddled it as part of a filth package called Faro's Famous Dozen.

A more unprincipled hodgepodge of lies, distortions, and forgeries can hardly be imagined. Soon after its publication Hamill himself repudiated his handiwork in a notarized confession running to one hundred and eighty-nine pages, a photostat copy of which lies before me as I write. Though he credits the worst fabrications to the publisher, he does not spare himself either. It was all the work of "ghouls," he says, eager for quick money through a sensational best seller. The garbage did not achieve best sellerdom, but its most outrageous lies took root and have proliferated ever since. Denounced by its author as a tissue of falsehoods, imaginary documents, and misquotations, the Hamill opus has remained the central reservoir of dirt for attacks on Hoover.

The other books derived from "the same polluted source," as Train put it. One of them, by a small-bore Tammany hanger-on and ex-policeman, John H. (known as Constitution) O'Brien, was based on the same "research" materials. It was O'Brien who first hatched the bright idea and raised the money to finance Hamill's work. Another book, by Clement Wood, was a straight rewrite of Hamill; a third, by Walter Liggett, likewise absorbed the worst errors and rawest lies of Hamill and O'Brien.

To add to the pretty picture, O'Brien sued Hamill, claiming that he had purloined the materials and was therefore "a thief, forger, and fraud." Hamill retorted no less elegantly. The malodorous details of their quarrel over spoils that weren't there are too complicated for me. Reading the press reports and documents one feels that he has stumbled into a diseased swamp. Yet between them these characters raked up the raw stuff on which anti-Hoover propaganda has fed ever since.

The liars might recant in tears, but the lies marched on and on. Specific charges and inventions might be forgotten, but the vague over-all impression that there was something fishy and discreditable about Hoover's background persisted. People with no special grudge will say offhandedly, "But wasn't Mr. Hoover mixed up in some Chinese scandal? Didn't he figure in some stock fraud affair?"

Even the President's boyhood, its Lincolnesque poverty and Quaker austerity, was treated with derision. Hamill mocked him for having "missed all the fun of childhood" and for "collecting the laundry" of other students in college. Wood sagely pointed out that "Hoover, alone of all our Presidents, belonged to a sect which permitted each member to be the final judge of his own actions, his own morality," which, he warned, "is an infinitely dangerous power to give to any man." From what sect the morality of Wood's rehash of the sordid Hamill hodgepodge derived was not clear.

If there was one thing beyond doubt, it was Hoover's pre-eminence as a practical engineer. His reputation for probity was among the most important reasons for his meteoric rise. As we have already seen, he constantly cautioned the public against get-rich-quick mining schemes. He made no secret of his contempt for promoters who practiced what he called "the science of extracting the greatest possible sum of money from some other human being." Every honor within the gift of his colleagues in the profession came to him as a matter of course.

But all the smear books insisted that he was a promoter and speculator rather than an engineer. The technique of his defamers was as simple as it was dishonest. They blamed him for every mining project that went sour before, during, or after he had any connection with it. Since he had been hired to investigate, operate, or salvage hundreds of mines, it gave them plenty of scope for misrepresentation.

The reader will recall an episode that reflected only glory on Hoover and on the firm with which he was associated as a young man: the million-dollar defalcation by a junior partner, on which Hoover and other members of the firm made good out of their own pockets. In the hands of the defamers even that was turned into a fable of frenzied finance in which Hoover was not the hero but the central villain.

As a practical engineer, it will be recalled, Hoover wrote and spoke against coolie labor and underpaid labor generally. Somehow the books stood this fact on its head and painted him as a slave-driving exploiter of cheap labor. Once he had described a horrifying situation in which "the disregard for human life permits cheap mining." The quoted phrase and others in his attack on such practices were wrenched out of context and presented *as if he approved the horrors he described!*

His fervent opposition to bolshevism and its Soviet practices the "authors" explained simply as bitterness over the loss of Russian mining properties in which he had a stake. Liggett was especially culpable on this score. Aside from the fact that Hoover had given up his Russian interests before the revolution, the implications are too vicious to be worth further discussion.

The "two-flags" part of the Hamill fabrication, endlessly exploited during the campaign, deserves mention. Echoes of it can still be heard. Work abroad, wherever the accidents of geology lead him, is in the nature of the mining engineer's calling. It was always as an American, introducing American methods, surrounded by American associates, that Hoover worked in China, Australia, Africa, Russia, Latin America, wherever metals were stored in God's good earth. Because of this he was often referred to, as we have already noted, as "Hail Columbia" Hoover. His home, wherever he happened to live, seemed a bit of transplanted America, and Palo 'Alto was ever the magnetic center of his personal dreams and interests.

But it suited the purposes of Hoover's detractors to spread the two-flags legend. Some of them went so far as to allege that he became a British citizen. What is more, Hamill offered and the rest copied "documentary evidence"—his name on a local English voters' list. They merely forgot to mention that all house-owners and taxpayers were automatically inscribed on that list, whether they were Americans, Egyptians, or Patagonians.

The scurrilities did not make their authors rich. They had carried a bad thing too far. No one in his senses could believe that one mortal being had crowded so many crimes into one lifetime and "gotten away with it." After Hamill's repudiation of his book, it was withdrawn from circulation; leftover copies were apparently snatched up by the communist propaganda division, for they still show up now and then in Red bookshops.

It was in an atmosphere polluted by the Michelsons and the Hamills, fevered with rantings of snake-oil schools of economy, shadowed by fears, that the 1932 campaign took shape. Hoover had no hope of winning. The Democratic victory in Maine and the opinion polls left him no margin for self-delusions. Yet he made the best fight he could, in deference to duty.

Perhaps Republicans are not to be blamed for saving their cash in what they appraised as a hopeless contest. The Hoover forces disposed of only about a third as much money as their Democratic opponents. The President paid for radio time and traveling expenses out of his own pocket.

In their book *America in Midpassage,* Professor Charles A. Beard and Mary Beard point out that "Hoover had few ardent friends in Wall Street, which was supposed to be the nerve center of the economic system he was striving to resuscitate." They explain this fact by his attacks on market manipulations. His insistence on the senate probe of the Stock Exchange lost him the few ardent friends he might have retained in that general neighborhood. In addition, he had forfeited business backing by rejecting the N.R.A. scheme.

Thus the type of support which is roughly and inaccurately labeled Wall Street, in so far as it made itself felt in 1932, was on the Roosevelt side of the battle.

3

About the hardest thing to find in the Democratic party platform and in the speeches of the Democratic candidates in 1932 is a candid statement of the New Deal. Business and finance contributors to their campaign had little cause for apprehension—until after the election.

The American electorate that year voted against Hoover and for Roosevelt overwhelmingly, but they certainly did not vote for the New Deal. Indeed, if words have any meaning, if election speeches are anything more than trickery, they voted *against* the New Deal. The most emphatic pronouncements of the Democratic candidates, as a matter of fact, sound like a preview of anti-New Deal slogans in subsequent campaigns.

The governor of New York and his Texas running mate concentrated their fire on excessive spending and deficits in the Hoover administration. In specific, unambiguous terms they asked for a mandate to reduce government expenses by 25 per cent, to trim down debts, to balance the budget. "On my part," said Governor Roosevelt, "I ask you very simply to assign to me the task of reducing the annual expenses of your national government." "When we come into power," Garner exclaimed, "we'll give the country a demonstration in real economy."

Too much spending and lending by Hoover, Democratic orators repeated a thousand times, were responsible for the country's continuing ills. "Their failure to balance the budget of a family of 120,000,000 people is the very bottom of the economic troubles from which we are suffering," Garner declared. How were the voters to surmise that Hoover would be the last President in sixteen years who would even try to balance that family budget? How were they to guess that in yielding to the plea to "throw the spenders out!" they were bringing in a philosophy which assumed that deficits were a good thing for a nation? "It certainly makes life more easy and governing more popular for

Presidents," Hoover was to remark in retrospect about the new fiscal philosophy.

Governor Roosevelt tried to keep himself on a plane of reason above the crackpot economic ranters who made up a large part of his entourage. "It is the habit of the unthinking to turn in times like this to the illusion of economic magic," he warned, and identified "a huge expenditure of public funds by the Federal Government" as the prime illusion in this category. Here, at random, are other quotations from the governor's campaign speeches:

Now, to bring about government by oligarchy masquerading as democracy, it is fundamentally essential that practically all authority and control be centralized in our National Government. The individual sovereignty of our States must first be destroyed. (March 2.)

Let us have the courage to stop borrowing to meet continuing deficits. . . . Let us have equal courage to reverse the policy of the Republican leaders and insist on a sound currency. (July 30.)

I share the President's complaint against regimentation; but, unlike him, I dislike it not only when it is carried on by an informal group, amounting to an economic Government of the United States, but also when it is done by the Government of the United States itself. (August 20.)

We are spending altogether too much money for Government services that are neither practical nor necessary. And then, in addition to that, we are attempting too many functions. We need to simplify what the Federal Government is giving to the people.

I accuse the present administration of being the greatest spending administration in peacetimes in all our history. It is an administration that has piled bureau on bureau, commission on commission, and has failed to anticipate the dire needs and the reduced earning power of the people. Bureaus and bureaucrats, commissions and commissioners, have been retained at the expense of the taxpayer. (September 29.)

I regard reduction in Federal spending as one of the most important issues in this campaign. In my opinion it is the most direct and effective contribution that government can make to business. . . . Our Federal extravagance and improvidence bears a double evil; our whole people and our business cannot carry on its excessive burdens of taxation; second, our credit structure is impaired by the unorthodox Federal financing made necessary by the unprecedented magnitude of these deficits. (October 19.)

The Democratic platform specifically declares, 'We advocate a sound currency to be preserved at all hazards.' That is plain English. (November 4.)

Could anything be more sensible and orthodox? Could any-thing be more specific as a pledge against rash experiments? The views of certain of the people around Roosevelt might alarm his business backers, but clearly the candidate was reassuring them on this score. After all, the main targets of his oratory were pre-cisely those aspects of the Hoover administration which can be identified, in the perspective of time, as precursors of the New Deal.

Raymond Moley, in his memoirs, has revealed that in preparing for the campaign Roosevelt was urged by Tugwell and other left-wingers to come out for a huge public-works program. Roosevelt, he writes, "repeatedly shied away from this proposal," partly because Hoover had found it so hard to think up "good" projects, but "also because Roosevelt certainly did not, at that time, sub-scribe to the pump-priming theory."

The Republicans could only voice suspicion that under the orthodox Roosevelt phrases there lurked threats of reckless inno-vation. With a nod in the direction of Democratic congressmen who had sought to raid the Treasury, and another in the direction of the motley crew of brain trusters around Roosevelt's throne, the President warned that a solution "is not to be found in haphazard experimentation or by revolution. It must be through organic development of these (individualist) ideals. It must secure that co-operative action which builds initiative and strength outside of government." Because difficulties are stupendous, it does not fol-low "that we must turn to a state-controlled or state-directed social or economic system in order to cure our troubles."

Hoover could not pin his fears in this connection on the ortho-dox-talking candidate. He was relying on his intuitions. That they served him remarkably well is suggested by one warning which at the time he uttered it must have sounded far-fetched if not unfair. Governor Roosevelt said at one point in the campaign that the Republicans were in control of all branches of the government —"and I may add for good measure the Supreme Court as well." The President reacted as if he had touched a live electric wire.

"There are many things revealed by the campaign of our opponents which should give Americans concern for the future," he said. "One of the gravest is the state of mind revealed by my opponent in that statement. He implies that it is the function of the party in power to control the Supreme Court." If that were the case, he added later, "he is proposing the most revolutionary new deal, the most stupendous breaking of precedent, the most destructive undermining of the very safeguard of our form of government yet proposed by a presidential candidate."

The President also sensed terrible danger in another Roosevelt campaign assertion. "Our industrial plant is built," the governor declared. "The problem just now is whether under existing conditions it is not overbuilt. . . . Our task now is not the discovery of natural resources or necessarily the production of more goods, it is the sober, less dramatic business of administering the resources and plants already in hand. . . ."

That was the foundation stone of the extraordinary New Deal assumption that there was no more room in the United States for material progress; that America was "mature" and finished. This theory became the justification in later years of a cheerful defeatism that regarded ten million unemployed and twenty millions on relief rolls as natural and permanent. It sought to squelch the sense of adventure in American psychology and batten down the national hatches for a century of marking time.

President Hoover rejected this theory and this attitude in a tone of horror that was far beyond mere partisan emotion. "I deny that the promise of American life has been fulfilled," he exclaimed in Madison Square Garden, "for that means we have begun to decline and fall. No nation can cease to move forward without degeneration of spirit."

The President's addresses are available in book form. For Americans with sufficient historical curiosity they make fascinating reading. Hoover was not fooled by the orthodox gestures, seeing through them to the core of menace. "My countrymen," he declared, "the proposals of our opponents represent a profound change in American life—less in concrete proposal, bad as that may be, than by implication and by evasion. . . . This election is not a mere shift from the ins to the outs. It means deciding the direction our nation will take over a century to come."

Hoover devoted himself largely, of course, to an analysis and

defense of his administration. In his first campaign address, accepting the renomination, he said:

"Two courses were open. We might have done nothing. This
would have been utter ruin. Instead, we met the situation with
proposals to private business and the Congress of the most gigantic
program of economic defense ever evolved in the history of the
Republic. We put them into action.

"Our measures have repelled these attacks of fear and panic.
We have maintained the financial integrity of our Government.
We have co-operated to restore and stabilize the situation abroad.
As a nation we have paid every dollar demanded of us. We have
used the credit of the Government to aid and protect our institu-
tions, public and private.

"We have provided methods and assurances that there shall be
none to suffer from hunger and cold. We have instituted measures
to assist farmers and homeowners. We have created vast agencies
for employment. Above all, we have maintained the sanctity of
the principles upon which this Republic has grown great.

"In a large sense the test of success of our program is simple.
Our people, while suffering great hardships, have been and will
be cared for. In the long view our institutions have been sustained
intact and are now functioning with increasing confidence of the
future. As a nation we are undefeated and unafraid. Government
by the people has not been defiled."

4

There is substantial agreement that the depression had been
arrested and an upturn achieved around the middle of 1932. The
economic situation in Europe was visibly stiffened; in nearly all
the great commercial nations recovery continued upward from
that point for the next two years, and Hoover's leadership was
widely credited for this conquest of chaos. In the world as a whole
the battle against depression seemed to have been victorious. Only
in a few countries was the tendency reversed—and most sharply
in the United States.

Said the Democratic New York *Times* on June 16, 1934, "The
change for the better in the last half of 1932 is beyond dispute.

That this evident revival of confidence was suddenly reversed in February 1933 is equally true." Leonard P. Ayres, in *Economics of Recovery,* attested that "the corner was turned in the country in the summer of 1932"; the most important factor in stopping that recovery in America while it continued abroad, he added, "was political in nature." Professor Irving Fisher, in a speech on December 28, 1933, declared: "We should have been further on the road to recovery today had there been no election last year. Recovery started under Mr. Hoover but . . . a recession [came] because of fear over political uncertainties."

The Department of Commerce under Roosevelt was understandably cautious in its judgment. Yet its review for 1933 said that in 1932 "business in the more important commercial nations of the world was showing a tendency to recovery. . . . In the United States business improved substantially from July until September and held firm without much definite tendency either way in October and November. . . . The relatively long interval between the election and the inauguration of the new President proved unsettling to business and was a factor militating against further immediate improvement."

Walter Lippmann on June 18, 1936, wrote that Hoover and his associates "had hold of the essence of the matter in the spring of 1932 when . . . they arrested the depression." The National Industrial Conference Board, November 10, 1934, said: "The facts presented in the chart bring out clearly that the first steps toward recovery were taken in the year 1932." Edmund Platt, a former vice-chairman of the Federal Reserve Board, declared (New York *Times,* July 4, 1933): "If 1932 had not happened to be a presidential year, the recovery begun then might have continued without any serious interruption."

Wilbur and Hyde present the proofs that the beginnings of a real recovery were under way:

In the months of August, September, and October 1932, bank failures had almost ceased while banks reopened were more than suspensions. The great flow of gold the months previous to July reversed itself into an enormous inflow. The whole banking structure greatly strengthened. Wholesale commodity prices and farm prices advanced steadily through July, August, and September. Cotton and wheat advanced over 20 per cent. United States cotton manufacturing advanced from 51.5 per cent of mill capacity in July to 97 per cent in October. Domestic wool consumption advanced from 16,500,000 pounds in May to 46,100,000 pounds in September. The Federal Reserve Board's index of industrial production swept upward from 56 in July to 68 for both September and October.

The constructive policies of Hoover which had by long and patient effort coaxed this result into being were ended on November 8, when Roosevelt was chosen by a 57 per cent vote of the electorate. From that day until the next March 4 Hoover was President in name only. His word was worth no more—perhaps less—than that of any private citizen. There is nothing more impotent than a lame-duck administration.

People watched and listened to only one man, the President-elect. Unfortunately they heard nothing to still their panicky fears and suspicions that, orthodox campaign talk notwithstanding, the country was headed for alarming monetary, economic, and social experiments. As signs of business and financial jitters multiplied, as the precious margins of improvement crumbled, President Hoover, the press, spokesmen for economic bodies pleaded with Roosevelt to do a simple thing: *merely to assure his country that he intended to abide by his campaign promises.*

This he refused to do. The more menacing the growth of fear, the closer we came to panic, the more obdurately he retreated into silence. He was jovial, high-spirited, bubbling over with flippancies, but would not lift a finger to head off the worst collapse the country had yet experienced.

Pressed by newspapermen on the first specific issue confronting him, the question of international debts, he laughed and wise-cracked, "That's not my baby." He flatly rejected Hoover's earnest, pleading invitation that he join in supporting the stabilizing processes in the world. Editorial comment was shocked. Roosevelt, said the New York *Times,* "obviously displayed more tact than courage." The Detroit *Free Press* said, "It is highly unfortunate that Governor Roosevelt was unable to bring himself to meet the President halfway. . . . Mr. Roosevelt had an opportunity unique in the history of the American presidency and he failed to grasp it." The Baltimore *Sun* warned that though "the baby" is not Roosevelt's it "may soon develop into an unruly stepchild lodged permanently under his roof and disposed to play with matches."

In instructing the Democratic Congress what to do and what not to do, Roosevelt acted the role of Chief Executive from the day of his election. On December 29, for instance, he did not scruple to instruct the Democratic Congress to oppose measures for balancing the budget being urged by the President. But when the need to quiet public apprehensions and sustain national morale was involved, he took the technical tongue-in-cheek view that until inauguration day he was a private citizen who should not intervene.

History may ask why even a private citizen, having the power to allay careening fears, did not use it. Could it be that he shared the belief, voiced indiscreetly in the far left flank of his motley entourage, that "the worse the better"? Could it be that he approved the political logic which held that the lower the base at which the new regime started, the brighter its record would seem —and the readier a despairing people would be to countenance broken campaign covenants and extreme experiments?

He was fully aware of the consequences of his studied silence on the very questions on which he had been most eloquent until election day. Charles Michelson has written, "The President-elect told me on one occasion that the bank crisis was due to culminate just about inauguration day. . . . Naturally *he did not care to have the dramatic effect of his intended proposals spoiled* by a premature discussion of them in advance of their delivery."

The italics are mine. One hopes that Michelson went too far. It is hard to believe that any American, and a President-to-be in particular, would put "dramatic effect" above the chance to help halt a dizzy plunge into a financial abyss. That the plunge did enhance the drama of the inaugural is not in itself conclusive proof that it was intended that way by those who might have stopped it and did not even try.

Roosevelt was a three-in-one personality, according to Michelson; a fanatic idealist, a stubborn Dutchman, and a practical politician. "The practical politician was on the job when the Hoover proposition was broached," he declared. The proposition was nothing more than an earnest, humble plea that Roosevelt deny the rumors which were sending hordes of depositors to draw money out of banks and prompting smart insiders to send their cash out of the country—foresight which soon netted them 60 per cent profits. If Michelson was right, "practical politics" has rarely been expressed with such reckless cynicism.

"The panic and setback of the last period could have been easily prevented," Hoover would write as ex-President. It is one of those things that can never be proved with absolute finality. Perhaps even Roosevelt's intercession would not have arrested the panic started by his election. But one thing is certain: If Roosevelt and his brain trust had *planned* to push the country over the brink in order to take over at the lowest possible point, they would have behaved no differently. They did not merely refrain from doing or saying anything that would bolster confidence; they did and said precisely those things which shook confidence and confirmed fears.

Individuals and business organizations began to protect themselves as best they could against what his associates were already calling "the Roosevelt Revolution." Billions of dollars were hastily transferred abroad. Cash was withdrawn from the banks at a rate which few of them could sustain even in normal times; in the final weeks as much as $200,000,000 a day was taken out and hoarded. Thousands of depositors demanded payment in gold—indicating that they were not simply doubting the stability of the banks but the stability of the American dollar. Matters were scarcely improved when news got around—without effective denial—that prominent Democrats, presumably better informed than other citizens, were transporting large sums abroad; these presumptive insiders shared in the 60 per cent bonanza when the dollar was in fact devalued.

As more banks suspended, as more businesses closed their doors in those fantastic final months, Hoover made a dozen appeals to the incoming President, publicly and privately. The more urgent his tone, the more time Roosevelt took in answering—and every answer was a cold No.

"Unwilling to admit that co-operation cannot be established between the outgoing and incoming administrations," Hoover suggested new plans, new formulas. He was willing to settle on any statement that might help ward off the final blow. For him there could be no thought of personal pride, or politics, or appearances. Through intermediaries he even offered to transmit to Congress any proposals Roosevelt himself might wish enacted; bad news would be better than the prolonged uncertainty which bred panic.

If Roosevelt was smilingly tight-lipped, the strange aggregation of panacea-peddlers he had gathered around him were not. Their hints of new currencies and unlimited spending fed the swollen fears. Not once did the President-elect repudiate them. Even when the press quoted him personally on plans for tinkering with money, and the dispatch was read into the *Congressional Record,* he failed to make a denial.

It was a time of hysterical rumor and demagogic incitation. Father Coughlin was holding forth on the radio. The magazines and the air waves were filled with wild talk about revolution and the need for a "dictator" to save the nation. Not since the War between the States had there been more desperate need for counsels of faith in America. A message of reassurance from the newly elected President would have cleared the air. Evidently he did not want it cleared.

A bombshell was tossed into the unsettled post-election situation when Congress, on the insistence of Vice-President-elect Garner, proceeded to make public the lists of loans extended by the Reconstruction Finance Corporation. A Democratic "rider" to the R.F.C. bill had authorized such publicity; President Hoover had signed the bill notwithstanding, on explicit promises that the authority would never be exercised. Business and labor leaders rushed to Capitol Hill to beg that this disastrous step be avoided. They failed to stop the insanity.

In retrospect nobody, probably not even Garner, would defend that act of vandalism. The New Deal itself quickly voided the publicity rider. In that fevered time publication of the fact that a bank had sought and obtained an R.F.C. loan was accepted by jittery depositors as evidence of weakness, precipitating a run. At least a thousand banks closed under pressure touched off by this loan publicity. Many an institution which might have weathered the storm with R.F.C. help feared to apply for it—knowing that the resultant publicity would hasten the run they wanted to avoid. After his resignation, vice-chairman Pomerene of the Federal Reserve Board told The Associated Press: "It was the most damnable and vicious thing that was ever done." For it operated to turn the danger of a bank panic into a certainty. Could it be that this was the covert purpose of the stratagem?

Then, in mid-February, came the news that Senator Carter Glass had refused the post of Secretary of the Treasury in Roosevelt's cabinet. Glass was a "sound money" man; his action amounted to a confirmation of the country's worst fears in the matter of currency and tax experimentation. The jitters grew apace.

The incoming crowd was cheerful and cocky about the cumulative troubles. What some of the men around Roosevelt said among themselves inevitably reached the White House; their jubilant chatter played variations on the shocking, the incredible theme, "the worse the better." They were all "practical politicians," apparently.

Several weeks before the inauguration, for example, Professor Rexford Guy Tugwell was lunching with James H. Rand, Jr., a prominent Roosevelt supporter. According to Rand's later account, Tugwell informed him cheerfully that the banking structure would soon collapse and added, "We should worry about anything but rehabilitating the country after March 4."

A final plea to Roosevelt was sent by the President in a handwritten letter on February 18. It began with these words:

"A most critical situation has arisen in the country of which I feel it my duty to advise you confidentially. I am therefore taking this course of writing you myself and sending it to you through the Secret Service for your hand direct, as obviously its misplacement would only feed the fire and increase the dangers.

"The major difficulty is the state of the public mind, for there is a steadily degenerating confidence in the future which has reached the height of general alarm. I am convinced that a very early statement by you upon two or three policies of your Administration would greatly restore confidence and cause a resumption of the march of recovery."

Roosevelt did not respond for ten days—ten days that shook the national economy almost beyond repair—and his answer was one more No. He claimed that he had replied immediately but that his missive had been "mislaid." Unfortunately there were a few discrepancies in the claim which opened the alibi to doubt.

Hoover did everything humanly possible to avert the banking disaster everyone saw coming. He appealed, in vain, to Congress to take action on the bankruptcy law which had been gathering dust for a year; to repeal the publicity menace in connection with the R.F.C. law; to expand the R.F.C. loan limits; to make more federal funds available for the relief of skyrocketing distress. Congress, of course, waited for signals from the new boss, and they did not come. Hoover was in almost continuous day-and-night session with financial and Treasury officials. The Advisory Council of the Federal Reserve and influential newspapers joined him in begging Roosevelt to reaffirm his election pledges.

In the final days, when Secretary of Interior Wilbur pointed out that in view of Roosevelt's stubbornness the battle was lost anyhow, the President exclaimed:

"We will fight until 10:49 A.M. March fourth, when I leave for the Capitol. We must try everything, not once but a dozen times."

Whether the new regime planned it that way or not, the great cave-in came with miraculous exactitude on the last morning of Hoover's term. Those who wished to take over at the lowest point had their way with a vengeance, at incalculable cost in substance and in suffering to the country. Those who wanted the most calamitous base possible for future calculations of New Deal achievements had their wish. And always thereafter, indeed, they used March 4, when Roosevelt was sworn in—not November 8, when he was elected—as their base in making invidious comparisons.

The panic which Hoover had warded off five times thus came at last, when he no longer had the prestige and the power to stop it. Whatever may be said of the preceding years, certainly the final catastrophe had more to do with the incoming than the outgoing administration. But the blame for that too—for that especially—was loaded on Hoover's shoulders.

I have not done justice to those terrifying four months. A correspondent who covered the grim story, Lawrence Sullivan, wrote a book about it which he called *Prelude to Panic*. Anyone who doubts that the responsibility for the climactic tragedy rests squarely on the Roosevelt administration will find in its pages a hundred distressing proofs aligned for easy reading and understanding.

The public could not know all the facts at the time. In the great glad din of the New Deal era those who tried to tell the facts could not make themselves heard. One of them, of course, was the ex-President himself. On December 16, 1935, he would say:

"What happened on March 3, 1933, was an induced hysteria of bank depositors. The banking structure at large subsequently proved to be sound. . . .

"The truth is that the world-wide depression was turned in June–July 1932 all over the world. That was before the election of the New Deal. That is supported by scores of leading American economists, businessmen, and public leaders. It is supported by the economic publications throughout the world. . . .

"After the election of the New Deal we began a retreat. Only in the United States was there an interruption. We were the strongest and should have led the van. And we lagged behind for two years. The other countries of the world went forward without interruption. They adopted no New Deal. Apparently those nations did not hear that the mechanics of civilization came to a dead stop on March 3, 1933.

"It did not come to a stop even in the United States. It was meddled with. We have not got over it yet. But why did we have a panic of bank depositors in 1933? Because they were scared. We had no bank panic from the crash of the boom in 1929. We had no panic at the financial collapse in Europe in 1931. We had no panic at the most dangerous point in the depression, when our banks were weakest, in the spring of 1932. There was no panic before the election of November 1932. When did they become frightened? They became scared a few weeks before the inauguration of the New Deal, on March 4, 1933.

"What were they frightened of? They could not have been scared by the outgoing administration which had only a few days to run. They were frightened by the incoming New Deal. Why were they scared of the New Deal? Because soon after the election large numbers of people awoke to the fact that promises given in the campaign would be violated. . . .

"The banking structure was not insolvent. After the banks were closed it was found that the solvent banks, measured by deposits, comprised 92 per cent of the banking strength of the country. The President [Roosevelt] himself stated they were sound. Subsequently more banks were found sound and reopened. And beyond this, important banks wrongfully closed by the New Deal, such as in the Detroit area, are now paying out 100 per cent to depositors.

"It was the most political and the most unnecessary bank panic in all our history. It could have been prevented. It could have been cured by simple co-operation."

That was a serious charge the ex-President made—perhaps the most sensational that a former President had ever made against a succeeding administration. But he was not heard. Ten thousand official and voluntary press agents of the New Deal shouting hallelujah drowned him out.

In 1947, fourteen years after he had ceased to be President, I asked Hoover this question: "In the perspective of time, if you knew then what you know now, would you have changed any of your major policies as President."

He did not need to ponder that one. Evidently he had answered it in his own mind innumerable times.

"No," he said. "I am convinced of the essential correctness of my administration's policies. We definitely had the depression licked, but the election of the New Deal reversed the trend and perpetuated the depression. It was to be many years before conditions approximating the summer and early autumn of 1932 would be attained again. The processes of liquidation had been about completed at that time. Other nations continued their march to recovery. Ours was forced back by fear of the unknown and suspicions which came true quickly after March 4.

"As to relief policies, I believed then and even more so now, after the experience of the New Deal years, that we were right in keeping it on a local basis and keeping it out of politics. Centralized federal monopoly of relief brought with it bureaucracy, waste, and political trading on human misery. The cost of relief went up twice and threefold as soon as it was made a football of politics. The instincts of charity and mutual help, all the vast local resources and spiritual leverages, were never again used."

Dr. Ray Lyman Wilbur, former president of Leland Stanford University, was Secretary of Interior in Hoover's cabinet; Arthur Mastic Hyde, ex-governor of Missouri, was Secretary of Agriculture. In their joint study of *The Hoover Policies* they venture a forecast based on intimate knowledge of the administration of which they were a part:

History will record that despite many handicaps President Hoover guided the Nation safely through perilous times and placed it on the road to recovery in 1932. It will also record the effective care of distress, the unparalleled industrial peace of the times, and the fidelity to national obligations.

It will record that Hoover originated and developed more new government policies for the correction of business abuse and the advancement of economic life than any President up to his time. It will record that it was Hoover who laid the foundations for an era of social progress in this country. It will record that with these great accomplishments he held to Constitutional Government and to the fundamental ideals of free men. Above all, it will record him as the American Leader of these principles in his time.

CHAPTER XX

Ordeal by Abuse

LITTLE HAS BEEN SAID ABOUT THE personal life of Herbert Hoover as President, but in truth he allowed himself neither time nor thought for a personal existence. Driven by a keyed-up consciousness of crowding perils, he made of his days a treadmill and reduced sleep to four or five hours a night. The camp at Rapidan where he often spent his week ends became just another White House, without surcease from pressures. Again and again eager plans for a family holiday in California were washed out by a new inundation of trouble. Scarcely had he repaired one dyke with infinite travail when another and yet another gave way.

His two sons now grown to tall, personable, intelligent manhood; his charming daughters-in-law; the three grandchildren whom he adored; the First Lady—all of them respected the heaped-up anxieties under which Hoover labored. In addition they must conceal from him their own special anxiety, which was for his health under the punishing pace he was maintaining.

Because they had no relish for the glitter and pageantry of the great office, residence in the White House was for them all a discipline rather than a thrill. As a matter of principle they evaded publicity, or even the semblance of exploiting their name and address. Mrs. Hoover was one of the ablest, most keen-minded first ladies in the annals of the presidency. If she did not register sharply on the country's mind, it was because she willed it that way. She had the gift of self-effacement.

She ran the household with grace and tact and wisdom. Knowing her husband's need for affection and companionship, she saw to it that a few of the men who called him Chief, whose lives were woven into his own since the epic days of Belgium, were frequently in the White House and at Rapidan. They were less a brain trust than a heart trust, bringing the President the sympathy and generosity of spirit he could find neither in the country nor in his own party.

For Mrs. Hoover and the children the exodus from the White House was a species of release, despite all the tragic overtones of the occasion. Hoover's dream of a normal family life in relative leisure at Palo Alto, postponed for twenty years, was coming true. The slump had worked havoc with his savings, but enough remained for their modest needs and tastes, especially now that Herbert, Jr., and Allan were doing well in their own careers.

If they counted on real seclusion, on a holiday of the spirit as well as the body, they were quickly disillusioned. Immense effort and fortune had gone into the task of turning Hoover into a symbol of iniquity. Those who had made the investment had no intention of discarding their costly masterpiece. Propaganda in a carnival mood, complete with angels and devils, was becoming one of the main functions of government; the symbolic Hoover was too valuable a stage property at the demoniac end to be allowed to retire in peace.

The attack on the ex-President was pressed with new fervor, new financing, new vindictiveness. The do-nothing myth was improved, enlarged, and embellished; new wings were constantly added to the old structure and stocked with fresh horrors. The foulness washed up to Hoover's very doorstep; the mockery and the misrepresentation overflowed his years. Day after day the shyness and sensibility which are the marks of his nature were outraged by name-calling and garish accusations.

It ceased to be a political attack and became a persecution, a self-righteous and pharisaic crucifixion. He could not open a paper or turn on a radio or go to a public place without the risk of stupid insults. He saw his words and acts and noblest intentions twisted into caricatures.

A few pathetic reports of scandals in the Hoover administration ballooned skyward and deflated with a bass whistle. One of these referred to an R.F.C. loan to a Chicago bank in which General Dawes had an interest. It made a sputtering noise and collapsed in nothingness. The loan, it turned out, was not only legitimate but commendable. It had been urged and endorsed by the Democratic members of the R.F.C. in the interests of the whole Chicago bank setup. And every dollar of it had been returned.

Another of the attempts was scandalous enough, and tragic, but not in the way the balloonists had planned.

In 1930 the Postmaster General had renegotiated all air-mail contracts with aviation companies, to standardize rates and procedures. Costs to the government were reduced, routes were consolidated, and other reforms effected. But suddenly, more than three years later, the public was apprised that its interests had been traduced by Hoover's Post Office Department. In February 1934 President Roosevelt canceled all air-mail contracts without the formality of hearings or investigation and ordered the Army to fly the mail.

When Colonel Lindbergh, among others, warned the President that the Army was not equipped for the job, the White House denounced him as "just a publicity seeker." Unhappily Lindbergh was right. Twelve army officers were killed in those flights.

A Senate investigation of the contracts, for all its eagerness to justify Roosevelt and expose his predecessor, could find no proof of malfeasance. Meanwhile Postmaster General James Farley was made the "goat" for the twelve killings. Years later he revealed that he had protested to Roosevelt against the investigation as well as against the issuance of statements in his name without his consent.

The last mistake of the investigation was to announce a foray on the character of the ex-President's elder son. Young Herbert had developed a system of ground-to-plane radio communication, as a result he was hired at $100 a week as chief engineer of an air transport company which, like all such companies, flew some mail. His father did not even know about this until the Michelson office began to circulate innuendoes. The young man thereupon tried to resign but was dissuaded by his father and the company.

When the Senate Committee announced plans to summon Herbert, Jr., he released to the press a copy of his letter of resignation in 1930. There the innuendoes were so thoroughly smashed, the true facts were so clearly set forth, that the committee changed its mind about calling him. An upsurge of public resentment against the whole show forced the Administration to reinstate the contracts. The smear that failed had cost twelve innocent lives.

The Dawes bank and air-mail affairs were the closest the New Deal came to "exposing" the previous administration. A special section was set up in the Department of Justice to explore the Hoover term, but its energetic digging netted exactly nothing.

Their very failure to solve the economic problems, it seemed, impelled the new masters to derogate the old. They could prove that things were tolerable now only by showing that they were intolerable under Hoover. It was suddenly discovered, almost as an afterthought, that millions had starved before March 4, 1933; but no one bothered to explain why this minor matter had been kept secret during the campaign. Battalions of new satraps in the empire of federal relief, if only to justify their demands for more and more billions of dollars, had to exaggerate the distress that prevailed before their own arrival on the scene.

The New Dealers had promised rashly that everyone would be back at work by Labor Day, 1933. But in the spring of 1936 there were a million more unemployed than on the day Roosevelt was elected President. Rarely, during his first two terms, did the total dip below ten million. This central failure, which made a sour joke of the boasts of success, had to be veiled with elaborate ballyhoo. It had to be blamed on capitalists, economic royalists, Liberty Leaguers, Republicans, recalcitrant Democrats, old and new species of reprobates—and of course on the king demon of them all, Herbert Hoover.

There was no American so humble that he was not provided with someone or something to hate. Every fireside chat set up a few more lightning rods to deflect popular angers from the government to some group of citizens. There were no more jobs now than under Hoover—but there were more excitements, slogans, schemes, accusations. A hundred noisy agencies now flourished where only one had bloomed unseen and unheard. New legions of officeholders tossed confetti billions into the air and everyone, businessmen included, scrambled for the gaudy stuff. There was no end of "must" orders to a supine Congress and of "directives" to a confused citizenry. Every new commission set up in the business of legislating for some area and acting as judge and jury in enforcing its own laws. A new industry grew up: the sorting and interpretation of government edicts—exegesis of Official Writ.

The White House, once a home and a place of work, came to resemble a three-ring circus. Its denizens, from the dog up, made headlines and newsreels and radio skits. They sold soap, insurance, gossip, newspaper columns, articles, airplanes. Never had such a barking and screeching and cooing issued from Washington to delight a fun-starved populace. Never had court favorites reigned in glory and resigned in disgust with such syncopated publicity. There were Tommy the Cork, Henry the Morgue, Sammie the Rose, Harry the Hop, and a hundred others to give a continuing depression the aspect and the feel of a national mardi gras. Showmanship became a synonym for statesmanship.

The preceding administration—for that matter all preceding administrations—seemed drab and stodgy, especially it seemed stingy, by contrast. In its old-fashioned concern for constitutional methods and limitations, moreover, it seemed a pettifogging and timid spoilsport. Now the old constraints were off. The sky was the limit. Everything was bigger, better, more openhanded—the appropriations, the federal pay rolls, the relief rolls, the national debts, the political promises. And the budgets were kept from being too unbalanced by the elementary trick of listing new expenditures in a separate "emergency" column.

Thus life could be simplified and everyone could join heartily in "Happy Days Are Here Again." Few Americans, looking back, could quite forgive the austerity of the Hoover administration, its constant beefing about expenses, its sentimental appeals to moldy ethics. Poor Hoover was a gloomy Gus who treated disasters as if they were disastrous, when in fact—as was now being made manifest—depression could be barrels of fun.

2

Hoover departed from the White House in a time of sorrow and anguish. The fates, with some hefty mortal help, had contrived to bring the national house down in rubble around his ears. Why shouldn't the cheerful saviors, dangling their bag of tricks, show their contempt by removing the Secret Service guards from Hoover's trivial person?

That insult to the presidency set the tone for all the years that came after. Hoover was not a Chief Executive who had laid down heavy burdens but a felon driven from the scene of his misdoings. The Michelson Mills pushed the old line of anti-Hoover goods and added bright new numbers. But the outfit lost its monopoly. Dozens of new smear plants, complete with spook departments, came into being. And about 1935 the communists and their graded fellow travelers pitched into the job.

We should not underestimate the role of the communists in the persecution. They had been past masters in the science of character murder when the brain trusters were still apprentices. This was a period which I called in a book about its lunacies *The Red Decade*. It was then smart to be Red. It was liberal to be illiberal the communist way. Comrades infiltrated the schools, the churches, the press, publishing, radio, every corner of American life. They could pulverize a reputation more rapidly and deftly than any other group in the past.

For a while they lambasted the Roosevelt administration as vigorously as its predecessor. F.D.R. figured in their poison-pen "literature" as a "fascist . . . financial dictator . . . imperialist" given to "shameful demagogy" and "drastic attacks upon the living standards of the masses . . . terrorization of the Negro . . . systematic denials of civil rights."

But about the middle of 1935 everything changed. Moscow had adopted its "democratic" united-front line, with the Trojan horse as its proud emblem. In France and other countries this was bodied forth in popular-front governments. In America, where political communism was too weak to demand a place in a coalition regime, it operated indirectly through stooges and "sympathizers" and the new breed of totalitarian liberals. Let me quote from *The Red Decade*:

We witnessed the unfoldment in this country of an amazing *unofficial Popular Front government*—unrecognized, unadmitted, independent of the administration, yet operating energetically within the New Deal framework. It added up to the most potent and ubiquitous influence in Washington, a half-clandestine government-within-the-government, arrogantly open in some spots on some occasions but conspiratorial in essence. . . .

With every passing month the penetration was deeper, the entanglement closer. The leaders of this sub-rosa power were for the most part not in office themselves, but worked through hundreds of big and little officials deployed through the length and breadth of the mushrooming New Deal bureaucracy. . . .

Certainly all but a few of the upper-bracket New Dealers maneuvered into giving aid and comfort to this foreign lobby were merely victims of their own high-minded enthusiasms. At worst they were dupes of an amateur Machiavellism which reconciled them to any associations for noble ends. The Stalinist slogans of the period were so beguiling that the more befuddled officials—like the professors and literati and penthouse rebels—saw no harm in tagging along. The New Deal doors, politically and socially, were thus opened wide to the temporary Kremlin democrats. . . .

The Popular Front prospered in Washington through the snob appeal of the New Deal intelligentsia, and subcontractor braintrusters and pseudo-intellectual lawyers and writers-turned-politician. Certain Congressmen and especially the bored wives of politicians were thrilled and flattered by friendship with the polysyllabic sophisticates scattered through all the new bureaus, agencies, projects. It all fitted into the amorphous crusading fervor of the New Deal era. Political patronage was being lapped up greedily by boys and girls who talked Veblen, Spengler, Marx, and the Party line as glibly as the morning's news.

The whole show was a godsend for up-and-coming young lawyers, fluttery social workers, and capital ladies of a restless ripeness of years. They plunged into the ideological lingo and activities—all so excitingly unorthodox, edged with conspiracy and seemingly harmless . . .

The President sent messages of affection to Stalinist "front" conferences; his wife served as patron saint of the communist-controlled American Youth Congress; his cabinet members presided at red front meetings; the easiest road to a New Deal job—

especially in the lush fields of federal relief projects—was through helpful fellow travelers.

The government was neither more nor less blameworthy than the colleges, the magazines, the movie industry, and other branches of national life. Each of them had its contingent of open and camouflaged comrades who set its intellectual fashions. And the habitual reviling of Herbert Hoover was the one fashion that endured while others were amended or displaced.

"We'll hang Herbert Hoover on a sour apple tree," the comrades sang to the tune of "John Brown's Body." "We'll hang Herbert Hoover on a sour apple tree, when the revolution comes." Insulting cartoons of the ex-President became as standardized in the "liberal" press as any of the Party-line slogans. Every one of the vile inventions and forgeries of Hamill and his pornographic publisher was treated as if it were indisputable fact. As late as October 12, 1947, Hedda Hopper could report about one of the big political brains of Hollywood: "Katharine Hepburn turned down *B.F.'s Daughter* because the script called for her to read a line praising Herbert Hoover."

I have before me the July 10, 1944, issue of a Party-line smear sheet called *In Fact,* edited by an unhappy little man who works off his inferiorities by throwing mud at his betters. This issue is devoted to yet another smear of "Hoover, Merchant of Death." It presents as "inside news" a few shovelfuls of the decayed lies which Hamill had confessed to fabricating twelve years earlier.

Hoover, it records, called out the Army "to shoot down the American Legionnaires at Anacostia." He "started hating Russia when his oil, gold, and other mines were confiscated and he lost a billion dollars." He "persuaded the humanitarian Woodrow Wilson to support Mannerheim and the Finnish fascists." He "was making millions out of coolie labor" and believed that "the disregard for human life permits cheap mining." Readers of *In Fact* that week learned that "Every cent he [Hoover] has comes from the blood and sweat and tears of Chinese, Burmese, Russians, Nigerian Negroes, Mexicans."

Column after column of this putrescence—all of it typical of the anti-Hoover campaign from 1929 to this day. In Party-line publications it could be presented crudely. In the rest of the

American press, screen, and radio, wherever the New Deal and its fellow travelers infiltrated, Hoover-baiting was a shade more restrained. It came seasoned with satire. But taken together the attack convinced a whole new generation of Americans that their thirty-first President had been a monstrous exploiter, a sharp promoter, a hardhearted reactionary, and an enemy of the people.

The Republicans, alas, for the most part showed little courage or loyalty on this issue. Few of them believed the unclean absurdities about their recent standard-bearer; but even fewer had the manhood to defend him without reserve, as he deserved to be defended. They evidently suffered a loss of nerve and a blackout of self-respect. In the measure that Hoover was besmirched, they seemed eager to disavow him.

Their anxiety to dissociate themselves from Hoover may have reflected only a cheap expediency, but it looked like a plea of guilty to every libel on their last Republican administration. In the final analysis they were not only morally reprobate but politically self-defeating in disowning their last President.

They would have been in a sounder position, as well as better prepared to live with their private consciences, if they had brought to Hoover's defense the same energy that the Hoover-baiters brought to his persecution. Whether they liked it or not, he was in effect their candidate for the presidency in 1936 and 1940 and 1944. Every failure to defend him carried the fatal implication that the last Republican administration was indefensible. In confusion and in cowardice too many of them were content to do battle on the enemy's terms and on the enemy's grounds.

3

In a speech on December 16, 1935, Hoover alluded to "dark alleys of inspired propaganda" where "ideals and men are assassinated with poisonous whisperings." But there are few such references to his personal ordeal in the record of his years as ex-President. He made no public spectacle of his private dismay. He was aware that it was not Hoover the man—whom the smear brigades did not know or care to know—but Hoover the personification of a way of life who was under bombardment. His duty, as he conceived it, was not to defend himself, but to explain the philosophy of life which he had been forced by history to symbolize.

Before he entered political life, it will be recalled, he wrote a little book, *American Individualism,* in which he sought to define the liberal American pattern of thought. In the light of his twelve years in government, against the background of a contrary philosophy then dominant in American life, he set himself to enlarging that early definition. The result was a bigger book that he called the *Challenge to Liberty,* published in 1935.

Reading it in the knowledge of the personal vilification to which he was being subjected while he worked on it, the book seems remarkable for its calm, its charity, its deep-rooted faith in American destiny. There are in it few echoes of the raucous shouting, not a trace of the truculent abuse, which prevailed in those years. His personal ordeal seemed to him only a tiny fragment of the ordeal of mankind, forced in our time to face and resolve "the issue of human liberty."

The devaluation of individual rights in the United States, he explained, was only one phase of a world-wide crisis of the human spirit. In furious haste to bring under control sweeping social forces, "people and governments are blindly wounding, even destroying, those fundamental human liberties which have been the foundation and inspiration of progress since the Middle Ages."

Better than most of his contemporaries, he was aware of the need for social reform. Evil and injustice were rampant. "The great question before the American people," he wrote, "is not whether these dislocations and abuses can be mastered and these new and powerful forces organized and directed to human welfare, but whether they can be organized by free men. We have to determine now whether, under the pressures of the hour, we must cripple or abandon the heritage of liberty for some new philosophy which must mark the passing of freedom."

He identified regimentation by arrogant bureaucracy, "a vast centralization of power in the Executive," as symptoms of the disease afflicting liberty. "These are not partisan issues," he insisted. "They are the greatest issues of American life. . . . The hope of America and the world is to regenerate Liberty and its responsibilities—not to abandon it. . . . For twenty years I have been honored by my country with positions where contention with the forces of disintegration was my continued duty. I should be untrue to that service did I not raise my voice in protest, not at reform but at the threat of the eclipse of liberty. . . . No one with a day's experience in government fails to realize that in all bureaucracies there are three implacable spirits—self-perpetuation, expansion, and an incessant demand for more power."

There are in his pages no personal feuds and disparagements; no mocking of men's motives. He notes that some of the measures claimed as unique New Deal inventions were launched in his own administration and declares that "Many of the additional measures undertaken in these directions during the past months are admirable if properly administered." Referring to his unshaken conviction that relief of distress must remain local and personal, rather than an impersonal political function, he adds: "The moment the need exceeds the honest capacities of the local agencies, they must have support of the Federal Government as the final reservoir of national strength."

His strictures refer to means, not to ends: "Co-operation appraises its methods and consequences step by step and pays its bills as it goes. Bureaucracy rushes headlong into visions of the millennium and sends the bills to the Treasury." In troubled times, he knows all too well, people clamor for violent cures. But the ills of society "must often be cured by building up the cells of the economic body under careful nursing and antiseptics, rather than by surgery or patent medicines." There are evils, but "we do not need to burn down the house to kill the rats."

To people enamored of the word revolution and the slogans of hysteria he tenders the reminder that American liberalism, the respect for the individual entity, is the most revolutionary concept launched in two thousand years:

It is all old, very, very old, the idea that the good of men arises from the direction of centralized executive power, whether it be exercised through bureaucracies, mild dictatorships or despotisms, monarchies or autocracies. For liberty is the emancipation of men from power and servitude and the substitution of freedom for force of government. . . .

We cannot extend the mastery of government over the daily life of a people without somewhere making it master of people's souls and thoughts. That is going on today. It is a part of all regimentation. Even if the government conduct of business could give us the maximum of efficiency instead of least efficiency, it would be purchased at the cost of freedom. . . .

True Liberalism is found not in striving to spread bureaucracy, but in striving to set bounds to it. Liberalism is a force proceeding from the deep realization that economic freedom cannot be sacrificed if political freedom is to be preserved. True Liberalism seeks all legitimate freedoms first in the confident belief that without such freedom the pursuit of other blessings is in vain. . . .

We have in our lifetime seen the subjection of Liberty in one nation after another. It has been defeated by the untruth that some form of dictation by government alone can overcome immediate difficulties and can assure entry into economic perfection. That is the issue of our generation, not a partisan issue but the issue of human liberty.

The spark of liberty in the mind and spirit of man cannot be long extinguished; it will break into flames that will destroy every coercion which seeks to limit it.

It was in the faith expressed in these closing words of his book that Hoover as ex-President observed and analyzed the course of our nation. In public addresses and articles he dealt with one phase after another of the shifting and often contradictory improvisations called the New Deal. Taken together, his appraisal constitutes an earnest, comprehending, and penetrating study of the Roosevelt administrations.

The plan of this portrait of Hoover does not call for a statement of his specific criticisms of specific developments. A long book would not suffice for that—one hopes that Hoover himself will someday write it. I am concerned with the temper and direction of his criticism.

"Perhaps more than any other living person," he said in 1935, "I can sympathize with the President in his burdens. We could agree upon some acts of this administration, but we disagree upon profound principles of human liberty." If anyone, having read this far in my book, still brackets Hoover with know-nothing reaction, then I have failed to convey the essence of the man. It was Herbert Hoover who expressed fear that we may swing "from the foolishness of radicalism . . . to the selfishness of re-action."

In his running analysis of the New Deal, he cut through pretensions to realities. Four years after he had left the White House, for instance, he disposed of mountains of official claims with a few simple figures. Having increased expenditures by $14,000,-000,000, he pointed out, having expanded its bureaucracy by 160,000 persons, having created 5,000 paid committees and commissions, having devalued the dollar by 41 per cent—the New Deal showed a total reduction of unemployment at that point by 700,000. No amount of sloganized alibis could cover up that disproportion between the costs and what they purchased.

But his deeper quarrel was on the moral plane. What distressed him most was moral laxness in high places posturing as smart politics; the spectacle of a government devoting so much of its energies to self-eulogy and derogation of large segments of the citizenship; the growing cynicism toward the Constitution and the Supreme Court; the notorious manipulation of relief funds to mend political fences and win elections. He was shocked by the implications of a phrase like "you can't beat Santa Claus," and even more so by the amused complacency with which such things were accepted by the country. What he saw in deep sorrow was a lowering of standards in public life and a growing contempt for traditional national ideals.

"A nation is not great through its rivers or its ships on the sea or the deposits in its banks," he declared. "It is great by the moral fiber and character of its citizens. Nations die when those weaken."

4

The great debate on military intervention which agitated America for more than two years was never settled by the American people. It was settled by the bombs that fell on Pearl Harbor. That night Herbert Hoover, like thousands of other non-interventionists, announced that the debate was closed; that we were in the war and must unite to win it. He pledged his devotion to the cause of victory.

The emotional lesions of that war are too fresh, too raw, for reasoned judgments on its major issues. Honest, patriotic men who oppose their country's involvement in a war are placed in a difficult position when the war comes notwithstanding. That was the position of men such as the elder Senator Robert La Follette and Eugene V. Debs in World War I; of men such as Senator Burt Wheeler and Norman Thomas in the second.

Herbert Hoover expressed firm opposition to direct American participation in both those struggles. In 1917 a Democratic President did not hesitate to entrust Hoover with the number-one civilian war post, Food Administrator, and to make him a member of his War Council despite his prewar views. In 1941 and the years that followed another Democratic President barred Hoover from serving his country, though many of his closest associates urged in the name of national unity that the bars be lifted.

If all those who took the non-interventionist side of the great debate are to be eternally damned, damnation would swallow at least 75 per cent of the American people, including tens of thousands who died to guarantee victory. There were a few, no doubt, whose sympathies were with the Germans and more who were neutral. But the majority of the American people ardently wished the defeat of Germany and were eager to hasten it—but without joining the war in the military sense. Hoover was in this majority. So were President Roosevelt, Wendell Willkie and Henry A. Wallace, assuming they spoke the truth as late as November 1940.

"We will not participate in foreign wars and will not send our Army, Navy, or air forces to fight in foreign lands outside of the Americas. . . ."

These were President Roosevelt's words on October 25, 1940. They could have been Hoover's no less. On January 15, 1941, the former President wrote to Congressman Sol Bloom:

"I am in favor of extending every practicable aid, short of war, to Britain to enable her to maintain her independence."

He went as far as, and in some respects farther than, many of the loud interventionists in urging stepped-up production and expanded means of transportation to help the anti-Nazi belligerents. The question, as he saw it, was not whether Germany's defeat and a more democratic postwar world were desirable but whether these purposes could be compassed better by American entry into the war or by its non-combatant participation.

Hoover was convinced that England could not be beaten. "I do not believe—and most of our military authorities do not believe—that the British are going to be defeated in their heroic defense," he declared on October 31, 1940. Britian would come through safely, he insisted, "especially . . . if our industry furnishes them with all the guns and planes it is capable of producing."

This conviction has been made to look heinous by misrepresentation. Yet we find the Secretary of State at the time, Cordell Hull, attesting in his memoirs: "The President and I believed Britain could and would resist the Nazi attack successfully. . . ." Alluding to the fear of a British defeat, Hull declares that "neither Lothian nor I contemplated this at all." Lord Lothian was the British Ambassador in Washington.

The clamor for military intervention against which Hoover objected must be appraised in relation to that belief which Roosevelt, Hull, the British plenipotentiary all shared with Hoover that the danger of British collapse was remote. Hoover, indeed, held that America could be *more* helpful by remaining out of the military struggle and devoting itself exclusively to producing the sinews of victory. He argued that to the extent that we diverted manpower for military action and industrial capacity for equipping our own forces, we impaired our effectiveness as an arsenal.

When the Nazis took on Russia in June 1941, six months before the United States was pushed into the conflict, confidence in British victory was raised to a certainty. There seemed even less reason, therefore, for our military involvement. The Soviets, after terrific initial losses, halted the German invaders outside Moscow by November. The ultimate defeat of Hitler, now engaged on two fronts and faced with a rapidly growing contribution of American munitions, seemed a matter of time.

The purely ideological aspect of the struggle, as far as Hoover was concerned, ceased to have any reality: "Collaboration between Britain and Russia will bring them military values, but it makes the whole argument of our joining the war to bring the four freedoms to mankind a gargantuan joke."

Hoover refused to concede the absurdity that Hitler, by breaking his friendship pact with Stalin, had magically converted the Soviet despotism into a "freedom-loving democracy." He urged continued and expanded aid to Britain and acknowledged the military imperative of aiding Russia through Britain; but, he warned, "If we go further and join the war and we win, then we have won for Stalin the grip of Communism on Russia and more opportunity for it to extend in the world. We should at least cease to tell our sons that they would be giving their lives to restore democracy and freedom to the world."

At the same time Hoover felt deeply the need to block the spread of the war to the Far East. He was certain in his own mind—on the basis of intimate information—that Japan was eager to avoid conflict with the United States; and that almost until the last moment an amicable settlement virtually on American terms was possible.

A war with Japan, by siphoning American industrial and naval might from the Atlantic to the Pacific, seemed to him a risky weakening of the British position and a corresponding strengthening of Hitler's position. This view was shared by many British war leaders—probably it will appear, when the whole mystery-laden story of Japanese-American relations is finally told, that Winston Churchill was among them. They feared that extension of the war to the Pacific would postpone victory for years and, win or lose, would strip England of her Eastern empire.

Another belief, central in Hoover's thinking, should be underlined. It seemed to him that a triumph of American arms in Europe could not bring peace to that continent or enlarge the area of democracy. He faced up to the Soviet reality. The victory, he foresaw, would only shift the center of gravity of totalitarianism from Berlin to Moscow. By remaining outside the military orbit, by limiting itself to a decisive but non-combatant role, the United States could bring its prestige and its untapped military potential to bear in fashioning an enduring peace. The mere avoidance of an alliance with communism, he argued, would enhance our moral leverage in the postwar settlements.

These views he expressed explicitly and forcefully. Perhaps he was mistaken. A great deal more needs to be known and understood about the Pacific story which catapulted America into the conflict before a cocksure verdict will be anything more than an emotional verdict. Nothing has happened since December 1941 to convince Hoover that the world would not have been better off today had the alternative course which he urged been followed. A lot of things, indeed, have happened to fortify his pre-war convictions.

One need not share Hoover's war views to defend his right to hold them and the absolute, feckless, high-minded patriotism which was at their heart. He adhered to these views, within his lights and his logic, in the face of derision and abuse. If there is any merit in honesty and courage, he must be credited with both; unlike so many others who agreed with him until the 1940 election was over, he meant every word he uttered.

Surely no one can survey the postwar world—with half of Europe and Manchuria under the iron heel of communism, with the rest of Europe and China fighting desperately against the Red totalitarianism, with America pledging a big slice of its income to frustrate the plans of the Red imperialists, with the nightmare of a Third World War obsessing men's thoughts everywhere, with the ideals set up in the Atlantic Charter and in wartime propagandas trampled underfoot—no one can see those things and not feel an inner nudge of doubt.

Suppose Japan's minimum condition for peace—presumably continued mastery in Manchuria—had been accepted. Suppose the total American industrial potential had been thrown into the scales of the European war. Suppose the war had been won under those conditions. Could the world picture have conceivably been any uglier, any more menacing, than it is today? Could the threat of yet another and incalculably more devastating global struggle have been any sharper? That, we may be sure, is how historians, freed from the current emotional tensions, will speculate as they seek to solve the puzzles of our time. And the only certainty is that there will be almost as many conclusions as there will be historians.

Immediately after the sneak assault on Pearl Harbor the ex-President issued an unambiguous statement:

"American soil has been treacherously attacked by Japan. Our decision is clear. It is forced upon us. We must fight with everything we have. I have opposed the foreign policies of our government. I have believed alternative policies would have been better. But whatever our differences of view may be as to the causes which have led to this situation, those are matters to be threshed out by history. Today there is just one job before the American people. We must defeat this invasion by Japan and we must fight it in any place that will defeat it. Upon this job we must and will have unity in America. We must have and will have full support for the President of the United States in this war to defend America. We will have victory."

This was a pledge, offered by a man who had never broken one. I submit that the whole life's story of our only living ex-President dictated faith in the pledge; that his exclusion from the war effort was petty and ignoble. Thousands of others who had been no less outspoken against intervention before Pearl Harbor day were welcomed into the war effort. Indeed, men and women who had been anti-war not through conviction but simply on orders from a foreign power—who had changed their attitude only when the orders changed, with Hitler's attack on Stalin—were assigned to responsible war jobs. No such forgiveness and trust could be found in Washington for a man with Hoover's record of service to his fellow men!

From the first day of European hostilities in September 1939 Hoover thought of the sufferings of civilians. As a quarter of a century earlier, he was revolted by the "realism" which denied bread to innocent women and children, victims of the Nazi conquerors. His Belgian experience had convinced him that effective guarantees against misuse of food by the Germans was possible.

Year after year he struggled against terrific odds to bring some relief supplies to non-combatants, or at least to children, in Poland, Greece, Finland, France, Belgium, and Holland. He was under no illusions about the price he would pay for this in

stepped-up personal abuse. He knew that he was giving his detractors another stick—just then the stoutest stick of all—for
beating his reputation. But the knowledge, then the vindictive
proofs of this, did not deter him. He was guided by his Quaker
conscience.

He headed a Polish relief commission on invitation from the
Polish Government-in-exile. At the request of the Finnish Government, when the little country was violated by Soviet Russia at
the end of 1939, he directed an intensive Finnish Relief Fund
drive. The Belgian, Netherlands, and Norwegian exile governments also turned to him—until pressure from the British Government obliged them to disavow the relief work. "We received
imploring petitions from the relief committees which were organized inside these different countries, especially to save their children," Hoover has told me.

In November 1940 he organized the National Committee on
Food for the Small Democracies, which rallied hundreds of
religious leaders, educators, social workers: 1,400 prominent
Americans in all. General Pershing said on February 16, 1941:

"There is no doubt millions are in jeopardy unless they are
given aid from somewhere. From my own war experience and
some knowledge of problems involved, I have every confidence
that the salvation of these people can be worked out along the
lines proposed by Mr. Hoover, without military loss or benefit
to either side. The interest of this committee in maintaining
American ideals, and the friendship to America of these nations,
by saving these millions, is worthy of support."

American entry in the war did not alter the situation so far
as the need for aid was concerned; but it made Hoover's efforts
a hundredfold more difficult, more open to misunderstanding,
and deliberate distortion. Every pressure of self-interest—of ordinary self-protection—dictated that he abandon the unpopular
course. But he was one of the few who could hear the cries of
starved children under the thunder of explosives, and he would
not—being Hoover he could not—desist.

"The whole question," a Belgian newspaper said at the time,
"is whether the United Nations are fighting to liberate oppressed
peoples or to liberate a vast cemetery."

The results of his striving were pitifully small. Through private organizations like the Red Cross and the Friends he did provide some minor supplies. But it was not enough to save the new generation from vast suffering and death. The Allied leaders, rightly or wrongly, abandoned all the captive populations to Hitler's tender mercies. As Hoover, Pershing, and their fellows had warned, the Germans were adequately fed; only the conquered women and children went hungry.

Not long before his death, John Winant, former Ambassador to London and a partisan of the New Deal, made this statement about World War I: "I have often thought that if after the last war 2,000 of us out of the 2,000,000 who fought in France had volunteered to help the children of Germany, we might have avoided this war, because peace needs a personal caring as well as collective action." Certain it is that had the physical stamina of the captive peoples in this war been maintained, the recovery of their countries after the Nazi defeat would have been hastened, their resistance against the new totalitarian pest would have been fortified.

Hoover's critics on this issue, of course, were not content with claiming that his logic was wrong and his humane instincts misdirected. They assailed his motives and character. Super-patriots at fat banquets in hotel ballrooms, between hiccups, denounced him as a "Nazi lover" because he pleaded that a little milk and flour be allowed through the blockade for Greek or French babies.

But there were some who understood. An editorial in the *Christian Century,* issue of October 29, 1941, declared: "Out of the agony and bitterness of these days one great humanitarian figure is emerging in America. That is Herbert Hoover." In a time of unlimited hysteria, it went on, "This American has moved straight forward, refusing to give up his struggle to carry mercy and pity and friendship to the most hopeless victims of the war." Then it made the daring prophecy which I quoted earlier in this book:

"We believe that he is only now approaching the summit of his career."

5

It is possible, and even likely, that here and there in these pages I have been betrayed by ardor into overstatement. Ardor for justice. Yes, justice. A frayed, corny, and despised little word, but I offer it without apology to explain any lapse into hyperbole. Reading reams of unconscionable spite and malice aimed at Hoover, matching the man against the mean and sordid myth, one's sense of fairness is outraged, one is driven to a compensatory bias in his favor.

Not simply justice for a man brutally maligned but for the things his life connotes: the old-fashioned virtues, decencies, and loyalties. And the valor of renunciation. Hoover renounced immense wealth for public service, but that is a minor part of it. The major fact is that he has repeatedly renounced popular acclaim for principle, for duty as he conceived it. As President, then as ex-President, he has never revised or reversed himself under the terror of organized vituperation; he has never yielded to the temptation of doing the politically profitable thing against his own logic and conscience.

There seems to me no danger that this book (or others certain to come as Hoover is reappraised in historical perspective) will launch a counter-myth of perfection. The man's human failings are too much in evidence for that. There is nothing flamboyant and melodramatic about his personality to win and hold man in the mass. He fits into none of the conventional hero patterns. The hallmark of his character and career is integrity, and that is not exactly a quality to whip up popular adoration.

Hoover is admittedly without much talent as a politician. He has generated a cult of devoted admirers without trying; he could not have built a personal machine of power if he had tried. There simply is not enough flexibility, not enough gift for cutting moral corners, in his make-up. If assuring one's re-election at any cost, by hook or crook, by maneuvering people and manipulating issues, be the primary test of success in the White House, then he was a flop in that office.

His failure has been in the area of public relations. He has not "sold" himself to the electorate. Myriad opportunities to please and flatter and amuse the masses went by the board; not in his feelings but in his manner he has been aloof from the madding crowd. The mere fact that his enemies have managed so well to conceal his qualities and motives under masks of their own making is proof of that failure.

But more and more of the masks are being removed. Already it is clear that sober historical revaluation of the thirty-first President will disclose the essential man under the accidental and artificial externals. Except at the lunatic left, a new appreciation of Hoover, sometimes grudging, sometimes embarrassed, often contrite, is increasingly in evidence. America has reason to be gratified by this fact—for its own sake, not for Hoover's sake.

He has crowded three great careers into one lifespan: as engineer, humanitarian, and public servant. It would be against nature if he had not made many serious mistakes and some blunders. The important truth, however, is that none of these mistakes or blunders has been in the domain of morals and motives. None of them has been the result of selfishness or greed or malice. The mistakes charged against him, where they stand up at all, reflect on his judgment or his techniques—never on his character.

There is ample room for argument, in the case of Hoover as of any great public figure, about the wisdom of this or that policy; the validity of this or that conviction. There is no room for argument about his good will, his good intentions, his selfless dedication to his fellowmen and his country.

What has impressed me profoundly as I studied the data of his life is Hoover's wholeness and genuineness. There is nothing phony, nothing petty, nothing spurious in his story. He has not lived with an eye on opinion polls and intellectual fashions. His beliefs and conduct have derived from his philosophy of life. And that philosophy itself—whether one shares it fully or not—has not been an improvisation of expediency or a rationalization of self-interest. It is deep-rooted in the American soil. It has evolved naturally, honestly, consistently in the American experience. It is integral with our national heritage.

Rarely has such a capacious intelligence as Hoover's been combined with such a great heart and robust spirit. Even more rarely, the democratic process being what it is, has a man so richly endowed reached the presidency.

Herbert Hoover is a great monolithic figure. Time is rapidly washing off the mud with which he has been bespattered. The granite of integrity underneath is becoming obvious even to the less perceptive of his countrymen.

Bibliography

COREY, HERBERT, *The Truth About Hoover*. Houghton Mifflin, 1932.

CROWTHER, SAMUEL, *The Presidency vs. Hoover*. Doubleday, Doran & Co., Inc., 1928.

DEXTER, WALTER FRIAR, *Herbert Hoover and American Individualism*. Macmillan, 1932.

EMERSON, EDWIN, *Hoover and His Times*. Garden City Publishing Co.

HERBERT HOOVER, *Principles of Mining*. McGraw, 1909.

The New Day, Campaign Speeches of Herbert Hoover. Stanford University Press, 1928.

A Boyhood in Iowa. Aventine Press, 1931.

Hoover After Dinner. Scribner's, 1933.

American Individualism. Doubleday, Doran & Co., Inc., 1934.

The Challenge of Liberty. Scribner's, 1935.

Addresses upon the American Road, 1933-38. Scribner's, 1938.

Further Addresses upon the American Road, 1938-40. Scribner's, 1940.

Addresses upon the American Road, 1940-41. Scribner's, 1941.

America's First Crusade. Scribner's, 1942.

Addresses upon the American Road, 1941-45. D. Van Nostrand Co., 1946.

HOOVER, HERBERT, AND COOLIDGE, CALVIN, *Campaign Speeches of 1932*. Doubleday, Doran & Co., Inc., 1933.

HOOVER, HERBERT, AND GIBSON, HUGH, *The Basis of Lasting Peace*. D. Van Nostrand, 1945.

IRWIN, WILL, *Herbert Hoover, a Reminiscent Biography*. Century, 1929.

JOSLIN, THEODORE G., *Hoover Off the Record*. Doubleday, Doran & Co., Inc., 1934.

KELLOGG, VERNON, *Herbert Hoover, the Man and His Work*. Appleton, 1920.

LANE, ROSE WILDER, *Making of Herbert Hoover*. Century, 1920.

MICHELSON, CHARLES, *The Ghost Talks*. Putnam, 1944.

MITCHELL, BROADUS, *Depression Decade*. Rinehart, 1947.

MOLEY, RAYMOND, *After Seven Years*. Harper's, 1939.

MYERS, WILLIAM STARR, AND NEWTON, WALTER H., *The Hoover Administration, a Documented Narrative*. Scribner's, 1936.

REEVES, EARL, *This Man Hoover*. A. L. Burt Co., 1928.

SULLIVAN, LAWRENCE, *Prelude to Panic*. Statesman Press, Washington, 1936.

WILBUR, RAY LYMAN, AND HYDE, ARTHUR MASTIC, *The Hoover Policies*. Scribner's, 1937.